SUBSTANCE
&Style

Instruction and Practice
in Copyediting

Revised

Mary Stoughton

EEI

Grateful acknowledgment is made to the following for permission to reprint:

Exercises 1 and 5 used with permission from Margherita S. Smith.

Exercise 6 adapted from an excerpt from *Editing the Small Magazine* by Rowena Ferguson, copyright 1976, and used with permission from Columbia University Press.

The articles "The Acrobatic Apostrophe" (*The Editorial Eye*, January 1994) and "Cracking the Code: Making Verbs Agree with Collective Nouns" (*The Editorial Eye*, July 1992) reprinted with permission of Dianne Snyder.

The article "Who Said That? On Handling Quotations" (*The Editorial Eye*, October 1993) reprinted with permission from Edward D. Johnson.

The article "Not by Intuition Alone: Taking Stock of Editing Habits" (*The Editorial Eye*, January 1995) reprinted with permission from Diane Ullius.

The article "The Considerate Editor: The Art of Criticizing Colleagues" (*The Editorial Eye*, August 1994) reprinted with permission from Catharine Fishel.

EEI Books
66 Canal Center Plaza, Suite 200
Alexandria, VA 22314-5507
Phone: 703-683-0683
E-mail: books@eei-alex.com

EEI publishes other books on editorial topics. For a free catalog, call 800-683-8380. Books may be purchased at quantity discounts for educational or business purposes. Please call or write to the address above for pricing information.

Second Edition

Stoughton, Mary, 1942–
    Substance & style : instruction & practice in copyediting / Mary Stoughton. — 2nd ed.
        p.   cm.
    Includes bibliographical references and index.
    ISBN 0-935012-18-4 (pbk.)
    1. Copy-reading.   I. Title.
PN162.S75   1996
808'.06607—dc20   96-14711
                                                                        CIP

Cover design by Sharon Rogers, EEI

96 97 98 99 00 01 / 10 9 8 7 6 5 4 3 2 1

Table of Contents

Foreword

There are as many kinds of editors as there are editorial jobs. The bond among us is that we're all editors, facing a common problem: how to make the written word say what the author intended it to say.

This book is addressed to two groups of people: those who think they would like to be editors and those who find themselves in the position of having to edit without having had the training to do so. The first category cuts across all ages and walks of life; fascination with words is usually a lifelong affliction. The latter applies to those who work on publications of any sort (newsletters, newspapers, journals, fact sheets, catalogues, brochures—the list is endless); those who need to polish documents of any kind (letters, proposals, reports, research papers, and so on); and those who have discovered that having to communicate on paper brings a whole set of problems that knowledge of subject matter doesn't solve.

We devised this book as a self-help study guide; after each topic is discussed, there are exercises to test your skill. For readers who want more practice, additional exercises and answer keys appear in appendix A. We also included a glossary of common grammatical and editorial terms. If you persevere, you'll absorb the basic skills you need for copyediting; then you must apply them on the job.

You'll probably have to adapt the editing guidelines in this book to fit your own situation. If you work exclusively on-line, you won't need to spend much time on editorial marks; if you always work on short articles with immediate deadlines, you probably won't be able to make the three "passes" (or readings) we recommend. The judgments you make and the principles you apply, however, are still editorial ones covered by the discussions in this book.

We not only teach you to make copyeditor's marks, we also teach you why: the rule of grammar or the style decision that dictates each choice. In addition, we discuss those times when it's best to leave something alone.

This book grew out of a class that I teach for EEI, formerly Editorial Experts, Inc., a publications consulting firm in the Washington, DC, area. EEI has been teaching workshops on publications since 1981. The class on copyediting, which I've taught since 1986, has introduced hundreds of people to the subject. This revised edition of the book contains, among other changes, more information on on-line editing, an updated style guide matrix, and an updated reference list.

EEI produces an award-winning newsletter on publications standards and practices called *The Editorial Eye*. Over the years, many articles on editing as a profession have appeared in *The Eye*; we gathered a few of these articles—some lyrical, some acerbic—into appendix D. They shed light on what editors do and why most of us would not choose to do anything else.

Mary Stoughton
Alexandria, VA
January 1996

Acknowledgments

Many people at EEI had a hand in this book, reviewing sections of it in various stages, suggesting material for it, or contributing to the exercises. Some of the exercises and some of the discussion on hyphens and dashes are based on work done by Margherita S. Smith, who graciously gave me permission to use it. I also want to acknowledge the contribution of Alison W. Reier, who spent countless hours poring over the words and organizing and reorganizing the material, especially the style matrix in chapter 11. She caused me to reexamine carefully and thoughtfully the focus and thrust of the book. Finally, I want to thank Mara T. Adams, without whom there would have been no book.

The book belongs to the author.
—Maxwell E. Perkins

INTRODUCTION TO COPYEDITING:
What It Is and What It Isn't

1

Editor: One who revises, corrects, or arranges the contents and style of the literary, artistic, or musical work of others for publication or presentation; one who alters or revises another's work to make it conform to some standard or serve a particular purpose. (Webster's Third International Dictionary)

Good editing should be invisible; editors, however, are not. Ask an author about editors as a breed and the response may be prefaced with a snarl. All too often the relationship between authors and editors is adversarial. Both feel constrained to be defensive, although it needn't be so. Ideally, authors and editors complement each other, each striving to produce the perfect manuscript.

The stereotype of the editor/author relationship was captured by a cartoon in *The New Yorker* that showed two men with muttonchop whiskers sitting at a table. One, holding a manuscript, is saying to the other, "Come, come, Mr. Dickens, it was either the best of times or the worst of times. It could not have been both." An author produces the perfect sentence and the editor quibbles over trifles; editors are "comma people," as opposed to authors, who are "content people." Like most stereotypes, this one contains a grain of truth. Authors in general are more concerned with content and editors with its expression. As a division of labor, this one is as valid as any other.

This book addresses a particular kind of editing called copyediting. Copyeditors examine a manuscript sentence by sentence. By the time a copyeditor gets the manuscript, larger decisions, such as additions, deletions, or reorganizations, have already been made by other editors or reviewers.

Copyediting is different from substantive editing, which is concerned with those larger decisions. A copyeditor examines a manuscript for spelling, grammar, punctuation, consistency, and conformity to style. As one long-time editor put it, "The ultimate goal is to produce a sentence that sounds as if it could have been written no other way....You, the editor, are a bridge between two people, the person who has written and the person who will or may read."

Copyeditors take a manuscript and polish the language; they strive to make the author's meaning as clear as possible, to save readers from editorial inconsistencies that at best distract them from the content and at worst cloud the author's meaning. Copyeditors make sure that a manuscript will stand up to the scrutiny of both the author's peers and the general public. The copyeditor is often the last line of defense against absurdities that creep into print and embarrass the most diligent among us.

Editing in general and copyediting in particular are skills you learn by doing. However, most editors share common traits—a love of the written word, an appreciation of language in all its richness, a desire to see order emerge from chaos in the form of a manuscript that sings or speaks from the heart. The intellectual challenge is always there, but more than anything else, editing is fun—so much fun that it's easy to get carried away.

To copyedit, you first need to know how to mark a manuscript so that the author can absorb your suggestions and the keyboarder who will make your revisions can understand at a glance what needs to be done. This book will teach you how to make the marks, but it will also discuss why you make them and when you make them. Conversely, it will set some general guidelines for when you'd best leave a manuscript or a passage alone.

Definitions

Writing to specification (as opposed to creative writing) means starting from an idea, with no manuscript or with notes alone; it includes research, interviews, consultations, draft preparation, and revisions.

Substantive editing includes reorganizing, rewriting, writing transitions and summaries, helping plan schedules, attending meetings, and consulting with authors and publishers.

Copyediting means reviewing a "finished" manuscript (copy) for spelling, grammar, consistency, and format. Copyeditors also check the completeness, accuracy, and format of tables, bibliographies, references, and footnotes. Copyediting doesn't usually include rewriting or reorganization, but it does mean eliminating wordiness and reviewing the content for logic.

Proofreading consists of checking the final keyboarded version (proof) against the manuscript version to find typographical errors and deviations from typesetting or word processing instructions. Proofreaders query (question), but normally don't change, editorial errors and inconsistencies.

As with any other task, it's important to know how copyediting fits into the larger picture. This understanding makes instructions more relevant and can even determine the level of effort expended. Copyeditors aren't expected to redo the work of the author and substantive editor, but rather to polish and complete it. Everyone works together to produce a harmonious whole.

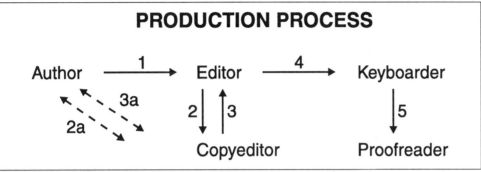

What is the copyeditor's role in the production process? An author writes a manuscript, which will be published in some form—book, report, brochure, pamphlet, or the like. The publisher gives the manuscript to an editor (1), who reads it and makes suggestions and revisions. The copyeditor (2) polishes the language, corrects the grammar, and may also have to query the author (2a) about obscure points or unclear or missing material. When the editing is finished (3), the manuscript may return to the author for approval (3a) or go to a keyboarder after the editor has checked it (4). Then a proofreader checks the keyboarded version against the edited version (5) to be sure that the two are the same.

Because editors need to be very familiar with the rules of the language, this book incorporates a review of grammar and punctuation and includes examples and alternate solutions. Exercises will teach concepts and test skills. Often there's no right or wrong answer; some solutions are simply better than others.

No editor can function without the basic tools of the trade: a dictionary and a style manual. Editing often means ensuring conformity to a style, and this book will attempt to sort out the various ones, by comparing some commonly used styles on such points as punctuation, abbreviation, and numbers. It will also discuss what a style decision is and how it differs from a rule of grammar. Once you understand what a style decision is, you can then resolve whatever question has arisen. But familiarity with a particular style comes only with constant use.

As an editor, you needn't be a perfect speller; very few people are. But you must develop a discerning eye; a misspelled word should *look* wrong to you even if you don't really know how to spell it. Thus a spelling pretest follows. Doing this exercise will show you where you stand now. An answer key follows.

EXERCISE 1: SPELLING TEST

Instructions: Cross through every misspelled word and write out the entire word with the correct spelling in the blank provided.

_____ The occurrence of a misspelled word in print is totaly

_____ impermissible. The affect is disastrous, an embarrass-

_____ ment to the printer, a distraction to the reader, and a

_____ slurr on the writer's competence. Misspelling is a sign

_____ that the role of the proofreader has been slighted or

_____ misunderstood. Although the proofreader is principly

_____ committed to seeing that the proof follows the copy

_____ accurately, there is a further committment to preventing

_____ the author, editor, or printer from looking rediculous.

_____ A practitioner of proofreading is never presumtuous in

_____ correcting (or--better--querying) an incorrect spelling.

_____ Let no conscientious proofreader wholey acquiesce to

_____ the rule of "follow copy" in regard to spelling.

Instructions: Choose one of the two letters in parentheses to complete the word.

1.	comput_r	(e;o)	7.	inadvert_nt	(e;a)
2.	deduct_ble	(a;i)	8.	indispens_ble	(a;i)
3.	defend_nt	(a;e)	9.	m_mento	(e;o)
4.	depend_nt	(a;e)	10.	resist_nt	(a;e)
5.	dissen_ion	(s;t)	11.	sep_rate	(a;e)
6.	super_ede	(c;s)	12.	tox_n	(e;i)

ANSWERS

The occurrence of a misspelled word in print is ~~totaly~~   _totally_

impermissible. The ~~affect~~ is disastrous, an embarrass-   _effect_

ment to the printer, a distraction to the reader, and a   _____

~~slurr~~ on the writer's competence. Misspelling is a sign   _slur_

that the role of the proofreader has been slighted or   _____

misunderstood. Although the proofreader is ~~principly~~   _principally_

committed to seeing that the proof follows the copy   _____

accurately, there is a further ~~committment~~ to preventing   _commitment_

the author, editor, or printer from looking ~~rediculous~~.   _ridiculous_

A practitioner of proofreading is never ~~presumtuous~~ in   _presumptuous_

correcting (or--better--querying) an incorrect spelling.   _____

Let no conscientious proofreader ~~wholey~~ acquiesce to   _wholly_

the rule of "follow copy" in regard to spelling.   _____

1.	comput**e**r	(e)	7.	inadvert**e**nt	(e)
2.	deduct**i**ble	(i)	8.	indispens**a**ble	(a)
3.	defend**a**nt	(a)	9.	m**e**mento	(e)
4.	depend**e**nt	(e)	10.	resist**a**nt	(a)
5.	dissen**s**ion	(s)	11.	sep**a**rate	(a)
6.	super**s**ede	(s)	12.	tox**i**n	(i)

For words such as *dissension* or *memento*, your dictionary may list more than one spelling. Always use the first or preferred spelling. Because dictionaries vary, be sure to use the one your client or employer prefers. Also, assume nothing. Don't automatically change the word *materiel* to *material* or *tranches* to *branches*: Check the context and look it up.

If you want more practice in spelling, turn to appendix A, exercise 1.

The good editor has the confidence to say no to any author who would compromise the medium's standards, and the humility to recognize when those standards are transcended.

—Arthur Plotnick

GRAMMAR:
If You Don't Know It, You Can't Correct It

2

Unlike spelling, which needn't be perfect in these days of spell checkers that spot and offer alternatives for possible errors, grammar is at once more immediate and less susceptible to automatic correction. A sentence that's grammatically unclear or badly written jars the ear of the listener or the consciousness of the reader.

Good editors share a love for and an appreciation of language. You have to like words to edit well, but you also have to know how the language works—why certain constructions are allowed and others aren't. Further, it's important to remember that the written word is more formal than the spoken word. The difference between the two is less distinct than it used to be, although some strictures remain. Should this distinction strike you as artificial, remember that in some languages (French, for example) entire tenses are no longer spoken, just written.

As an editor, you need to hone your skills to be able to find and fix those amorphous problems that weaken prose. You also need to know the names of faulty constructions, so that you can explain your editorial changes to an author. Some grammatical points will always be obscure. But as a copyeditor, you should generally notice most misplaced modifiers, most unclear antecedents, and most agreement problems after even a cursory reading. Exercise 2 is a pretest to give you an idea of the grammatical problems you'll encounter as you work. You'll find sentences that are wordy, and sentences with subject-verb disagreements, misplaced modifiers, and unclear (or missing) antecedents for pronouns. Rewrite or reorder the words to fix the problems you find, remembering always that you must *not* change the meaning.

Answers and explanations appear in the answer key, which follows the pretest. All the subjects in the test are discussed in detail elsewhere in this book.

EXERCISE 2: SENTENCE CORRECTION

Instructions: After each sentence, write the name of the grammatical and other problems you find. Then reorder words or rewrite sentences as needed to correct that problem.

1. Unhappy and depressed, the movie made me feel worse.

2. They only ate what they wanted to eat.

3. Without his wife, his life became onerous.

4. When the artist finished the painting of the boat, he immediately covered it with varnish.

5. My mother has a friend who is very tall.

6. She was unaware of the fact that mice are born hairless.

7. The president said he expected everyone to support the offensive at the press conference last night.

8. Of all the quilts submitted, Laura's design was the most unique.

9. Hopefully, I have completed my income tax form correctly.

10. He thinks that he'll take a shower, and after that go to bed.

11. Lord Byron was young, well born, and had nice manners.

12. He hated politics and all elected officials were considered dishonest by him.

13. My favorite foods are: pizza, popcorn, and watermelon.

14. The congregation is not rich, but they certainly are generous.

15. If he was as clever as he is bold, he would be very successful.

16. It is she who suffers from depression.

17. Neither the coach nor the players is going.

18. Would Scarlett O'Hara have been happier if she would have married Ashley Wilkes?

19. Shakespeare's sonnets are about lovers who agonize over it.

ANSWERS

It's important to have corrected these sentences, but it's essential to know why they need correction and also how to defend the changes you've made. Following are the edited sentences, showing the correct marks and explanations of the problems needing correction.

1. *Because I was* ^ ~~U~~nhappy and depressed, the movie made me feel

   worse.

   Misplaced modifier (a word or phrase not logically or grammatically describing what it was meant to): As the sentence was originally written, the movie was unhappy and depressed.

2. They (only ate) what they wanted to eat.

   Misplaced modifier: Here the word *only* modifies *what they wanted*, not *ate*.

3. Without his wife, his life ~~became~~ *he found* ^ onerous.

   Misplaced modifier: *His life* wasn't *without a wife; he* was. Such constructions are common in conversation but unacceptable in print.

4. When the artist finished the painting of the

   boat, he immediately covered it with varnish.

   Unclear antecedent (a substantive word, phrase, or clause referred to by a pronoun): What does the word *it* refer to—the painting or the boat? Actually, it could be either. If the answer isn't clear from the context, you as an editor would have to query the author.

5. My mother has a (friend ~~who is~~ very tall).

6. She *didn't know* ~~was unaware of the fact~~ that mice are born

   hairless.

   Wordiness: Some words could be cut out of these sentences with no loss of meaning, and *was unaware* has a simpler equivalent.

7. The president said he expected everyone to support the offensive at the press conference last night.

Misplaced modifier: You're permitted to doubt that the offensive took place at the press conference.

8. Of all the quilts submitted, Laura's design was ~~the most~~ unique.

Modification of absolutes: Some words, such as *unique*, denote an absolute quality that can't carry a qualifying adjective such as *more* or *most*. Either something is unique or it's not. *Critical* is a similar sort of word, one that's modified regularly and incorrectly. A situation is critical or it's not: *Very critical* and *extremely critical* are redundant.

9. *I hope* ~~Hopefully,~~ I have completed my income tax form correctly.

Incorrect modifier: *Hopefully* used as an independent comment has crept into contemporary speech. Like *obviously* and similar terms, it's meant to modify the entire sentence. Some grammarians, however, consider this usage incorrect and prefer that *hopefully* be changed to *I hope* in this example.

10. He thinks that he'll take a shower, and ~~after that~~ go to bed.

Wordiness and incorrect punctuation: *Take* and *go* are two equal parts of the predicate forming a compound verb. A comma shouldn't separate the parts of a compound verb.

11. Lord Byron was young, well born, and ~~had nice~~ *well* manner*ed*.

Faulty parallelism: Similar constructions must be treated similarly. The words following the verb weren't all predicate adjectives.

12. He hated politics and ~~all~~ elected officials

~~were~~ (considered) dishonest ~~by him.~~

Faulty parallelism: The two independent clauses weren't parallel in structure.

13. My favorite foods are; pizza, popcorn, and

watermelon.

Incorrect punctuation: The colon is incorrect; use it only after a complete sentence.

14. (The congregation) is *or Although* not rich, ~~but they~~

certainly ~~are~~ *is* generous.

Incorrect antecedent: Although the sentence is perfectly comprehensible to readers, *they* has no antecedent. *Congregation,* the intended antecedent, is singular; *they* is plural.

15. If he ~~was~~ *were* as clever as he is bold, he would be

very successful.

Incorrect mood (the manner in which the action of the verb is conceived by the writer): This sentence should contain a subjunctive verb (condition contrary to fact), one of the few remnants of this form in the language. He's obviously *not* as clever as he is bold.

16. ~~It is~~ she ~~who~~ suffers from depression.

Wordiness: The sentence should be revised unless the extra words are truly there for emphasis or to distinguish this person from another who doesn't suffer from depression.

17. Neither the coach nor the players ~~is~~ *are* going.

Subject-verb disagreement (*neither...nor* or *either...or*): When these forms are used, the verb agrees with the subject nearest to it—in this case, *players.* The verb must be plural.

18. Would Scarlett O'Hara have been happier if she
    had
    ~~would have~~ married Ashley Wilkes?

> **Too many conditionals** (*would haves*): One will suffice. Only the *if* clause needs a subjunctive verb. Scarlett didn't marry Ashley; thus, the situation is contrary to fact.

19. Shakespeare's sonnets are about *People* ~~lovers~~ who
    agonize *about being in love* ~~over it~~.

> **Implied antecedent** (a usage common in everyday speech but not acceptable in writing): *It* refers to an imbedded idea, which must be spelled out.

The errors in these sentences are typical of the problems you'll find while editing. You'll also be faced with style questions (*one* or *1*, *exercise 10* or *Exercise 10*), as well as tables, charts, and references. The following chapters are designed to prepare you for anything and to help you become that bridge between author and reader.

Editing is not an exact science; it is an
art guided by instinct and enhanced by
training and the tools of the trade.

—Mary J. Scroggins

COPYEDITING MARKS: Getting Started

3

Editorial marks are a sort of shorthand that has evolved over time. These marks are not universal, but they're nearly so. They save the editor untold hours of writing detailed instructions. Nonetheless, if you don't use the marks clearly and correctly, your work can generate needless revisions, raise costs, and cause annoyance.

Clear, professional-looking marks also impress authors and help lend credence to the editor's suggestions. Further, no keyboarder should have to make a "best guess" at what an editorial mark means. These days, it's easy to make changes and produce another printout, but it's also easy to forget that each additional iteration costs time and money. In the publishing world both are usually in short supply.

The marks that follow are standard for editors. Some organizations use slightly different ones for particular purposes. If your office uses variants, by all means conform, but keep in mind that someone else (an "outside" author or keyboarder, for instance) may not understand your notation.

Editors and proofreaders use the same marks, but use them differently. Editors mark in the text line, because the keyboarders need to read every line as they work. Proofreaders, working at a later stage in the editorial process, mark in the margin, so the keyboarder making corrections need only run an eye down the margin to see what to do.

Delete one character, several letters, or a whole word with a looped cancel mark (⌐), which supposedly evolved from a medieval α (for *delendo—get rid of*). If you want to delete an entire passage, box it in and draw an X through it.

Delete

> Delete this ƒletter.   Delete this letter.
>
> Delete this ~~word~~ word.   Delete this word.

To close up space entirely, use this mark (⌒), often called close-up hooks.

Close up

> tooth‿paste   toothpaste
>
> tooth‿brush   toothbrush

Using only the top half of the mark means to decrease the space, or to leave a word space, or to take out any extra space, depending on the context.

```
Now       is the time.  Now is the time.
```

Delete and close up

When you combine the delete symbol with the close-up hooks, you get a mark that looks like this: ⌿ . Use it when you want to delete a letter in the middle of a word or at the end of a word, just before a punctuation mark.

```
Noow is the tiyme.       Now is the time.

Now is the timer.        Now is the time.
```

Insert

When you want to insert a letter or a phrase, use a caret (ʌ). Always place your insertions above the line, and always place the caret precisely where you want the insertion to be.

```
                    all good
Now is the time for ʌ men    Now is the time
                             for all good men
```

A brace (‿) under the insertion helps direct the eye to the proper place.

```
      is the
Now ʌ time               Now is the time
for all good men         for all good men
```

If you're inserting a letter at the beginning or end of a word, you must use close-up hooks as well. To some people this practice seems superfluous, but without the hooks it's often impossible to tell where such insertions belong in very heavily edited copy. For example, what did the editor intend here, *fields* or *snow*?

```
       s
field ʌ now
```

The use of close-up hooks would have told you.

```
       s
field ʌ now              field snow

       s
field ʌ now              fields now
```

If you want to add space rather than a word, use a caret and a space mark (#). Some editors draw a line to separate the two words rather than using the symbol:

```
       #
Insert ʌ space           Insert space

Insert/space             Insert space
```

A slash through a capital letter means that the letter should be lowercase. If you wish to lowercase several letters in a row, you can use a slash with a "hat" on it.

    L̸owercase   lowercase

    L̸OWERCASE   lowercase

To make a lowercase letter or word uppercase, put three lines under the letters to be changed.

    capital   Capital

    all caps   ALL CAPS

Small caps are capital letters that are only as big as lowercase letters; they're often used for acronyms, such as VISTA, or combined with regular capitals for names in signature lines. To mark for small caps, use two lines under the words or letters.

    Robert E. Brown   ROBERT E. BROWN

    Robert E. Brown   Rᴏʙᴇʀᴛ E. Bʀᴏᴡɴ

Some people choose two lines to indicate regular caps, but such usage isn't standard.

The underline symbol (_____) is used to signify both italics and underscore. To differentiate between the two forms, write the instruction (*ital* or *score*) in a circle in the margin. Keyboarders know not to enter or "set" anything circled in the margin. Circle all instructions, specifications, or queries, so that no one will put them into the text by mistake.

(ital)   The Sound and the Fury   *The Sound and the Fury*

(score)   The Sound and the Fury   The Sound and the Fury

To remove italics, put a series of hatch marks through the line, or put a delete mark at the end. The latter, however, is very easy to miss in heavily edited copy.

    remove italics

    remove italics

Boldface

To indicate boldface, use a wavy line (⁓) and to remove it, use hatch marks or write and circle , which means *lightface*.

Boldface ⁓	**Boldface**
Remove boldface ⁓⁓⁓	Remove boldface
Remove boldface	Remove boldface

Transpose

The transposition mark looks like this: ⁓ . You can use it to transpose both letters and words.

Trnaspose	Transpose
words Transpose	Transpose words

You can also transpose around something that you've left untouched, although it's often better to rewrite the words. Be sure to keep transpositions easy to read and don't make transpositions within transpositions.

go boldly to where no man has gone

To go boldly to where no man has gone

To boldly go where no man has gone

Replace

To mark for replacement, slash through the incorrect letter and put its replacement above the line. To replace an entire word, cross it out and write the correction above it to avoid any possibility of misunderstanding.

a slash	slash
splash srlash	splash

Spell out/Use the other form

If you want to use the complete word instead of an abbreviation, circle the abbreviation. Circling also indicates that you want the other form.

7	seven
Co.	Company
GM	General Motors

Note that the circle works both ways:

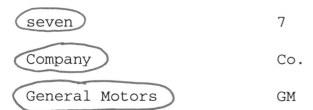

seven	7
Company	Co.
General Motors	GM

If the circled text results in an ambiguous instruction, write out what you want. For instance, does *Calif.* become *CA* or *California*? Is *GM* *General Motors* or *General Mills*? Is *VA* *Virginia* or the *Veterans Administration*? In none of these cases will your keyboarder know what to do (except perhaps from context, and good operators generally see words, not context).

A symbol called the pilcrow (⁋) is used to denote the beginning of a paragraph. This sign, which dates back to Middle English, is universally understood. Some editors use a sign that looks like an *L* (∟) to mark a paragraph break, but this mark is too often lost in heavily edited copy and therefore is used less often.

Paragraph

⁋ Need a new paragraph   ∟Need a new paragraph

Conversely, if you don't want a paragraph where one already exists, then you mark to run on (⌐). You can use the same symbol to mark the end of a considerable deletion as well.

Run on

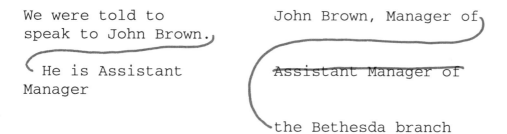

We were told to
speak to John Brown.

He is Assistant
Manager

John Brown, Manager of

~~Assistant Manager of~~

the Bethesda branch

To move material to an adjacent line, brace or circle the passage and show with an arrow where you want it to go.

Transfer

Be sure your marks and instructions are clear
and accurate when you want to move material
to an adjacent line from one place to another.
Brace or circle material to be moved.

Box material to be moved to a different position on the same page and run an arrow to the new position.

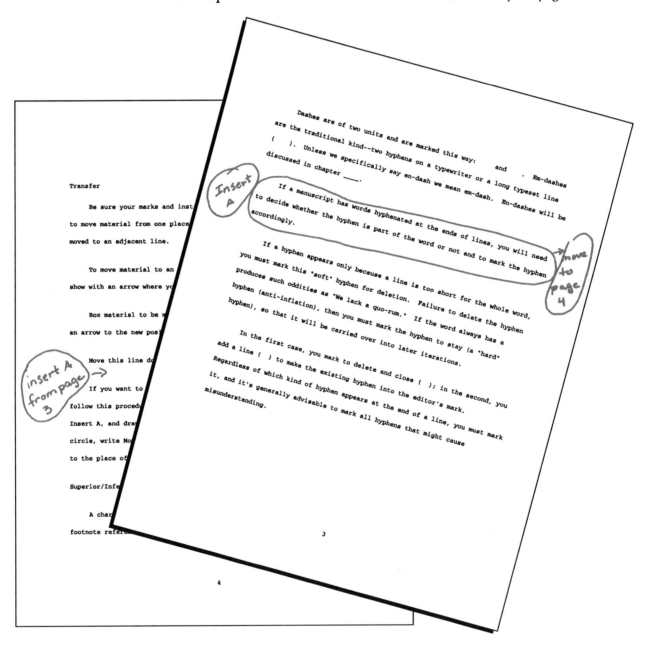

Move this line down.
Copy marked this way is easily read by the word processing staff.

If you want to move material to another page, say from page 3 to page 4, follow this procedure: On page 3, circle the material to be moved, label it *Insert A*, and draw an arrow pointing toward the right-hand margin. In a circle, write *Move to page 4*. On page 4, draw an arrow from the left margin to the place of insertion and write in a circle, *Insert A from page 3*.

A character that goes above the line (superscript), as in a formula or foot-note reference, is marked this way: ∨ .

footnote↓   footnote[1]

A character that should go below the line (subscript) is marked this way: ∧ .

H2O H_2O

A **comma** is marked this way: ⌃ . The caret makes the mark stand out on the page and indicates that it goes below the line.

The **period** looks like a bull's-eye: ⊙ . Without the circle, the period can be mistaken for a random dot on the page.

The **semicolon** and the **colon** can also have carets, ⌃ / ⌃ , although some editors use the marks alone, ; / : , or circle them ⦶ ⦶ .

Apostrophes and **quotation marks** are placed in upside-down carets to indicate their placement above the line: ∨ and ∨ .

Question marks and **exclamation points** use the traditional handwritten symbols ? and ! .

The **hyphen** looks like an equal sign: = . This is the traditional mark, although a single line is used as well.

Dashes are of two sorts and are marked this way: ⊤ₘ and ⊤ₙ . **Em-dashes** are the traditional kind: two hyphens if a software code isn't used or a long typeset line (—). Unless we specifically say en-dash, we mean em-dash. En-dashes will be discussed in chapter 10.

If a manuscript has words hyphenated at the ends of lines, you'll need to decide whether the hyphen is part of the word or not and mark the hyphen accordingly.

If a hyphen appears only because a line is too short for the whole word, you must mark this "soft" hyphen for deletion. Failure to delete the hyphen produces such oddities as "We lack a quo-rum." If the word always has a hyphen (anti-inflation), then you must mark it to stay (a "hard" hyphen), so that it'll be carried over into later iterations.

In the first case, you mark to delete and close (⌢); in the second, you add a line (−) to make the existing hyphen into the editor's mark. Regardless of which kind of hyphen appears at the end of a line, you must mark it, and it's generally advisable to mark all hyphens that might cause misunderstanding. (Marking hyphens is discussed further in chapter 4.)

```
He opened the tooth‾
paste tube.

You should install child=
proof locks on these doors.
```

Here is an example of each of these punctuation symbols correctly marked by an editor.

comma	Yes⌃
period	he said⊙
semicolon	I was late⌃ therefore I lost.
colon	We will discuss the following⌃
hyphen	tamper‗proof seal
apostrophe	Mind your P⌄s and Q⌄s.
quotation marks	⌄Go,⌄ he said.
question mark	Did you say that?
exclamation point	Down!
em-dash	The brothers⸺Manny and Moe⸺
en-dash	1939‒1945

Stet

Finally, if you edit in ink and later discover that you've made a mistake, you use the stet symbol (*Stet*), which means to ignore the correction and let the original stand. (*Stet* comes from Latin and means *let it stand*.) To stet a word, put a series of dots under it and write the word *stet* in a circle next to what you want to keep.

```
Little Bo Peep has lost her sheep⸮  Stet
                                ......
```

Sometimes an editor must indicate where material should appear on the page or in a table. If you want a line to begin at the left margin (*flush left*), you use this mark: ⌊. If you want the line to be moved to the right margin (*flush right*), you use this mark: ⌋. If a head, for example, should be centered, you put the two marks together like this: ⌋⌊ . Another way to ask that material be centered is to use this symbol: (ctr) .

```
Copyediting ⌋

          ⌊ Date

⌋ Chapter 1 ⌊
```

To align, or make margins or columns even, you use two parallel lines. But be sure to say in a marginal notation how you want the column or the passage aligned if it isn't obvious. (For example, write "align on the decimal" and circle the instruction.)

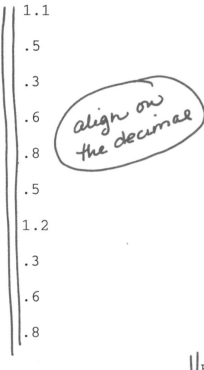

```
‖ 1.1
  .5
  .3
  .6
  .8
  .5
  1.2
  .3
  .6
  .8
```

```
        ‖ French
Ita‖ian
Ger‖an
```

To indent, you can use the pilcrow (⁋) or a small box to indicate a 1-em space (a space that's the same size as the capital letter M). In the old days of movable type, an em-space or em-quad was a standard measurement; although the standard has been replaced, the notation remains. Here are examples of each of these marks.

⁋ `In the beginning`

□ `In the beginning`

Instructions: Now that you've mastered copyediting marks, you're almost ready to tackle a simple manuscript. First, however, complete the following exercise by making the correct copyediting marks.

Delete	frequently
	ham and and eggs
Close up	nation wide
Delete and close up	worldywide
Insert the correct letter	editr
Lowercase	chairman of the Board
	CHAIRMAN OF THE BOARD
Capitalize	mexico
Italics	*ital* The Economist
Boldface	as soon as possible
Transpose the first two words	the Place period at the end.
Spell out	9 of the soldiers
New paragraph	¶
Hard hyphen	seventy-seven
Soft hyphen	develop-ment
Stet—let it stand	*stet* The news is ~~very~~ bad.
Align	black blue red yellow green

ANSWERS

Delete	̶ffrequently
	ham a̶n̶d̶ and eggs
Close up	nation wide
Delete and close up	worldy̶wide
Insert the correct letter	edit̶r
Lowercase	chairman of the B̶oard
	C̶HAIRMAN OF THE BOARD
Capitalize	mexico
Italics	The Economist (ital)
Boldface	as soon as possible
Transpose the first two words	the Place period at the end.
Spell out	(9) of the soldiers
New paragraph	¶
Hard hyphen	seventy= seven
Soft hyphen	develop̶ ment
Stet—let it stand	The news is v̶e̶r̶y̶ bad. (stet)
Align	black
	blue
	red
	yellow
	green

Instructions: Make the correct editing marks in the following lines and paragraph. The answers follow. If you aren't comfortable using copyediting marks, review the preceding sections. It's all right to have to verify an occasional mark, but you must master the basics before you can proceed.

A. Follow the line-by-line instructions and check your answers.

1. Change to all caps.

    Practice in marking copy

2. Change to caps and lowercase (initial caps).

    PRACTICE IN MARKING COPY

3. Change to italics.

    Practice in Marking Copy

4. Mark for caps and small caps, centered.

    Practice in marking copy

5. Mark for lowercase italics, flush right.

    PRACTICE IN MARKING COPY *(ital)*

6. Mark for boldface, flush left.

    Practice in Marking Copy

ANSWERS _____

1. Practice in marking copy

2. PRACTICE IN MARKING COPY

3. Practice in Marking Copy

4. ⌉Practice in marking copy⌐

5. PRACTICE IN MARKING COPY ⌉

6. ⌈Practice in Marking Copy

B. Read the paragraph through quickly and then use editing marks to carry out the instructions. Remember to mark within the text.

Line 1—Mark a 1-em paragraph indent. Transpose the letters to correct the spelling error.

1. Educators had better mind their own langauge if

Line 2—Delete the repeated word.

2. they are going to to move toward a solution

3. rather than compound the problem. The prize for

Line 4—Delete *the field of.* Add the word *writing* after *educational.*

4. dubious achievement in the field of educational writing

Line 5—Delete the three extra words.

5. went to a vacuous display of Pennsylvania college

6. professor for a vacuous display of word spinning

Line 7—Delete the repeated letters and close up the space.

7. that seemed to be more representatative of the

8. prose we encounter every day than a national

Line 9—Correct the spelling error.

9. record for educational gobbledyggok.

Line 10—Mark a 1-em paragraph indent. Transpose the letters to correct the spelling error.

10. Jargon is a problem in our own patr of the field

Line 11—Delete the *al* from *educational* and mark to close the word up to its comma.

11. of educational, and it is commented on by the

12. reviewers of the four books on instructional

Line 13—Delete the italics from *issue.*

13. theory discussed in this Highlights issue. In

Line 14—Add an *s* to *field.*

14. most field, it is the words that help to make

Line 15—Lowercase the letters of the last word.

15. the specialists Special.

1. ☐Educators had better mind their own langauge if

2. they are going to to move toward a solution

3. rather than compound the problem. The prize for

4. dubious achievement in ~~the field of~~ educational writing

5. went to a ~~vacuous display of~~ Pennsylvania college

6. professor for a vacuous display of word spinning

7. that seemed to be more representatative of the

8. prose we encounter every day than a national

9. record for educational gobbledyggok.

10. ☐Jargon is a problem in our own path of the field

11. of educational, and it is commented on by the

12. reviewers of the four books on instructional

13. theory discussed in this Highlights issue. In

14. most field, it is the words that help to make

15. the specialists sPecial.

Instructions: Use editing marks to correct the following sentences, and then check your answers against the key. Each sentence highlights a particular problem. Although only one solution is given for each sentence, some variations will certainly be correct. Just be sure that you corrected the problem identified in the solution and that you didn't introduce new errors or change the meaning.

1. Catch all misspellings and tpyos.

2. No sentence fragments. Fix run-on sentences, they're hard to read.

3. The cause of the problems in many sentences
   is
   are subject-verb disagreement; subject and
   have
   verb has to agree in person and number.

4. A pronoun must agree with its antecedent.

5. Catch unclear pronoun references For example,
   correct the copy when the pronouns this and
   that are used loosely; careful readers are
   confused by this.

6. Working carefully, dangling participles and
   all misplaced modifiers need correction.

7. You dislike finding fault, but when one sees
   careless shifts of pronoun case, he or she
   can't help complaining.

8. If you have done your job as copyeditor, you ^have
   improved the copy by removing unnecessary verb
   tense shifts.

9. Use the semicolon properly; always use it
   where it's appropriate; and never where it's
   not appropriate.

10. Reserve the apostrophe for it's proper use,
    and omit it when its not needed.

11. Avoid commas, that are not necessary, but be
    sure to put a comma between the two parts of a
    compound sentence.

12. Avoid un/necessary hyphens.

13. Nonparallel construction is faulty,
    undesirable, and ~~don't permit it.~~ *not permitted*

14. ~~Do not~~ leave ~~in~~ *out* words that are ~~not~~ necessary.

15. Strike out redundant tautologies.

16. If you go over your work a second time, you
    will find ~~on going over it~~ that a great deal
    of repetition can be avoided by ~~going over~~
    ~~your work and editing again.~~

17. Smothered verbs are an addition to wordiness; when possible, attend to the improvement of clarity by the replacement of nouns with verbs.

18. In most technical writing, the passive voice is to be avoided.

19. Watch for good word use; steer clear of incorrect forms of verbs that have snuck into the language.

1. Catch all mis~~p~~spellings and t~~y~~pyos.

2. ~~No~~ Don't use sentence fragments. Fix run-on sentences;

   they're hard to read.

3. The cause of the problems in many sentences

   ~~are~~ is subject-verb disagreement; subject and

   verb ~~has~~ have to agree in person and number.

4. A pronoun must agree with ~~their~~ its antecedent.

5. Catch unclear pronoun reference~~.~~s For example,

   correct the copy when the pronouns this and *(ital)*

   (ital) that are used loosely; careful readers are

   confused by ~~this.~~ such usage.

6. Work~~ing~~ carefully; to correct dangling participles and

   all misplaced modifiers ~~need correction.~~

7. You dislike finding fault, but when ~~one~~ you sees

   careless shifts of pronoun case, ~~he or she~~ you

   can't help complaining.

8. If you ~~have done~~ did your job as copyeditor, you

   improved the copy by removing unnecessary verb

   tense shifts.

9. Use the semicolon properly; always use it where it's appropriate, and never where it's not appropriate.

10. Reserve the apostrophe for it's proper use, and omit it when its not needed.

11. Avoid commas, that are not necessary, but be sure to put a comma between the two parts of a compound sentence.

12. Avoid unnecessary hyphens.

13. Nonparallel construction is faulty and undesirable; and don't permit it.

14. Do not leave in words that are not necessary.

15. Strike out redundant tautologies.

16. If you go over your work a second time, you will find on going over it that a great deal of repetition can be avoided by going over your work and editing again.

17. Smothered verbs are an addition to wordiness; when possible, attend to the improvement of clarity by the replacement of nouns with verbs.

18. In most technical writing, ∧ ^avoid^ the passive voice⊙ ~~is to be avoided.~~ ¶

19. Watch for good word use; ^avoid^ ~~steer clear of~~ ¶ incorrect forms of verbs that have ^crept^ ~~snuck~~ into the language.

If you want more practice in marking, turn to appendix A, exercise 2. If you're ready to tackle a longer piece, continue to chapter 4.

An author's greatest fear is to appear, as a result of revision, less than brilliant. The good editor convinces authors that **without** revision their genius will be obscured.

—Arthur Plotnick

COPYEDITING:
Working With Text

4

The more you edit, the easier it becomes. Although at first you may feel that there are too many things to remember, most of the rules and shortcuts eventually become automatic. Don't be overwhelmed. Even experienced editors don't notice or expect to catch every mistake the first time they go through a manuscript. Most editors plan to work through a manuscript at least twice; they want to make three passes if possible.

Until your editing skills are honed, you may want to approach a manuscript by doing one task at a time. For example, devote the first reading to purely mechanical points like spelling, sentence structure, and punctuation. On the second pass, pay more attention to style issues and make sure that your marks are correct. The third time through, pay careful attention to content: Check to see that the piece reads well and that you've respected the author's basic intent and style. During this whole process, but especially during the last pass, you must concentrate. If your mind wanders, you won't be able to edit well.

When you get a manuscript, always check to see that the pages are numbered. If they're not, number them in sequence, beginning with the title page. If you add pages, give them the number of the preceding page plus *a*, *b*, *c*, and so on—for example, 10a, 10b, 10c—and note this number on the preceding page ("p. 10a follows"). If you delete a whole page, mark it with a diagonal line the length of the page. Leave the page in place so that the keyboarder or the author won't look frantically for a "missing" piece of paper or be stuck with text on screen and no place to put it.

Whether you edit in pencil (red or black) or ink depends on whether the material needs to be photocopied or faxed. Some editors hesitate to use pen because it's harder to change the marks once they're made, but it's often better for copies or faxes.

To prevent needless queries, put a check over an unusual spelling or usage. The check means that you verified the rarity.

> ✓
> `Brzezinski`
>
> ✓
> `quark`

Take care of the manuscript; make sure that there's a protection copy (paper or diskette) of anything you send in the mail. Even courier services occasionally lose things.

Don't write vertically on the page. If you create a maze of insertions and deletions or if your handwriting is illegible, rekey; if you rekey, proofread. Similarly, don't print in block letters; distinguish between caps and lowercase. Don't use a capital letter when you want lowercase. Remember that someone will have to interpret your changes. The harder you make this task, the greater the probability of error.

One trick of the editorial trade is to examine layout (the appearance of the piece) and format (indentions, headings, lines, etc.) in a separate pass through the copy. Do all main heads look the same? Are subheads consistent? Are all the paragraphs similarly indented? Are lists consistent or do some start with *1.* and others with *1)*? Do all the tables have the same format, or do they vary unnecessarily? It's extremely difficult, if not impossible, to check format as you edit; you'll overlook too many errors if you try to do too much at once.

When the manuscript you need to edit is as short as the one in exercise 6, it helps to read it through before you make a mark on the page. Such a cursory reading gives you a sense of the author's approach and the content of the piece. The title, appropriately enough, is "Copyediting." For all its typos and omissions (introduced solely for the exercise), the text clearly describes both the copyediting function and your role as copyeditor.

Instructions: Copyedit this article. Pay attention to matters of consistency and to careless errors the author and keyboarder made in preparing this draft. Fix nonparallel constructions; at least query content problems. Watch for grammatical problems and unnecessary passive voice. Use proper editorial marks to show changes. Take as long as you want and try to catch all the errors. Use a dictionary to choose among alternative spellings.

This piece has several headings; decide whether they're main headings or subordinate headings. Distinguish between them by calling main headings A-heads *and subordinate headings* B-heads. *Put A or B in a circle next to each one. (The paragraphs have been numbered to make it easy for you to check your editing against the answer key.)*

COPY-EDITING

1. Copyediting, sometimes called copyreading, is one of the final steps in the edittorial process. To copyredit means to bring a Manuscript in line with goodEnglish usage; make it sytlistically consistent; and, by making minor minor modifications, to enhance it readabilitie. Let us consider of these functions in turn.

2. EnglishUsage. In the English language, there are no absolute rule of grammar, only practices of good usage which are collated and standardize by recognized experts who produce Grammers, dictioneries, and style books. Therefore, the aim of the copy editor is for reasonable, not absolute correctness? English sas a living language is contuna continually changing. A construction that was "bad in

grand fathers day may be permitted today and become "Good" tomorrow. A case in in point is the practice of not ending a sentenxe with a preposition. Today, only the real purists among grammararians insist on following thhat practice ABSOLUTELY. Aboiding a preposition at the end of a often cuases it to be prim, stodgy and stilted. A pertinant old chestnut is credited to Winston Churchills. When he was with confronted with the rule, he wanted to know if would be supposed to say: "That is something up with which i will not put." Many semicolloquial but very communi cative verbs include prepositions. Put up with, of course, one of them.

3. Another exampel of change in usage concerns the split infinitive--an infinative with a word, usually an adverb, inserted between "to" and and the rest of the verb. Split infinatives that are awkward, stilted, and unneccessary should be avoided. however, should transferring the word or wordssplitting an infinative cause a sentence to be

ambiguous, that sentence should either be left as is or recast.

4. The copyeditor must be attentive about various other points, including confusion in the sequence of tenses; lack of agreement in number between subject and verb; and use of pronoun whose ante cedents are not well established. These require a vigilant eye. The primary purpose of the copy in making a manuscript grammatical is to clarefy menaning, not to make the language reach the language reach a given standard of grammarical "purity. Therefor, effectiveness of communication is more important than considerations of grammar. Some authors employ a style that in colloqual to the point of infringing on good usage, although there doubt as to meaning never. For a copyeditor to try to "clean up" a manuscript of such an author is a violation of the author intent and integrety. as an artist. Other writters use a truncated cr staccatto style that does not comform to the conventions of sentence

structure. Here again the copy editor does not interfere or tamper with the authors basic.

5. <u>Consistant Style.</u>   This function of copyediting concerns such questions such as spelling, punktuation, the use of phypens, quotation marks, and italics. Every manuscript willrequire some corrections of this kind. Probably no author scrutinizes the manuscrip with the same care as a copyeditor, becasue the authorcs interest main is content. And some authors, even those who turn in highly acceptable copy, are weak in spelling and the fine points English usage. It is the copyeditors job to be proficient in these matters. Dont be too hesitant or too lazy to look up questionable points or those you don8t know. In fact, if you study you're style book, your eye will be come more alert to things in manuscrip that should be corrected.

6. Readability. This function does not refer to the overall reabibility of the manuscript; it should be assume that judgement on this point was made when the manuscript was excepted. The copyeditor checks certain detales to see

whether minor modifications would bring about improvement in communication. The details which should be checked are the first sentence or paraGraph, to see that the lead is a good one; the conclusion to see that the piece adds up well; and paragraphing and sentence structure through out the paragraphing and sentence structure.

7. The copyeditor should also watch for overly involv sentences. The simply inserting a period and a subject to make two sentences out one will sometimes en hance readability without cramping or changing the writer's stile. There are some writers, even good ones, who are addicted to the "There is" or "There Are" construction. Forms of the verb "to be" are usually weak in a setnence. such sentences may be reconstruct so as to bring foreward a stronger very verb. Part of the copyeditor's job is to check quotations for accuracy.

Copyright

8. It is important also to make sure that no infringements of copy right willl be involved in prnting quotations.

MARKING

9. In reading and marking both copy and proof, the editor use a number os standaerd copyeditor's marks, a kind of shot hand understood by editor's and printer's alike. You should become familiar with these marks as quickly can. Fascimile pages showing edited copy appear in most style books, in many dictioneries, and in grammar texts.

10. Meaning: In all copyediting, be sure not to change in anyway the content of an article or to modefy the authors ideas or style. The temptation of the neophite is to make too many changes in copy. Use your pencil spairingly and have sound reasons for every mark you make and you'll be a good copyeditor.

(Adapted from *Editing the Small Magazine* by Rowena Ferguson. Reprinted with permission.)

Here's a key to the exercise; explanations and some other editing solutions begin below, and then follow parallel to the marked key.

The first style decision you had to make in this exercise was how to treat the title, *Copyediting*, used here as a noun. The one-word form shown is accepted by many dictionaries. The main thing to remember is to be consistent in your treatment of words.

Heads

To mark the head, *Copyediting*, print a capital *A* next to the head, and circle the letter, so that it won't be set: Ⓐ . Because you're already looking at heads, find *English Usage* at the beginning of the second paragraph. This head is subordinate to the first, in that *English Usage* is a topic subsumed by that A-level head. Mark *English Usage* with a *B*, and circle the letter. *Consistent Style, Readability, Copyright, Marking,* and *Meaning* also are B-level heads, to be marked accordingly. As a copyeditor, you may or may not be responsible for adding design specifications, such as paragraph indents, italics, or run-in heads. However, you'll always be expected to mark the level of heads, so that whoever does the formatting can see how many levels there are.

1. Copyediting, sometimes called copyreading, is one of the final steps in the editorial process. To copy-edit means to bring a Manuscript in line with good English usage; make it stylistically consistent; and, by making minor minor modifications, to enhance its readabilitie. Let us consider each of these aspects functions in turn.

Ⓑ

2. English Usage. In the English language, there are no absolute rules of grammar, only practices of good usage which that are collated and standardized by recognized experts who produce Grammers, dictioneries, and style books. Therefore, the aim of the copy editor is for reasonable, not absolute, correctness. English as a living language is contuna continually changing. A construction that was "bad" in grand father's day may be permitted today and become "Good" tomorrow. A case in in point is the practice of not ending a sentenxe with a preposition. Today, only the real purists among grammararians insist on following that practice ABSOLUTELY. Avoiding a preposition at

Paragraph 1: Fix the obvious typographical errors; remember to mark them with delete symbols and close-up hooks, as necessary. Note the unnecessary capital letter and the spacing error. Next, fix the nonparallel construction (two phrases in a series of three contained the word *to;* the middle item didn't). Either insert *to* in the second phrase as shown or delete it from the third (*modifications, enhance its readability*). Then take out the doublet or repeated word. Doublets are easy to miss, although they are less common now that word processing systems beep their outrage when a word appears twice in succession. To correct the last sentence of the paragraph, insert the word *each* or delete the word *of.* Also replace *functions,* which doesn't convey the proper nuance. Copyediting is a function; these three items are aspects, phases, aims, or parts of the job.

Paragraph 2: *English Usage.* You've already marked the head level; be sure to insert the letterspace. Make *rule* plural to agree with its verb, *are.* Use a caret and close-up hooks to attach the *s* to *rule.* You need the same sort of insertion to attach a *d* to *standardize.* Change *which* to *that* to introduce the restrictive clause, one that limits the meaning of the clause that precedes it. (For a discussion of restrictive clauses, see chapter 9.) The rest of the sentence contains mechanical (spelling and capitalization) errors. Especially note, however, the presence of the serial comma after *dictionaries.* You may delete this comma or leave it in: The use or omission of serial commas is a style decision. Whatever decision you make here you must follow consistently throughout the manuscript.

Then you must decide how to treat *copy editor.* In *Webster's Third New International Dictionary,* it appears as two words, but the distinction between *copyediting* and *copy editor* seems odd. Sometimes, consistency rules as it does here. Therefore, we made *copyeditor* one word. In the same sentence, the word *for* becomes extraneous if you insert a comma to set off the phrase in apposition (explaining *reasonable*). The single comma after *reasonable* is incorrect. Appositives are usually (but not always) set off by commas; see chapter 10. The sentence wasn't a question, so replace the question mark with a period. Note that, when you delete the *s* at the beginning of *as,* you don't need to delete the space; a simple delete symbol suffices at the beginning of a word.

Add a closing quotation mark after the word *bad* or underscore or italicize such usage. However you handle emphasis within a manuscript, be sure to do it consistently for similar uses, such as the complementing word *good.* *Grand fathers* needs close-up hooks and an apostrophe. For the apostrophe, be sure to place your caret carefully, so that the apostrophe will end up before the *s* and not after it.

The next sentence contains a doublet and a misspelling. The *real purists* sentence has two more misspellings (both of which require delete symbols and close-up hooks) and a whole word capitalized. Lowercase *ABSOLUTELY* by using the slash with a "hat" that continues to the end of the word.

the end of a ^sentence often cuases it to be prim,
stodgy,and stilted. A pertinant old chestnut
is credited to Winston Churchills. When he
was with confronted with the rule, he wanted
to know if would be supposed to [asked whether he should] say; "That is
something up with which i will not put." Many
semicolloquial but very communicative verbs
include prepositions. Put up with, of course, is
one of them.

3. Another exampel of change in usage concerns
the split infinitive--an infinative with a
word, usually an adverb, inserted between "to"
and and the rest of the verb. Split
infinatives that are awkward, stilted, and
unneccessary should be avoided. however,
should transferring the word or wordssplitting
an infinative cause a sentence to be
ambiguous, that sentence should either be left
as is or recast.

4. The copyeditor must be attentive about [to] various
other points, including confusion in the
sequence of tenses; lack of agreement in
number between subject and verb; and use of

After fixing *Aboiding*, note that a word was omitted. Use a caret to insert it, transpose the letters in *cuases*, and insert the serial comma, if that's your chosen style.

The *chestnut* phrase carries the uncommon meaning of an old joke or story and is unnecessary to the sense of the text. Nor does it contribute to the paragraph. Because the accompanying sentences are somewhat wordy anyway, edit a little more heavily.

```
Winston Churchill, when confronted with the
rule, asked whether he should say, "That is
something up with which I will not put."
```

Carefully note all the marks in this passage, especially the delete symbol and close-up mark at the end of *Churchills*, and the comma after *say*. A direct quotation is usually preceded by a comma, not a colon, unless the citation is long (an extract) and block-indented rather than marked with quotation marks.

As for changing *i* to *I*, remember that, except for obvious typos (which this one is), you should leave quoted material alone. Some journals and newspapers follow a "don't-embarrass-your-contributor" policy and readily admit to changing quotations. As a rule, however, it's best to get permission before making such changes, which can have legal and ethical ramifications.

For consistency, delete the italics and put the phrase *put up with* in quotation marks. If you chose to italicize *bad* and *good* earlier, italicize this phrase as well. Just be sure that you treat emphasis in the same way throughout the piece. Complete the paragraph by adding *is*; carefully place a caret at the appropriate place in the line.

Paragraph 3: The first sentence contains a transposition, a substitution to correct a misspelling, a doublet, and an em-dash notation. Automatically marking dashes and hyphens to prevent any misunderstanding is a good habit. The next sentence contains another misspelling; a serial comma that should be retained or deleted, depending on the choice you made earlier; and an extra letter.

The last sentence in the paragraph also contains several errors: *However* needs an initial capital letter, two words are run together, *infinitive* is misspelled again, and the word *either* needs to be moved so that the *either* and the *or* are followed by similar constructions.

```
...that sentence should be either left as is or
recast...
...that sentence should either be left as is or be
recast...
```

pronouns whose antecedents are not well
established. These require a vigilant eye.
The primary purpose of the copy in making a
manuscript grammatical is to clarefy
meaning, not to make the language reach the
language reach a given standard of
grammatical "purity." Therefor, effectiveness
of communication is more important than
considerations of grammar. Some authors
employ a style that in colloquial to the point
of infringing on good usage, although there
doubt as to meaning never. For a copyeditor
to try to "clean up" a manuscript of such an
author is a violation of the author intent
and integrety as an artist. Other writters
use a truncated or staccatto style that does
not comform to the conventions of sentence
structure. Here again the copy editor does
not interfere or tamper with the author's basic.

5. Consistant Style. This function of
copyediting concerns such questions such as
spelling, punctuation, the use of phypens,
quotation marks, and italics. Every manuscript
will require some corrections of this kind.

Paragraph 4: Persons are not *attentive about;* they are *attentive to,* or, perhaps better, *they attend to.* The semicolons in this sentence can be replaced by commas; the general rule is to use semicolons to separate elements in a series when there is interior punctuation or when the elements are long. In this sentence, the items are relatively short, and the distinction is not crucial. Delete *in number;* the phrase is redundant. The only thing subject and verb agree on is number. *Pronoun* needs an *s* with close-up hooks (because the *s* goes at the end of the word), and *ante cedents* needs to be closed.

The next sentence contains a pronoun without an antecedent: What does *these* refer to? The nearest plural noun is *antecedents,* which are not what the sentence is about. *Problems* will work, although other words, such as *points* or *issues,* will do as well.

Complete the word *copyeditor* so the following sentence has meaning. Three words are misspelled in that sentence: For two of them, substitution alone is sufficient; for the third, you need to delete and close up. Delete the doublet as well. To complete the sentence, note that *purity* has a beginning, but not an ending, quotation mark. You could just as easily delete the beginning quotation mark as add an ending one; the difference is a subtle shift in emphasis.

The next sentence has only one spelling error: *therefore* needs an *e.* The two misspellings in the following sentence are easy to correct, but the last phrase requires a little thought. Some rewriting would be helpful, but with *is* and a transposition, the sentence does makes sense.

```
Some authors employ a style that is colloquial
to the point of infringing on good usage, al-
though the meaning is never in doubt.
```

Author needs an *'s* twice in the next sentence (in the first case, because of the transposition), and there are two other errors: a misspelled word and an extra period. *Writters* and *staccatto* require delete symbols and close-up hooks; two other misspellings require only substitution.

In the last sentence of the paragraph, add an apostrophe to form the possessive for *author* and add a word to complete the thought.

Probably no author scrutinizes the manuscript with the same care as a copyeditor, because the author's main interest is content. And some authors, even those who turn in highly acceptable copy, are weak in spelling and the fine points of English usage. It is the copyeditor's job to be proficient in these matters. Copyeditors should be neither too hesitant, nor too lazy to look up questionable points or those they don't know. In fact, Copyeditors who study their style book will become more alert to things in manuscript that should be corrected.

6. B Readability. This aspect does not refer to the overall readability of the manuscript; it should be assumed that judgement on this point was made when the manuscript was accepted. The copyeditor checks certain details to see whether minor modifications would improve communication. The details that should be checked are the first sentence or paragraph, to see that the lead is a good one; the conclusion, to see that the piece adds up well; and the paragraphing and

Paragraph 5: For the head, *Consistent Style,* which you have already marked with a circled *B*, correct the misspelling, delete part of the underscore (it's too long), and delete part of the space following the period.

The text, again, is discussing an aspect, not a function; the other problems are obvious, except perhaps for the addition of *and.* The key reflects one possible treatment of the items in a list; the sentence might be even clearer if semicolons were used:

```
This aspect of copyediting concerns such ques-
tions as spelling; punctuation; and the use of
hyphens, quotation marks, and italics.
```

Add a space mark (⟋) at the beginning of the next sentence. You may think that spacing is corrected automatically, but that correction is unlikely: Keyboarders don't make corrections that aren't marked. Spacing errors continually reappear until someone marks them.

The errors in the *Every* and *Probably* sentences are obvious and easily corrected. Note the *t* with the close-up hooks, the two transpositions, and the apostrophe in *author's.* In the next two sentences, the errors are also quite clear, but the last three sentences of the paragraph are choppy, with a change in person. Up to this point, the whole manuscript has been in the third person; copyeditors do this, and then they do that. *You* has not been used until now. To make the text consistent, edit the sentence into the third person.

```
Copyeditors should be neither too hesitant nor
too lazy to look up questionable points or
those they don't know.  In fact, copyeditors
who study their style books will become more
alert to things in manuscripts that should be
corrected.
```

The other corrections in the sentences are mechanical.

Paragraph 6: You've already marked *Readability* with a circled *B*.

Readability isn't a function either; edit to *aspect* or something similar. Of the next four misspellings, only *judgement* warrants comment: American dictionaries list *judgment* as the preferred spelling; use it instead of its variant.

The next sentence has a smothered verb (*would bring about improvement* readily becomes *would improve*). *Which should be checked* is a restrictive clause, limiting the meaning of *details.* Use the word *that* to introduce the clause, and don't set it off with commas. Last, you need to make the elements in the sentence parallel.

sentence structure through out, the
to see that the parts work well together
~~paragraphing and sentence structure.~~

7. The copyeditor should also watch for overly
involv*ed* sentences. ~~The~~ simply inserting a
period and a subject to make two sentences out *of*
one will sometimes en hance readability
without cramping or changing the writer's
st*y*le. ~~There are~~ some writers, even good
ones, ~~who~~ are addicted to the "There is"
or "There Are" construction. Forms of the
verb "to be" are usually weak in a setnence.
such sentences may be reconstruct*ed* ~~so as~~ to
bring foreward a stronger ~~very~~ verb. Part of
the copyeditor's job is to check quotations
for accuracy.

(move OK?)

These sections are not mentioned in lead paragraph. Add an explanation or delete?

Ⓑ ¶ Copyright⊙

8. It is *important* *also* to make sure that no
infringements of copy right will be involved
in prnting quotations.

Ⓑ ¶ MARKING⊙

(OK as edited?)

9. In reading and marking ~~both~~ *the* copy ~~and proof,~~
~~the~~ editor*s* use a number of standaerd
copyeditor's marks, a kind of shot hand
understood by editor's and printer's alike.

Paragraph 7: The first two sentences contain simple errors. Be sure that you made your marks correctly. Then look at the third sentence; deleting *There are* produces a much stronger sentence. The rest of the corrections here are straightforward.

The last sentence (about checking quotations) doesn't belong in this paragraph or in a section called *Readability*. As a matter of fact, it may not even belong in this text, because it isn't mentioned in the lead or first paragraph of this exercise, the one that discussed *English usage, stylistic consistency,* and *readability*. That paragraph didn't say a word about *Copyright* (or about the following sections, *Marking* and *Meaning*).

One of the rules of good writing is that a lead paragraph outlines what the text intends to discuss or prove. There should be no surprises for the reader. As a copyeditor, you can only point out such a discrepancy, either to the author or to your supervisor. You shouldn't rewrite, unless given permission to do so. Therefore, write a note in the margin or on a query sheet to explain the problem.

You've already marked the B-level head, *Copyright.*

Paragraph 8: The editorial corrections in this paragraph are mechanical.

Marking. This head, now labeled *B,* may not belong in the piece either, as the query notes.

Paragraph 9: Note that deletion of the words *and proof* changes the meaning of the first phrase. As a copyeditor, you should probably query rather than delete this phrase, but you know that the editor doesn't normally see proof, but rather works on the copy earlier in the production cycle. Otherwise, the corrections in the sentence are fairly mechanical. Be sure to fix the change in person also.

Editors
~~You~~ should become familiar with these marks as

quickly ~~can~~ as possible. Fascimile pages showing edited

copy appear in most style books, in many
a
dictionaries, and in grammar texts.

10. Meaning: In all copyediting, editors should be sure not to

change in any way the content of an article or

~~to~~ modify the author's ideas or style. The

temptation of the neophyte is to make too many

changes in copy. Copyeditors should, their ~~Use your~~ pencils sparingly

and have sound reasons for every mark ~~you~~ they make.

~~and you'll be a good copyeditor.~~

Paragraph 10: *Meaning.* Here's another B-level head that, according to the lead paragraph at least, doesn't belong. Aside from the misspelled words and the spacing errors, you need to fix the change in person throughout the paragraph, especially the imperative in the last sentence. The solution in the key shifts the meaning somewhat, but without the imperative there's no good way to capture the injunction of the original.

Check the key to make sure you understand all the marks and the reasons for them. If anything is unclear to you, review chapter 3.

Don't be discouraged if this exercise took you a long time. Aim for accuracy, not speed. The exercises in this book require more work and more marks than an ordinary manuscript. Remember also that you'll pick up speed as you gain practice.

On average, an experienced copyeditor can edit about six pages of double-spaced text an hour. It will take longer to edit a poorly written manuscript and extensive references, footnotes, or tables.

As an editor, you should plan to make at least three passes through a manuscript, although you won't always have the time. You'll develop your own approaches to a manuscript and your own shortcuts.

The publications world is full of deadlines; there never seems to be enough time, even when a manuscript is short. Journalists and proposal writers and editors are especially pressed and can seldom give a manuscript more than one reading. You'll catch about 75 percent of the errors on one pass. By slowing down and being very careful or by choosing to ignore certain issues, you can probably raise that figure to 80 percent. The trade-off here is time (or money) versus thoroughness; and the answer depends on the situation.

It helps if you can put a manuscript aside for a little while and make a final pass later. Though such scrutiny is rarely possible, another editor should look over the work when you finish; another pair of eyes will always find some error that managed to creep in or slip by.

The copyeditor's role

What do copyeditors do? First and last, they follow instructions. They determine the author's meaning and clarify it where possible. They never change the meaning; where the meaning is ambiguous, they query. They bring problems or issues to the attention of the author or their supervisor. They attempt to make a manuscript be all that the author meant it to be.

What sorts of problems do copyeditors look for?

- Errors in grammar, punctuation, spelling, and sentence structure: basically, departures from the hard-and-fast rules of the English language.

- Style problems in the largest sense: wordiness, nonparallel construction, poor word choice, and excessive use of the passive voice.

- Style decisions dictated by the choice of a style manual: treatment of numbers, capitalization, abbreviations, and so on.

- More difficult issues: bias, sexism, inaccuracies, inconsistencies, misquotations, illegality (use of copyrighted material without permission).

This description is by no means exhaustive, but it does highlight duties and responsibilities.

The following section contains a list of copyediting tasks that should help you focus your efforts for each pass through the manuscript. This list is fairly extensive; not all the entries apply to every manuscript. Someone, probably the editing manager or supervisor, should examine each project and determine the level of effort required and time allowed.

The editor's checklist you'll find at the end of this chapter contains all the points discussed here. Such a checklist eliminates detailed and sometimes confusing verbal instructions and provides a record for both the editor and the manager. Use the checklist to organize your own editing assignments.

General Procedures Required on All Jobs

- Write neatly and legibly.

- Use standard editing marks.

- Show additions and changes above the lines, not below.

- Make an alphabetical list of all words in the manuscript about which you have made a choice of treatment (hyphens, caps, abbreviations, etc.).

- Number all pages sequentially. Indicate added pages by adding *a, b, c,* etc., to the preceding page number.

Minimal Copyediting Tasks on All Jobs

Any copyeditor always addresses the points listed below. Notice that re-writing and reorganization are not allowed. Copyediting is a limited function; the checklist helps restrain copyeditors from doing too much.

1. Review and correct spelling, grammar, and punctuation.

2. Correct inconsistencies in capitalization, compounding, number style, abbreviations, use of italics or underscores, and sequence of anything alphabetical or numerical.

3. Point out, but do not rewrite, awkward, turgid, confusing sections.

4. Point out, but do not fix, major organizational problems.

Additional Copyediting Tasks

For specific jobs, you may be assigned any or all the parts of this section.

5. Check heads in text and tables against the table of contents.

   Not all manuscripts have a table of contents, nor do they necessarily require one. However, if there is a table of contents, its entries must match the text headings exactly. If you find a discrepancy and can't determine which version—text or table of contents—is correct, you must query the author.

6. Make table of contents.

   Editors are sometimes asked to compile a table of contents or a list of tables or figures after editing. If you have this task, find out from the author or supervisor how detailed the contents should be. Then list the titles and headings exactly as they appear in the text. An easy way to differentiate A- and B-heads is by indenting:

   Introduction

   Background

   Method

   Experiments

7. Format.

   Renumber footnotes. Renumber pages. Mark heads (A, B, C; 1, 2, 3, etc.).

   Always check to see that footnotes are sequential; substantive editing may have eliminated or added some footnotes so that the rest need to be renumbered. Copyeditors are also expected to mark head levels: Main heads are level A or level 1, subtopics or subheads are level B or level 2, and so on. Rarely does a manuscript have more than four levels of heads. When you come to a head, decide which level it is and place an A or B or whatever in a circle next to the head. Eventually, the designer or supervisor will tell the keyboarder how to treat each level. (For example, all A-heads may be boldface, initial caps, centered; all B-heads may be flush left.) Copyeditors usually don't have to instruct keyboarders on format except in the most general terms.

8. Mark end-of-line hyphens.

   As discussed in chapter 3, a hyphen can appear at the end of a line for two reasons: when an unhyphenated word is broken because it's too long to fit on a line (soft hyphen) and when a hyphenated word is broken at the hyphen (hard hyphen) for the same reason.

   Before the class was dismissed for the day, the professor outlined for us the process of calci-fication.   (*soft hyphen*)

   or

   I was pleased that he had improved his self-image by cultivating good work habits.
   (*hard hyphen*)

End-of-line hyphens cause problems—as text moves, soft hyphens are supposed to go away; hard ones are to be retained. The problem, of course, is that the hyphens that are supposed to be dropped frequently aren't; the ones that are supposed to remain frequently don't; every hyphen you see merits a second look.

Although word processing programs distinguish between soft and hard hyphens, the keyboarder must sometimes enter an extra code for a hard hyphen.

Some authors, designers, and keyboarders sidestep the problem by deciding that the text will have no words broken at the ends of lines, thus producing text with a *ragged right* margin. Also, material that is to be sent over a modem to be typeset or set from disk probably won't have end-of-line hyphens.

9. Put into a specific style: __GPO __Chicago __Other.

   Not all manuscripts require that you follow a particular style manual; for some, it's sufficient that the copy be internally consistent. (Chapter 11 discusses style in depth.)

10. Put all tables into consistent, proper form; ensure parallelism within and among tables.

    The best way to ensure parallelism within and among tables is to look at them together, away from the text. With the tables side by side on your desk, compare their format. Are the titles set up the same way? Do the headings match, or are some caps and lowercase and some all caps? Are there rules in some but not in others? If you have specifications for the tables, were they followed? If not, make the tables consistent.

    Looking at all the tables together increases your efficiency. You don't have to remember what the earlier ones looked like; you simply compare them.

    Be sure that the title reflects the material in the table accurately. Check all math; query if your answers deviate from the author's.

11. Check parallelism throughout the text; revise when necessary to make elements in a series parallel. Be sure all lists are consistent in format.

    Most people instinctively want to fix parallelism problems. Pay special attention to lists.

12. Check pronouns to make sure all have clear antecedents; replace them with nouns or rewrite as needed.

Agreement of pronouns and their antecedents gives rise to many questions. Patterns that are acceptable in speech aren't always acceptable in writing, although authors may state (and rightly) that the meaning is clear. From a grammatical point of view, however, the noun that a pronoun is meant to replace is often not clear; in these cases, clarification by the author or the editor is essential.

13. Check passive constructions; whenever appropriate, try to replace with active voice.

Some authors are especially fond of the passive voice (in which the subject of the sentence isn't the doer of the action, but rather is acted upon). Although passive voice has a clearly defined place in the language, the passive voice is less forceful than the active. Notice that the checklist says to replace with active voice *whenever appropriate*. The active voice isn't always appropriate, nor is it possible to rephrase every sentence to accommodate the active voice. (See chapter 6 for a full discussion.)

14. Eliminate smothered verbs. Rewrite to break up noun strings.

This item deals with word choices; smothered verbs are those buried in a sea of nouns, like *make reference to* instead of *refer* or *make a study of* instead of *study*. Noun strings, on the other hand, are just that: nouns used as modifiers as in *District employee residency law requirement*. What does this phrase mean? After three readings, you're still not sure. Smothered verbs and noun strings obscure meaning; eliminate both, except in technical or scientific writing where noun strings are sometimes part of the idiom and can't be replaced without loss of meaning. (See chapter 12 for a discussion of smothered verbs and noun strings.)

15. Remove first person (*I* and *we*) throughout the manuscript except in the preface or foreword.

Many manuscripts written in the first person are very effective. Some, however, have an *I* thrown in only once in a while. As copyeditor, you'll often be instructed to remove such references.

16. Eliminate sexist language.

Whenever possible, you should replace nouns and pronouns of gender with neutral, nonsexist terms: *Salesman* becomes *salesperson*, *newspaperman* becomes *journalist*, and so on.

17. Explain unfamiliar acronyms and abbreviations at first mention.

Technical writing especially is full of such shortened forms. As a rule, use the complete form at first mention, with the acronym or abbreviation in parentheses following it. In subsequent references you can use the shortened form alone or you may wish to employ the long form occasionally.

18. Substitute one word for many, short words for long.

This straightforward injunction asks you to eliminate wordiness and, where possible, to prefer the plain word. Simple language isn't always preferable, but it often is. (See chapter 12.)

19. Make sure each table, chart, or footnote is called out and arranged in correct sequence.

The existence of every table, chart, or footnote must be noted in text before the referenced item appears. The first text reference is termed a *callout*. Often, with revisions or editing, paragraphs are moved or merged, and callouts get scrambled. To associate callouts with their figures quickly and accurately, copyeditors should note the first mention of each table, chart, or footnote (*T.1* or *fn 1*, for example) in the margin or else use a highlighter to mark the item. Always circle such notations, so no one incorporates your notes into the text by mistake.

20. Check cross-references for accuracy and consistency.

If the text refers the reader to appendix A for information or an explanation, you must verify that there is indeed an appendix A and that appendix A contains what was promised. If the author cites Smith 1986 in the text, be sure the reference list also contains this citation. The spelling of the author's name and the date of publication must match exactly.

Checking references usually requires a separate step and is very time-consuming; but if reference citations are inaccurate or incomplete, the author risks being thought careless. However good the content, it will not stand up to scrutiny if the references are sloppy.

21. Put bibliography and footnotes in consistent format.

Arrange references, bibliography, and footnotes according to a particular format (style). Style manuals give extensive rules for the treatment of these subjects. (See chapter 13.)

Heavier, More Substantive Editing, Rewriting, and Related Tasks

This section concerns more substantive tasks than those normally assigned to a copyeditor, although you may be instructed to do some of the tasks listed here, such as numbers 22 and 23.

22. Check math, numbers, problems, answers to questions in exercises.
23. Check descriptions of tables in text against information on tables themselves.
24. Review whole manuscript for sentences, paragraphs, portions that can be eliminated.
25. Add or delete heads and subheads as necessary.
26. Check organization and reorganize if necessary.
27. Rewrite awkward, turgid, confusing sections.
28. Review logic of arguments; look for weak points.
29. Write transitions.
30. Write summaries for chapters, sections, or the entire document.
31. Check accuracy of content (editor is expected to be familiar with subject).

Manuscript _____   Editor _____
Date _____   Reviewer _____

Editor's Checklist

A. General Procedures Required on All Jobs

- Write neatly and legibly.
- Use standard editing marks.
- Show additions and changes above the lines, not below.
- Make alphabetical list of all words in ms. about which you have made a choice of treatment re: consistency in hyphens, caps, abbreviations, etc.
- Number all pages sequentially. Indicate added pages by adding a, b, c, etc., to the preceding page number.

B. Minimal Copyediting Tasks on All Jobs

1. ____ Review and correct spelling, grammar, and punctuation.
2. ____ Correct inconsistencies in capitalization, compounding, number style, abbreviations, use of italics or underscores, and sequence of anything alphabetical or numerical.
3. ____ Point out, but do *not* rewrite, awkward, turgid, confusing sections.
4. ____ Point out, but do not fix, major organizational problems.

C. Additional Copyediting Tasks Specified for This Job

5. ____ Check heads in text and tables against table of contents; make the same or query.
6. ____ Make table of contents. _____Make list of tables.
7. ____ Format. _____Renumber footnotes. _____Renumber pages. _____Mark heads (A,B,C; 1,2,3; etc.) _____Add keyboarder/typesetter instructions. Other: _____
8. ____ Mark end-of-line hyphens to be deleted or retained.
9. ____ Put into a specific style: GPO_____ Chicago_____ Other_____
10. ____ Put all tables in consistent, proper form; ensure parallelism within and among tables.
11. ____ Check parallelism throughout text; rewrite when necessary to make elements in series parallel. Be sure all lists are consistent in format.
12. ____ Check pronouns; make sure all have clear antecedents; replace with nouns or rewrite.
13. ____ Check passive constructions; whenever appropriate, try to replace with active voice.
14. ____ Eliminate smothered verbs. _____Rewrite to break up noun strings.
15. ____ Remove first person throughout manuscript. _____Remove except for preface/foreword.
16. ____ Eliminate sexist language.
17. ____ Explain unfamiliar acronyms and abbreviations at first mention.
18. ____ Substitute one word for many; short words for long.
19. ____ Make sure all referenced matter (tables, charts, footnotes, etc.) follows its first callout.
20. ____ Check cross-references for accuracy and consistency.
21. ____ Put bibliography and footnotes in consistent format: Chicago_____APA_____Other_____

D. Heavier, More Substantive Editing, Rewriting, and Related Tasks

22. ____ Check math, numbers, problems, answers to questions in exercises.
23. ____ Check descriptions of tables in text against information on tables themselves.
24. ____ Review whole manuscript for sentences, paragraphs, portions that can be eliminated.
25. ____ Add or delete heads and subheads as necessary.
26. ____ Check organization and reorganize if necessary.
27. ____ Rewrite awkward, turgid, confusing sections.
28. ____ Review logic of arguments; look for weak points.
29. ____ Write transitions.
30. ____ Write summaries (_____for chapters/sections; _____for entire document).
31. ____ Check accuracy of content (editor is expected to be familiar with subject).

Word-carpentry is like any other
kind of carpentry: you must join
your sentences smoothly.

—Anatole France

SUBJECTS AND VERBS: They *Will* Agree

5

A sentence has two parts: a subject and a predicate. The subject, in the form of a noun or pronoun, identifies what the sentence is about, and the predicate contains a verb—an action word (*run*) or a description of a state of being (*is*). Most nouns, pronouns, and verbs in the English language have singular and plural forms. The subject determines whether the verb should be singular or plural; agreement means that a singular subject takes a singular verb and a plural subject takes a plural verb. How could anything so straightforward cause difficulty?

Many factors combine to obscure the relationship between a subject and its verb. Inverted sentences and collective nouns tend to mask their subjects; prepositional phrases coming between a subject and verb confuse the issue. Here are some basic rules.

1. The following pronouns take singular verbs.

anybody	every	no one
anyone	everybody	one
each	everyone	somebody
either	neither	someone
	nobody	

Each of the projects is done.

Everybody likes Suzy.

Anyone who wants to come is welcome.

One pronoun missing from this list is *none*, because *none* can take either a singular or a plural verb, depending on the context. When *none* means *not one*, it takes a singular verb; when it means *not any*, it takes a plural verb.

None of the apples is big enough.

None of the apples are Jonathans.

2. Plurals of Latin and Greek words take plural verbs.

```
criteria are            media are

curricula are           phenomena are

data are
```

Some newspaper styles specifically cite *data* and *media* (meaning the press, TV, etc.) as singular, because their traditional singular forms (*datum* and *medium*) no longer appear in that usage. *Criteria, phenomena,* and *curricula* are all plural, and *every* style treats them as plural, although you may see these words used (erroneously) as if they were singular.

3. *A number of* takes a plural verb; *the number of* takes a singular verb. Don't try to extend this rule to other nouns; it works only for *number*.

```
A number of people were at the craft fair.

The number of commitments we have prevents us
from accepting your kind invitation.
```

4. A compound subject takes a plural verb.

```
Blue and gold are her favorite colors.

Vanity and stupidity mark his character.
```

5. A compound subject joined by *or* takes a verb that agrees with the subject closest to the verb.

```
Supplies or money was always lacking.

Money or supplies were always lacking.

Adjustments or questions concerning your bill
do not relieve you of late-payment charges.
```

Pay attention to euphony when editing. If the plural verb "sounds" or "reads" better, transpose the order of the subjects, as shown in the *supplies or money* sentence.

6. Correlative expressions are used in pairs (*either...or* and *neither...nor*) and follow rule 5.

> Either the children or the dog is always clamor-
> ing for attention.

> Neither his brother nor his parents were will-
> ing to lend him any more money.

7. Some subjects appear compound but aren't. Prepositional phrases such as *in addition to, as well as,* or *along with* don't control the number of the verb.

> Vanity as well as stupidity marks his character.

The real subject here is *Vanity*, which is singular. Note that this sentence could also have commas.

> Vanity, as well as stupidity, marks his
> character.

8. Nouns that are plural in form but singular in meaning usually take singular verbs. Here are some examples; when in doubt, consult your dictionary.

> Bad news travels fast.

> Physics is required of all chemistry majors.

The following words are regularly treated as singular.

aesthetics	measles
astronautics	mumps
economics	news
genetics	physics
linguistics	semantics
mathematics	

And the following words are regularly treated as plural.

blue jeans   suds

scissors   trousers

slacks

9. Some nouns can take either singular or plural verbs. A few nouns that end in *ics*, such as *athletics*, *acoustics*, and *statistics*, are considered singular when referring to an organized body of knowledge and plural when referring to qualities, activities, or individual facts.

Statistics is challenging at all levels.

Statistics prove that women live longer than men.

Acoustics is recommended for all third-year students.

The acoustics in the theater are very good.

A collective noun defines a group that is thought of as a unit or functions as a unit. Collective nouns, when singular, require a singular verb; when a collective noun is made plural (*team, teams*), the noun requires a plural verb. Here are some examples of singular collective nouns.

army	crowd	herd	orchestra
audience	den	jury	platoon
band	faculty	league	public
chorus	family	majority	quartet
class	flock	membership	staff
clergy	gang	mob	team
community	government	navy	variety
council	group		

Ask yourself whether the group in question is functioning as a unit in the sentence: The group must behave as a group.

```
The team refuses to practice in the rain.

The jury decides whether a defendant is inno-
cent or guilty.
```

In the first example, the team is unanimously rebelling against getting wet. In the second one, the jury's decision must be unanimous. The jury must behave as a group, so the verb must be singular.

Note, however, that a singular collective noun that clearly refers to members of a group as individuals requires a plural verb.

```
The faculty have been assigned to various
committees.
```

All the members of the faculty are not on several committees; each member of the faculty has been assigned to one committee, or perhaps two. Look at another example.

```
The orchestra are going to their homes after
the performance.
```

The members of the orchestra don't all live in the same place; they're going in different directions, so the plural verb is necessary. If the plural noun seems awkward (and it often does), insert *members of* before the collective noun.

```
The members of the faculty have been
assigned to various committees.

The members of the orchestra are going to their
homes after the performance.
```

Collective nouns do have plural forms: The plural of *flock* is *flocks*. When such nouns are plural, you must use a plural verb.

```
Many flocks of birds fly south about the first
of October.
```

Here are some sentences to test what you've learned about subject-verb agreement. Work the following exercise and check your answers.

Instructions: Select the correct word to fill in the blanks. Fix anything else that's wrong (spelling, punctuation, incorrect word, etc.).

1. The Stars and Stripes ____ (was, were) raised at Iwo Jima.

2. There ____ (is, are) many a good shell to be found on that beach.

3. More than one argument ____ (was, were) cited by the defense attorney.

4. One of the unhappy children who ____ (comes, come) from that troubled family ____ (is, are) being treated for depression.

5. What kind of dietary restrictions ____ (does, do) your patients have?

6. Each of my children ____ (has, have) ____ (his, their) own strengths and weaknesses.

7. The data we have gathered from our samplings ____ (shows, show) that the voters, especially those in the Midwest, ____ (needs, need) to be reassured about recent changes in the tax laws.

8. Information about housing units that ____ (has, have) recently been released can be ordered from the Center.

9. So little consumer goods ____ (is, are) produced there that the standard of living remains low.

10. The media ____ (is, are) present in force outside the courtroom.

11. Mothers Against Drunk Driving, an organization of concerned citizens, ____ (is, are) soliciting funds to support ____ (its, their) efforts to influence legislation.

12. There ____ (is, are) fewer tickets available than there were last year.

13. The list of participants ____ (was, were) arranged in alphabetical order.

14. Steak as well as sausages ____ (was, were) served at the barbecue.

15. Imposition of restrictions on smoking, together with efforts aimed at educating the public, _____ (promise, promises) us a less polluted environment.

16. A number of résumés ____ (was, were) received at the office today.

17. The number of persons being treated at the clinic sometimes _____ (prevents, prevent) us from completing our billing on time.

18. To move into a new house and to make new friends _____ (requires, require) a great deal of effort.

19. Whether the House will pass the bill and whether the president will veto it, _____ (remains, remain) to be seen.

20. The complexity of the problem, and the need to keep pace with technology, _____ (presents, present) the company with many difficult choices.

ANSWERS

1. The Stars and Stripes <u>was</u> raised at Iwo Jima.

   One flag, familiarly called the Stars and Stripes, was raised.

2. There <u>is</u> many a good shell to be found on that beach.

   The *there is* (or *it is*) construction is usually unnecessary. Prose is much tighter without it. The subject of the sentence is *shell*, not *there*. You can thus edit one step further.

   Many a good shell is to be found on that beach.

3. More than one argument <u>was</u> cited by the

   defense attorney.

   More than one argument is the complete subject, which is logically plural. But what's really under discussion in this sentence is *one* presentation (which included arguments).

4. One of the unhappy children who <u>come</u> from that

   troubled family <u>is</u> being treated for

   depression.

   The subject of the main clause is *one,* so the main verb, *is,* is singular. In the subordinate clause, you have to determine the antecedent of *who* and make the verb agree with that word. The antecedent, of course, is *children.* It helps to pretend that the sentence starts with the *of* phrase.

   Of the unhappy children who come from that

   troubled family, one is being treated for

   depression.

   You needn't actually edit this way; just do the mental exercise to determine the correct verb form.

5. What kind of dietary restrictions <u>do</u> your

   patients have?

   The sentence is a question, and the subject follows the verb. The subject is *patients,* and therefore the verb must be plural. If this kind of sentence confuses you, turn it around.

   Your patients do have what kind of dietary

   restrictions.

6. Each of my children <u>has</u> strengths and

   weaknesses.

   You know, of course, that *each* is the subject and that *each* takes a singular verb. We deleted the pronoun because it was not necessary to show possession. If it is necessary, the pronoun must agree in number with its antecedent.

   Each of my children has *his* own strengths and

   weaknesses.

   Perhaps the parent in the sentence has only sons, in which case *his* is correct. Suppose, however, that this person has a child of each gender; then what should you use? Editors and society generally have been wrestling with this problem for several years, and the use of *their* in this case has become widespread. But *their*, a plural pronoun, can't refer to a singular antecedent. Sidestep the problem if you can. Here are some other solutions.

   Each of my children has (individual/particu-

   lar/specific) strengths and weaknesses.

   (Both/All) my children have their own

   strengths and weaknesses.

7. The data we have gathered from our samplings

   <u>show</u> that the voters, especially those in the

   Midwest, <u>need</u> to be reassured about recent

   changes in the tax laws.

   The word *data* is generally recognized as grammatically plural and thus requires a plural verb, but some journalistic style guides specify *data* as singular. If your organization relies on one of these guides, by all means use a singular verb, but remember that not everybody agrees. The subject of the subordinate clause is *voters*, which also needs a plural verb.

8. Information about housing units that <u>have</u>

   recently been released can be ordered from the

   Center.

   At first glance, it appears that *information* was released. Structurally and grammatically, however, the *units* have been released. The antecedent of *that* is *units*, so you need the plural verb. This sentence actually came from a directive issued by the Department of Housing and Urban Development; units were indeed released for occupancy, not information.

   Suppose for a moment that *information* was released. Can you rewrite the sentence to reflect this fact?

   Information that has been recently released

   about housing units can be ordered from the

   Center.

   Here, the antecedent of *that* is *information*, and the singular verb is correct. Everything depends on the context. But what about this sentence?

   Order information from the Center about hous-

   ing units that were recently released.

   Now the antecedent is *units*, and the plural verb is correct.

9. So few consumer goods <u>are</u> produced there that

   the standard of living remains low.

   The subject of the sentence is *goods*, which demands a plural verb. Note the change of *little* to *few*. *Little* refers to volume and *few* refers to numbers.

10. The media <u>are</u> present in force outside the

    courtroom.

    Media, of course, is plural, except in some journalistic styles.

11. Mothers Against Drunk Driving, an organization of concerned citizens, <u>is</u> soliciting funds to support <u>its</u> efforts to influence legislation.

The subject is one organization, soliciting as a group. The pronoun *its* also must agree with the singular antecedent.

12. There <u>are</u> fewer tickets available than there were last year.

Invert the sentence to find the subject. You may want to delete the words *there are*. Much depends on the flow of the rest of the paragraph, and it's hard to decide when the sentence is out of context.

13. The list of participants <u>was</u> arranged in alphabetical order.

The subject of the sentence is *list*, which is singular.

14. Steak as well as sausages <u>was</u> served at the barbecue.

Steak...was served. The intervening prepositional phrase doesn't affect the number of the verb.

15. Imposition of restrictions on smoking, together with efforts aimed at educating the public, <u>promises</u> us a less polluted environment.

The subject of the sentence is *imposition*. The intervening words don't change the number of the verb.

16. A number of résumés <u>were</u> received at the office today.

A number of takes a plural verb; the sense of the sentence is that many résumés were received.

17. The number of persons being treated at the clinic sometimes <u>prevents</u> us from completing our billing on time.

The number of takes a singular verb.

18. To move into a new house and to make new friends <u>require</u> a great deal of effort.

A compound subject joined by *and* (two infinitive phrases, *to move* and *to make*) requires a plural verb.

19. Whether the House will pass the bill and whether the president will veto it <u>remain</u> to be seen.

This sentence contains another compound subject joined by *and* (*Whether...and whether*), so you need a plural verb. The comma in the original is incorrect; a comma should never separate the parts of a compound subject, and normally a comma shouldn't separate a subject from its verb.

20. The complexity of the problem and the need to keep pace with technology <u>present</u> the company with many difficult choices.

You need a plural verb to agree with the compound subject—*The complexity* and *the need*. This sentence resembles the previous one; you should have deleted the commas.

In summary, subject-verb agreement isn't a simple topic; subjects hide among prepositional phrases or on the "wrong" side of the verb. As an editor, you must always be alert to hidden subjects. For more practice, turn to appendix A, exercise 3. Or you may continue on to chapter 6.

The difference between the right word and
the almost-right word is the difference
between "lightning" and "lightning bug."
—Mark Twain

ACTIVE AND PASSIVE VOICE: Who's Doing What

6

Verbs convey action in two ways—active or passive voice. If the subject of a sentence performs the action of the sentence (*John caught the ball*), the verb is in the active voice. If the subject receives the action (*The ball was caught by John*), the verb is passive.

Active voice tends to be more forceful and less wordy than the passive. The passive voice always has a helping verb and often contains the prepositional phrase *by* someone or something. Some editors automatically remove all passives.

You can, however, carry your dislike of the passive voice to extremes. The passive has its place and in some cases may even be preferred. If the emphasis is on the thing done, rather than on the doer, for example, use the passive voice. Here are some examples.

```
Medea killed her children.

The children were killed by Medea.
```

The first sentence emphasizes Medea. The second emphasizes her children, the victims.

```
He told me to get out.

I was told to get out.
```

The second sentence is much less forceful than the first. The passive voice here allows you to make a statement in a more tentative way than the active. When you read the passive, the emotional content is lacking. Editors want each sentence to carry its own weight, to tell clearly who did what to whom.

Intentionally or not, the passive voice often obscures the doer: No one takes responsibility for the action. Layers and layers of passives in a document make it difficult to determine accountability (or guilt). Events seem to take on a life of their own, with no one acting or reacting. In committees and representative bodies, bills are discussed, laws are passed, rumors are circulated, and no names are mentioned. The passive can guarantee anonymity. Sometimes this anonymity is inadvertent; sometimes it's exactly what the writer intends.

But the passive does have its place. In technical or scientific material, the actor (or researcher) may be unimportant: The emphasis is on the mice that were fed saccharin and observed to die. It may be best to leave such passives alone and focus on the procedures and the results themselves, unless you can edit to emphasize the mice: "The mice ingested..., measurable tumors appeared..., the mice died." But few scientific writers will yield that power to an editor.

The rhythm of the language or the flow of a paragraph may lend itself to the passive.

```
Though the night was made for loving
And the day returns too soon,
```

Think twice before you automatically excise a passive. Where does the author *want* the emphasis of the sentence? Editing requires weighing alternatives. With that thought in mind, do exercise 8. Remember that in the active voice, the subject is doing the acting. In the passive voice, the subject is being acted upon.

Instructions: Change the following sentences from passive to active voice. (There may be more than one correct way to rephrase each.) You may have to add a subject to do the acting, and you should also fix any other editorial problems you see.

1. ~~The~~ *The lobbyist wrote most of* regulation ~~was mainly written by the lobbyist~~.

2. *We are* ~~Consideration is being given to~~ *considering* your proposal. *We are considering*

3. *The company is organizing* A national network of technical assistance providers ~~will be organized~~.

4. *We are developing* *The agency* Publications ~~have been developed~~ to address changes in regulations.

5. Since that time, *the agency has issued* changes ~~have been issued~~ to amend the original publications.

6. ~~A series of technical seminars was sponsored~~ *The T & D ofc. sponsored a series of tech. seminars.* ~~by the Training and Development Office.~~

7. *Ms. Bellamy will* ~~Management of~~ *manage* the Credit Department ~~will be the responsibility of Ms. Bellamy.~~

8. *The new staff memb. will* ~~Implementation of~~ *implement* the guidelines ~~will be carried out by the new staff members.~~

9. *You* ~~It can be~~ reasonably expect ~~that~~ the program will ~~not~~ be evaluated ~~until~~ *in* 1999.

10. *Congress will call on* The Attorney General's Office and its representatives *will* ~~are going to be called upon~~ to give *their* ~~its~~ opinion.

11. ~~When~~ a member, *when he* ~~is~~ to be dropped from the union rolls, ~~he will~~ be notified by the appropriate authority.

12. Recommendations by the Zoning Commission for waivers (may ~~be~~ disapproved ~~by~~ the Board of Supervisors.

13. The date of entry into the school system will ~~be shown on~~ the transfer form.

ANSWERS

The lobbyist wrote most of,

1. The regulation ~~was mainly written by the lobbyist~~.

The lobbyist wrote most of the regulation.

You didn't have to add a subject because the prepositional phrase *by the lobbyist* named the subject for you.

We are *ing*

2. Consideration ~~is being given to~~ your proposal.

We are considering your proposal.

Here you needed to add a subject. The context normally dictates your choice; lacking a context, you could have picked any reasonable noun or pronoun.

The company will organize,   *providers of*

3. A national network of technical assistance~~ providers will be organized~~.

The company will organize a national network

of providers of technical assistance.

This sentence also required you to add a subject. In addition, you should at least consider eliminating the noun string as we've done. However, if *technical assistance providers* is commonly understood by your audience, don't change it.

The agency,

4. Publications ~~have been~~ developed to address

changes in regulations.

The agency has developed publications to ad-

dress changes in regulations.

This sentence seemed to have an official sound; hence, we used the more official subject (*agency*), although the word *we* certainly makes sense as well. If it isn't clear from the context who or what developed the publications or issued the changes, you must leave the sentence alone.

the agency

5. Since that time, changes ~~have been~~ issued to

amend the original publications.

Since that time, the agency has issued changes

to amend the original publications.

This sentence seemed to follow the last one. In this exercise, you have the leeway to add a subject; in a manuscript with no author guidance, you might have to leave the passive alone for lack of a subject.

6. A series of technical seminars was sponsored by the Training and Development Office.

   The Training and Development Office sponsored

   a series of technical seminars.

   The office that sponsors the series should be the subject.

7. Management of the Credit Department will be

   the responsibility of Ms. Bellamy.

   Ms. Bellamy will be responsible for managing

   the Credit Department.

   Here, replacing some of the nouns with verbs produces a more forceful sentence.

8. Implementation of the guidelines will be

   carried out by the new staff members.

   The new staff members will implement the guide-

   lines.

   As you see, removing the passive voice and correcting wordiness noticeably shorten the sentence.

9. It can be reasonably expected that the program

   will not be evaluated until 1999.

   This sentence is perhaps best left alone or, if the context gives a clue as to who is going to do the evaluating, changed only minimally.

```
A reasonable expectation is that we will not

be able to evaluate the program until 1999.
```

You may have been tempted to delete *expected* (or *expectation*), but such a revision might not be wise. Apparently, the 1999 date for the evaluation is not yet firm. The two words *reasonably expected* seem to constitute a sort of disclaimer.

Sentences like this are difficult to handle, and you must always be wary of subtly shifting the meaning.

Congress will call on,

```
10. The Attorney General's Office and its

    representatives ~~are going to be called upon~~ to
                an
    give ~~its~~ opinion.
```

```
Congress will call on the Attorney General's

Office and its representatives to give an opin-

ion.
```

We needed to choose someone to do the action. Congress is a likely subject, but it could just as easily be the president or another government agency.

In this sentence, did you notice that the second *its* didn't have a proper antecedent? Will the Office alone issue an opinion? Not according to the sentence. Some editing is therefore necessary. Another possible version, depending on the context, follows.

```
Congress will call on the Attorney General's

Office and its representatives to give their

opinions.
```

The appropriate authority,

11. ~~When~~ a member, *who about* is to be dropped from the union
    rolls, ~~he~~ ~~will~~ ~~be~~ ~~notified~~ ~~by~~ ~~the~~ ~~appropriate~~
    ~~authority~~.

    The appropriate authority will notify a member
    who is about to be dropped from the union
    rolls.

    Avoid the question of whether all the union members are male. Experienced editors develop creativity in sidestepping *he/she, him/her* constructions.

12. ~~Recommendations~~ ~~by~~ ~~the~~ ~~Zoning~~ ~~Commission~~ ~~for~~
    waivers ~~may~~ ~~be~~ disapproved ~~by~~ the Board of
    Supervisors. */that the Zoning Commission recommends.*

    The Board of Supervisors may disapprove waivers that the Zoning Commission recommends.

    This sentence required a little more editing. Other versions are certainly possible. Be sure that the flow of the edited sentence is better than the original and that the relationship among the parts is clearer.

Show

13. The date of entry into the school system ~~will?~~

~~be shown~~ on the transfer form.

Show the date of entry into the school system

on the transfer form.

The date of entry into the school system will

be shown on the transfer form.

The transfer form will show the date of entry

into the school system.

You can argue that the sentence is best left alone because there's no obvious subject. If the sentence is part of instructions, you can use the imperative, as shown in the first solution. If the text merely describes the information on the form, use the second.

Remember to weigh the alternatives carefully before you automatically change passive voice to active. If you want more practice with passive constructions, turn to appendix A, exercise 4. Or continue on to chapter 7.

E diting your own work is like removing your own tonsils—possible but painful.
—Anonymous

PRONOUNS: Case and Number Agreement

7

A pronoun is a word used in place of a noun; using a pronoun allows writers and speakers to avoid repeating the noun. Pronouns change their form (*case*) depending on their use in a sentence. English has three cases: nominative, objective, and possessive. Anyone who took high school Latin remembers cases; Latin has five. English, as it has evolved, has eliminated Latin's dative and ablative cases, as well as most other case forms—except those for pronouns. English uses the nominative case for subjects of sentences and for predicate nominatives. The objective case is for objects of prepositions and direct and indirect objects of verbs. The possessive case denotes adjectives.

CASE

Nominative	Objective	Possessive	
		(modifying)	(standing alone)
I	me	my	mine
you	you	your	yours
he	him	his	his
she	her	her	hers
it	it	its	its
we	us	our	ours
you	you	your	yours
they	them	their	theirs
who	whom	whose	whose
whoever	whomever		

Here are some examples of pronouns in each case.

Nominative case

```
Give this message to whoever answers the phone.
```

Whoever is the subject of the subordinate clause (*whoever answers the phone*) and is in the nominative case.

```
It was she who was late for school.
```

The predicate nominative *she* is the antecedent of *who*, which is the subject of the subordinate clause (*who was late for school*). Thus, both pronouns must take the nominative case.

```
He and his sister are going to camp for two
weeks.
```

The pronoun *He* is part of the compound subject.

Objective case

```
Allen Jones is the candidate whom we want to
support for the Senate.
```

Whom is actually the direct object of the verb *support* (we want to support *whom*); as a relative pronoun, *whom* forms a bridge between the two clauses in the sentence.

```
The race ended in a tie between you and me.
```

The two pronouns are the objects of the preposition *between*; they must be in the objective case.

```
The editor offered him the assignment.
```

Him is the indirect object of the verb *offered*, the object of the (understood) preposition *to*.

```
The editor offered the assignment (to) him.
```

Possessive case

```
Whose dog is barking?
```

```
The dog is chewing on its bone.
```

Whose is the possessive form of the relative pronoun *who*, used here to modify *dog*. *Its*, as a possessive, has no apostrophe.

It's is the contraction of *it is*; the apostrophe denotes a missing letter. Confusion of *its* and *it's* is quite common, as evidenced by this headline in a major newspaper: "At the top of *it's* class..."

```
      ʒ         ✓              O
   Do you object to my borrowing your dictionary?
```

Before a gerund (an *-ing* form of a verb used as a noun), use a possessive pronoun. Although *borrowing* is a verb form, its use here as a noun requires an adjective. *Your* shows possession of the dictionary.

```
             ✓              O
   Don't forget that it's mine.
```

Mine is a predicate adjective, a possessive, representing *my dictionary.*

Most of the time, your ear will tell you which form of the pronoun is correct. The use of *who* and *whom*, however, poses special problems. Maxwell Nurnberg, in his book *Questions You Always Wanted to Ask About English*, offers a workable, nontechnical solution to this problem, best discussed in the context of a sentence.

```
   Give me one example of someone (who, whom) you
   think was rewarded and not penalized for con-
   fessing.
```

Nurnberg's approach has three steps: First, consider only the words that follow *who* or *whom*. This approach leaves you with

```
   you think  __she__ was rewarded...
```

Notice that there's a gap in thought, emphasized here with the underlined space. Fill that gap with either *he* (*she*) or *him* (*her*), whichever is correct and makes sense.

```
   you think he was rewarded...
```

Replace *he* with *who* (the nominative case). This trick works every time.

```
   Give me one example of someone who you think
   was rewarded and not penalized for confessing.
```

Try Nurnberg's formula in exercise 9.

Instructions: Fill in the blanks with the correct pronoun (who or whom, unless otherwise specified).

1. They should give a trophy to _____ (whoever, whomever) the coaches choose as the most valuable player.

2. *Whom* do you think they'll choose to be May Queen?

3. It's not for me to say *who* should be punished for breaking the window.

4. The butler intoned, "*Who* may I say is calling?"

5. We'll send a complimentary copy of the directory to _____ (whoever, whomever) responds to the survey.

6. They asked the branch chief *who* on the staff might be the source of the security leak.

7. Senator Janeway is the man *whom* we want to nominate.

8. Moreover, we'll sell the house to _____ (whoever, whomever) meets our price.

9. Remember, it doesn't matter *whom* you like; it's _____ you know.

1. They should give a trophy to <u>whomever</u> the coaches choose as the most valuable player.

   The coaches choose <u>him</u>...

   The correct answer is *whomever*.

2. <u>Whom</u> do you think they'll choose to be May Queen?

   Questions are easier to deal with when you invert them.

   you think they will choose <u>her</u>...

   The answer is *whom*.

3. It's not for me to say <u>who</u> should be punished for breaking the window.

   Who is the subject of the verb *should be punished*.

4. The butler intoned, "<u>Who</u> may I say is calling?"

   In the movies, perfect secretaries and perfect butlers always say, *"Whom* shall I say is calling?"* but this version isn't correct. Apply Nurnberg's rule.

   I may say <u>he</u> is calling

   Or delete the phrase between the subject and the verb.

   <u>Who</u> is calling?

   Put this way, it becomes clear that *who* is correct.

5. We'll send a complimentary copy of the

   directory to <u>whoever</u> responds to the survey.

   The word *to* may be confusing.

   <u>he</u> responds to the survey

   Whoever is the subject of the verb *responds* and takes the nominative case. The whole clause *whoever responds to the survey* is the object of the preposition *to*.

6. They asked the branch chief <u>who</u> on the staff

   might be the source of the security leak.

   Drop the words between the subject and verb.

   <u>he</u> might be the source

   The subject is *who*.

7. Senator Janeway is the man <u>whom</u> we want to

   nominate.

   we want to nominate <u>him</u>

   Obviously, you have to use *whom*.

8. Moreover, we'll sell the house to <u>whoever</u>

   meets our price.

   Whenever a relative pronoun appears to be the object of a preposition, study the sentence carefully. *Whoever* is actually the subject of the subordinate clause, hence, the nominative case. Again, the whole clause is the object of the preposition.

9. Remember, it doesn't matter <u>whom</u> you like;

   it's <u>whom</u> you know.

   you like <u>him</u>...; you know <u>him</u>

   Both clauses require *whom*.

Remember that an antecedent is the word to which a pronoun refers; each pronoun should have a clear and immediate antecedent. Grammatically, a pronoun should refer to the closest noun that has the same number as the pronoun. An antecedent can be in a preceding sentence but not normally in a preceding paragraph. Here are some simple examples.

    My mother said she would call tonight.

    The child whom we hope to adopt is named
    Elizabeth.

    The insurance company dispatches its adjusters
    whenever disaster strikes.

In these examples, there's only one possible antecedent for each pronoun. Difficulties arise, however, when a pronoun can refer to more than one antecedent.

    Susan is a marvelous dancer and so is her
    sister. She has the lead in the senior play.

The first sentence in this example is clear, but whom does *she* refer to in the second sentence? Logically, the antecedent is probably *Susan*, but grammatically *she* refers to *sister*.

    There was a large walnut orchard behind our
    house. At dusk, the trees would be silhouetted
    against the sky. One summer day, however, it
    was bulldozed to make room for a car dealership.

In the third sentence, a problem arises with the antecedent of *it*. Logically, it's clear that the orchard was bulldozed, not the day or the sky. However, grammatically, either of those two words could be the antecedent of *it*. To make the sentence correct as well as clear, *it* should be replaced by *the orchard*.

Theoretically, the antecedent of a pronoun shouldn't be an idea: Everyone would agree with this. But what is the antecedent of *this* in the previous sentence? Not *idea*, but the concept that an antecedent shouldn't be an idea. Such usage is common in spoken English but not always acceptable in careful writing. Here are a few more examples.

```
My son plays football, which upsets his
grandmother.

Only 10 persons have turned in the assignment;
this is unacceptable.

Our son got second place in the science fair;
this made us very proud.
```

In each of these examples, the pronoun refers to an idea; football doesn't upset Grandmother, but the fact that her grandson plays does. If the sentence is perfectly clear, many editors leave such constructions alone, especially if changing them makes the sentence awkward or unnecessarily wordy.

We should make another point in this discussion of antecedents: An antecedent must be a noun, not a possessive adjective.

```
In Professor Walker's class, he discusses Ren-
aissance comedy.
```

What's the antecedent of *he*? It can't be *Professor Walker's*; that phrase functions as a possessive adjective. The sentence therefore has to be rewritten.

```
In his class, Professor Walker discusses
Renaissance comedy.
```

To repeat the rules, (1) a pronoun needs a clear antecedent, and (2) the pronoun must agree with its antecedent in number, gender, and person. A plural pronoun can't refer to a singular antecedent, nor can a feminine pronoun refer to a masculine antecedent. Adhering to these rules isn't as easy as it seems. Consider the following examples.

```
The restaurant has added eclairs and fruit
tarts to its dessert menu.

The employees voiced their protests.

Everyone entered her office and turned on her
computer.

Each dancer bowed as she left the stage.
```

```
Each cadet must present his rifle for
inspection.

Everyone should buy their color TV here.
```

Certainly, no one can object to the first two examples, but look at the third. Many people speaking informally use *their*, not *her*, in this instance. But *their* is plural and shouldn't be used with the singular antecedent *everyone*. Without digressing into a long discussion on neutral language, note that in bygone days the generic *he* encompassed men and women, as in the following examples.

```
He who hesitates is lost.

He who laughs last laughs best.

Everyone went into his office and turned on his
computer.
```

This solution is no longer considered acceptable, and the best way to solve the problem is to sidestep it.

```
People who hesitate are lost.

Those who laugh last laugh best.

People went into their offices and turned on
their computers.
```

In the fourth and fifth examples, remember that *his* or *her* alone is perfectly correct if the context shows clearly that persons of only one sex are involved.

If the sentence is referring to cadets at an all-male military school, *his* is proper and you should leave the pronoun alone. But many cadets at West Point and the Air Force Academy are women; you may need to recast the sentence.

This last example came from an advertising campaign and should be recast to avoid the problem.

```
Everyone should buy a color TV here.
```

All of the sentences in the following exercise are comprehensible when spoken but less acceptable in careful writing. The context will often direct you to the antecedent, but complex sentences or technical writing may seem unclear. In such cases, you must either query the author or, if the author is not available, leave the usage alone. With this injunction in mind, do exercise 10.

Instructions: Correct the following sentences and make sure that each pronoun has one clear, appropriate antecedent.

1. In any gathering they attended, John always
   monopolized the conversation; this ~~habit~~ annoyed his
   wife.

2. The person who cooks doesn't do the dishes,
   (which seems to be fair to me.) *I think this is fair.*

3. ~~We decided to~~ vacation ~~in Europe; this~~ seemed
   a European *on a*
   like a good idea at the time.

4. We bought *Chinese* take-out food ~~at the Chinese~~
   ~~restaurant~~, which was very expensive and
   tasted terrible.

5. Julie was accepted at Princeton, which greatly
   pleased her grandfather.

6. This army travels on ~~their~~ *its* stomach.

7. Anyone can do it if ~~they try~~ *she tries*.

8. Just before Christmas, everyone is running
   around spending ~~their~~ money.

9. Their ~~is a friendship spanning~~ three
   generations, ~~which~~ *friendship* is most unusual.

10. Don't drink and drive; this *activity* could be hazardous
    to your health.

ANSWERS

The context or the flow of a particular paragraph often dictates the choice of words or the form of the sentence. Sometimes, trying to eliminate ambiguity leads to a wordier, more awkward sentence. In each case you must decide whether the revision is in fact an improvement. Only some of the possible alternatives for the following sentences are listed here.

1. In any gathering they attended, John always
   monopolized the conversation; this *habit* annoyed his
   wife.

This sentence is clear as it stands, but you can also add the noun *habit*.

Alternative:

In any gathering they attended, John always

monopolized the conversation; this habit

annoyed his wife.

2. The person who cooks doesn't do the dishes,
   ~~which~~ *this division of labor* seems ~~to be~~ fair to me.

The person who cooks doesn't do the dishes;

this division of labor seems fair to me.

The antecedent of *which* is an idea, not the preceding noun. Thus for formal writing you need to add a noun and repunctuate the sentence. For informal writing, you could break the sentence after *dishes* and treat the rest as an aside.

Alternative:

The person who cooks doesn't do the dishes—

which seems fair to me.

3. We decided to vacation in Europe; ~~this~~ *the trip* seemed
   like a good idea at the time.

Again, the sentence is clear as it stands, but you could also change *this* to *the trip*.

Alternative:

We decided to vacation in Europe; the trip

seemed like a good idea at the time.

4. We bought ~~The~~ take-out food at the Chinese

restaurant, ~~which~~ was very expensive and

tasted terrible.

The take-out food we bought at the Chinese res-

taurant was very expensive and tasted terrible.

Alternative:

We found the take-out food from the Chinese

restaurant both expensive and unappetizing.

5. Julie ~~was~~ accept*ance* at Princeton, ~~which~~ greatly

pleased her grandfather.

This sentence is clear, but alternatives are also possible.

Alternatives:

Julie's acceptance at Princeton greatly

pleased her grandfather.

The fact that Julie was accepted at Princeton

greatly pleased her grandfather.

6. This army travels on ~~their~~ *its* stomach.

This army travels on its stomach.

7. Anyone *who tries* can do it. ~~if they try.~~

   Anyone who tries can do it.

8. Just before Christmas, everyone is running

   around spending ~~their~~ money.

   Just before Christmas, everyone is running

   around spending money.

   Eliminating the possessive adjective doesn't affect the meaning here.

9. Theirs is a friendship spanning three

   generations, ~~which~~ *such a bond* is most unusual.

   Alternatives:

   Theirs is a friendship spanning three genera-

   tions; such a bond is most unusual.

   Trying to compress the two clauses leads to a slight shift in meaning.

   Their friendship, which spans three genera-

   tions, is most unusual.

10. Don't drink and drive; this *combination* could be hazardous

    to your health.

    Don't drink and drive; this combination could

    be hazardous to your health.

The following exercise puts antecedent problems into the sort of material
that might appear in an advertisement or brochure.

Instructions: Read through the following exercise, noting pronoun problems. Circle each unclear antecedent and note any other problems. Most readers will find this piece comprehensible, although ungrammatical.

The first site plan in this series illustrates the most common layout for a neighborhood shopping center. They are one-story units averaging 600 feet and having six to eight stores which are usually constructed in suburban areas.

The best example of this kind of layout is the Marwick model, which is a tribute to his architectural prowess in this field. If you look at it, you will note that the drug and grocery stores are at either end. The others are in the middle. Loading docks are at the rear of these. This is as it should be, because no matter how effective your management program is, tenants are careless about their trash, and it will always be there, and that is an eyesore.

This model has easy ingress and egress and convenient, close parking spaces. Marwick takes care to build his centers so that handicapped persons can park there and use them. They do

not, however, block delivery service routes to
the rear of the building.

A word about drive-in banks—this tenant will
pay high rents when they are interested in
locating in a good center. The advantage is
that they will bring people to your center.
It will cause traffic snarls, though, especially on paydays, so you should plan ahead
and consider building it on the end.

If you use the Marwick and other models as
guides as you are planning, you will find that
it will help you to avoid these problems.

The first site plan in this series illustrates

the most common layout for a neighborhood shop-

ping center. (They) are one-story units averag-

square feet?

ing 600 <u>feet</u> and having six to eight stores

(which) are usually constructed in suburban

areas.

The best example of this kind of layout is the

can a model be a tribute?   whose?

<u>Marwick</u> model, which is a tribute to (his) archi-

what field?

tectural prowess in (this) field.   If you look

Is Marwick an architect, a builder, or a developer?

at (it), you will note that the drug and grocery

end of what?   which others?

stores are at either <u>end</u>.   The (others) are in

of what?

the <u>middle</u>.   Loading docks are at the rear of

(these). (This) is as (it) should be, because no

matter how effective your management

program is, tenants are careless about their

where?

trash, and it will always be (there) and (that)

is an eyesore.

model or site plan?
Shopping center built according to this model?

This <u>model</u> has easy ingress and egress and con-

to what?

venient, <u>close</u> parking spaces.   Marwick takes

care to build his centers so that handicapped

where? centers or spaces?

persons can park (there) and use (them). (They) do

not, however, block delivery service routes to
the rear of the building.

A word about drive-in banks—*this* tenant will
pay high rents when *they* are interested in
locating in a good center. The advantage is
that *they* will bring people to your center.
It will cause traffic snarls, though, especially on paydays, so you should plan ahead
and consider building *it* on the end.

singular - referring to a plural antecedent

end of what?

If you use the Marwick and other models as
guides as you are planning, you will find that
it will help you to avoid these problems.

Because so much ambiguity can exist, even in writing that is neither complex nor technical, you should always be alert to antecedent problems. Iden-
tifying them can be tricky, however, because spoken and written usage in
English diverge. Understanding a sentence's meaning doesn't normally
justify ambiguity. If antecedents are unclear, fix those you can and query
those you can't.

The English-speaking world can be divided into five categories: those who neither know nor care what a split infinitive is; those who do not know, but care very much; those who know and condemn; those who know and approve; and those who know and distinguish.

—H. W. Fowler

PARALLELISM: A Delicate Balance

8

Put simply, parallelism means that parts of a sentence similar in meaning are similar in construction. To achieve parallelism, writers and editors balance a word with another word, a phrase with another phrase, an infinitive with another infinitive, and so on.

Poets and public speakers use parallel construction extensively.

```
We cannot dedicate, we cannot consecrate, we
cannot hallow this ground.

I come to bury Caesar, not to praise him.
```

Here are some guidelines for parallel construction.

1. A noun and an infinitive aren't parallel.

```
The duties of the proposal manager were the
coordination of the production and to write
the executive summary.

The duties of the proposal manager were to
coordinate the production and to write the
executive summary.
```

It's better to say *to coordinate* than to introduce another smothered verb (i.e., *the writing of*).

2. A gerund and a noun aren't parallel.

```
You may earn extra credit by writing a report
or the submission of a completed reading list.

You may earn extra credit by writing a report
or submitting a completed reading list.
```

Two gerunds (*writing* and *submitting*) make the sentence parallel.

3. A gerund and an infinitive aren't parallel.

My daughter was more interested in <u>daydreaming</u> than <u>to do</u> her chores.

My daughter was more interested in <u>daydreaming</u> than in <u>doing</u> her chores.

To be parallel, *doing* must be used to balance *daydreaming*.

4. A noun and a clause aren't parallel.

The training director is responsible <u>for plan- ning</u> the curriculum and <u>that the courses should run smoothly</u>.

The training director is responsible for <u>plan- ning</u> the curriculum and <u>ensuring</u> that the courses run smoothly.

5. Items in a list should be made parallel.

The preflight checklist included the following:
- Secure the outside doors,
- All luggage must be stowed under the seats and not in the aisles,
- All seats must be in the upright position; and
- that the flight attendants should be seated.

Not only must all the elements in a list begin with the same part of speech, but the beginning capitalization and ending punctuation must also be con- sistent. You can correct the example as follows.

The preflight checklist included the following directions:
- Secure the outside doors.
- Stow all luggage under the seats and not in the aisles.
- Place all seats in the upright position.
- Tell the flight attendants to sit down.

All items now begin with a capital letter and verb and end with a period. The list is thus parallel.

6. An article or a preposition that applies to a series must either be used before the first item or else be repeated before each item.

```
The objectives were to cut off the enemy's
supply routes, demoralize the population, and
to support the existing government.
```

```
The objectives were to cut off the enemy's
supply routes, to demoralize the population,
and to support the existing government.
```

Add the word *to* before the second phrase (or delete it from the third) to make this sentence parallel.

7. Correlative expressions (*both...and, not only...but also,* and *either...or*) must be followed by the same construction.

```
Either you must follow the doctor's
advice or bear the consequences.
```

```
Either you must follow the doctor's
advice or you must bear the consequences.
```

```
Not only must you fill out your form
correctly, but also pay your taxes.
```

```
Not only must you fill out your form
correctly, but you must also pay your taxes.
```

```
Both the Senate and House of Representatives
agreed to the postponement.
```

```
Both the Senate and the House of Representa-
tives agreed to the postponement.
```

These general rules govern parallel construction. Most of the time, your ear will guide you. Parallelism pleases; the lack of it jars.

An exercise to practice what you've learned follows.

Instructions: Correct these sentences as necessary to make them parallel.

1. James likes to read, to swim, and playing soccer.

2. When you finish the test, check it for errors and that your name is [at] the top.

3. You will be advised when a court date is either set or the charges are dropped.

4. Not only did she scream at the children constantly, but she would also hit them.

5. Her Christmas list included a set of skis, a pair of boots, and money.

6. In this workshop, we will discuss the following topics:

   > The importance of location in commercial development

   > The elements that determine location

   > What about utilities?

   > Requirements for parking

   > Planning fringe space.

7. Either he should give up or try harder.

8. The successful applicant should present a
   professional image, impeccable credentials,
   and ~~should have a minimum of~~ six years of
   supervisory experience.

9. This retirement community offers ~~the~~ *the following:*
   ~~advantages of~~ a secure building, ~~the presence~~ *the opp to*
   of a congenial staff, transfer~~ring~~ to a
   medical facility if necessary, and giv~~ing~~ *away to* your
   for your loved ones peace of mind.

ANSWERS

The answers we give in the following key aren't the only possibilities; they're simply the ones that occurred to us.

1. James likes to read, to swim, and playing soccer. *(handwritten: "to" inserted before "playing", "ing" and "s" struck)*

   James likes to read, to swim, and to play soccer.

   Alternative:

   James likes reading, swimming, and playing soccer.

   Three infinitives or three gerunds solve the problem.

2. When you finish the test, check it for errors and that your name is at the top. *(handwritten: "see" inserted before "that")*

   When you finish the test, check it for errors and see that your name is at the top.

   Making both parts into imperatives seems the best solution.

3. You will be advised when a court date is either set or the charges are dropped. *(handwritten: "either that" above "when"; "is" struck; "has been" below "either" which is struck; "that" inserted; "have been" above "are" which is struck)*

   You will be advised either that a court date has been set or that the charges have been dropped.

   Remember that what follows *either* must also follow *or;* thus, the word *that* is repeated.

4. Not only did she scream at the children

    constantly, but she ~~would~~ also hit them.

    Not only did she scream at the children

    constantly, but she also hit them.

    If you want to convey the repetitiveness of the action, you should use the conditional (*would*) in both clauses:

    Not only would she scream at the children con-

    stantly, but she would also hit them.

5. Her Christmas list included ~~a set of~~ skis, a

    ~~pair of~~ boots, and money.

    Her Christmas list included skis, boots, and

    money.

    The word *money* doesn't lend itself to descriptors as the other terms do, so each word in the series needs to stand alone.

6. In this workshop, we will discuss ~~the~~ *Commercial development:*

    ~~following topics:~~

    ~~The importance of location in commercial~~

    ~~development~~

    ~~The elements that determine location~~

    ~~What about utilities?~~

    ~~Requirements for~~ parking

    ~~Planning~~ fringe space

```
In this workshop, we will discuss commercial

development:

        Location

        Utilities

        Parking

        Fringe space
```

Each item in this list needs to begin and end similarly and still make sense. The best way to approach such a list is to put the topic (*commercial development*) in the lead sentence. Notice the combination of the first two elements: Both discussed a facet of location.

This solution proposes no ending punctuation. Some style guides recommend internal and ending punctuation, and some don't. Nor is it essential that each item in the list begin with a capital letter. However, the elements (including their punctuation and capital letters) must be consistent among themselves. And although one publication may have several kinds of lists that may vary in style according to their complexity, the capitalization and punctuation (or lack of it) should be consistent within each type.

```
7.   Either he should give up or try harder.

     He should either give up or try harder.
```

Alternative:

```
     Either he should give up or he should try

     harder.
```

```
8.   The successful applicant should  have present  a

     professional image, impeccable credentials,

     and  should have  a minimum of six years of

     supervisory experience.
```

The successful applicant should have a professional image, impeccable credentials, and a
minimum of six years of supervisory experience.

9. This retirement community offers the following
   advantages: of a secure building, the presence
   of a congenial staff, transferring to a
   medical facility if necessary, and giving your
   loved ones peace of mind. for your loved ones

   This retirement community offers the following
   advantages: a secure building, a congenial
   staff, transfer to a medical facility if necessary, and peace of mind for your loved ones.

   Examples like this from the advertising world require a slightly heavier edit to make them parallel.

To summarize, parallel construction helps clarify meaning by imposing similar grammatical construction on parts of a whole. Parallelism can also emphasize ideas (or a relationship between them) and can keep complicated
sentences from being unnecessarily confusing. Lack of parallelism strikes a
sour note for listeners or readers and diminishes effectiveness. Appendix A,
exercise 5, will give you more practice in parallelism if you wish.

He that uses many words for the
explaining of any subject doth, like
the cuttlefish, hide himself for the most part in
his own ink.

—*John Ray*

MODIFIERS: They Dangle, Squint, and Get Lost

9

A modifier is a word, phrase, or clause that adds descriptive detail to another word, phrase, or clause. Modifiers can be adjectives, adverbs, appositives, or clauses.

Adjective:

> The <u>chattering</u> bird hopped swiftly across the grass.

Adjectival phrase:

> <u>Pale with fright</u>, Hansel and Gretel cowered in the corner.

Adverb:

> She looked <u>hopefully</u> through the employment ads.

Adverbial clause:

> <u>Although her work is good</u>, she needs to improve her attendance.

Appositive:

> John Wilkes Booth, <u>the brother of Edwin Booth</u>, shot Lincoln.

Clause:

> The dress <u>that she chose</u> made her look older.

The last example points to another characteristic of certain modifiers: They can be either restrictive (essential) or nonrestrictive (nonessential). A restrictive modifier limits the meaning of a term; without the modifier, the sentence could be ambiguous or could have a different meaning. Restrictive modifiers aren't set off by commas. Here are some examples.

Restrictive and nonrestrictive clauses

> The restaurant <u>that we went to</u> was very crowded.

The clause restricts *restaurant* to the one in which we ate.

> Scrooge was a man <u>who hoarded money</u>.

The clause restricts the meaning of *man*.

> The play <u>that I love best</u> is "Twelfth Night."

The clause restricts *play* to the one I love best, as opposed to all others.

Nonrestrictive modifiers are parenthetical in meaning. They add information but aren't crucial to the sentence; such modifiers are set off by commas.

> Ernest Hemingway, <u>who wrote many books</u>, committed suicide.

> The proposal, <u>which was 100 pages long</u>, was delivered on time.

The length of the proposal has no bearing on whether it was delivered on time, but the same sentence can be made restrictive.

> The proposal <u>that was 100 pages long</u> was delivered on time.

But the 125-page proposal was delivered late.

Generally speaking, the word *that* introduces a restrictive clause, and the word *which* introduces a nonrestrictive one. Although the *which/that* distinction may be disappearing, especially in spoken English, it's technically correct. In Britain, *which* is used for both kinds of modifying clauses, and formal and informal British writing reflects that fact.

If you aren't sure whether a modifier is restrictive or nonrestrictive, consider the context. If you're still in doubt, then query or leave the construction alone. Some modifiers can function either way; in such cases you have to determine the intended meaning. Look at these examples.

> Older persons who take many different kinds of medication are susceptible to cross-reactions.

> Older persons, who take many different kinds of medication, are susceptible to cross-reactions.

The modifier in the first sentence is restrictive; only certain older persons—those who take many kinds of medications—are susceptible to cross-reactions. The second sentence, however, says that all older persons are subject to cross-reactions because they all take many different medications.

> Americans whose diet is composed of 30 percent fat are prone to heart disease.

> Americans, whose diet is composed of 30 percent fat, are prone to heart disease.

The restrictive modifier in the first sentence here limits *Americans* to just those whose diet is rich in fats. The second sentence says that Americans in general are prone to heart disease; the fact that they eat too much fat is additional information.

Instructions: In the following sentences, decide whether modifiers are restrictive or nonrestrictive. Correct the sentences as necessary by adding or deleting commas or changing which *to* that.

1. This is the house which he rents. *[that]* R

2. A van is the type of automobile which caterers *[that]* prefer. R

3. The river, which used to be full of salmon, was polluted. N

4. The report which I compiled and sent to you, should help. N

5. The report on editing and grammar, which you did *[that]* for the style guide should help everyone write better. R

6. Mark wrote a poem about fall which was printed *[that]* in the school newspaper. N

7. The river, which ran through the city, was lined with marinas. N

8. The veil, which had been in the family for three generations, was made of ivory lace. N

9. Our offices, which are located on Canal Street, are easily accessible by bus.

10. The university ~~which he~~ *that* attends has an excellent physics department.

ANSWERS

1. This is the house ~~which~~ *that* he rents.

This is the most likely solution.

2. A van is the type of automobile ~~which~~ *that* caterers prefer.

This clause is restrictive, and so *that* is correct. *That* could also be omitted; the sentence would then be elliptical, with *that* understood.

3. The river, which used to be full of salmon, was polluted.

In the absence of a context, the most likely meaning is nonrestrictive.

4. The report ~~which~~ *that* I compiled and sent to you should help.

Alternative:

The report, which I compiled and sent to you, should help.

5. The report on editing and grammar ~~which~~ *that* you did for the style guide should help everyone write better.

6. Mark wrote a poem about fall*,*which was printed

   in the school newspaper.

7. The river*,*which ran through the city*,*was lined

   with marinas.

   Alternative:

   The river ~~which~~ *that* ran through the city was lined

   with marinas.

   Either way could be correct. In the first solution, there's apparently only one river. The second solution implies that there's another river close by that doesn't run through the city.

8. The veil*,*which had been in the family for three

   generations*,*was made of ivory lace.

   Alternative:

   The veil ~~which~~ *that* had been in the family for three

   generations was made of ivory lace.

9. Our offices*,*which are located on Canal Street*,*

   are easily accessible by bus.

10. The university ~~which~~ *that* he attends has an excellent

    physics department.

If you'd like to do another exercise on restrictive and nonrestrictive modifiers before you proceed, turn to appendix A, exercise 6. If you can easily distinguish between restrictive and nonrestrictive modifiers, continue on to misplaced modifiers.

Misplaced modifiers

A word or phrase placed next to a word that it can't sensibly describe is called a dangling modifier. Editors must be particularly alert to placement of modifiers, or absurdities will slip into print.

Dangling modifiers often appear at the beginning of sentences. Look at these humorous examples.

```
Running for the bus, his hat fell off.

Hissing furiously, the boy removed the kitten
from the tree.
```

However, dangling modifiers needn't be at the beginning of a sentence. They can also appear in the middle, where they seem to function ambiguously: They can modify either the preceding phrase or the following one. Here are some examples.

```
While she hesitated with gun poised he attacked.

The judge said Friday the probationary period
is over.
```

Who has the gun? A small detail to be sure. Did the judge make the statement on Friday or does the probation end on Friday? As the sentences stand, no one knows. Some grammarians call these problems squinting modifiers.

Other modifiers are misplaced; they stand near a word other than the one the writer or speaker intended them to describe. Adverbs such as *almost, merely, even, nearly, hardly, only,* and *just* are especially easy to misplace.

Look what happens when you misplace one of these adverbs.

```
I was just asking for a small favor.
```

As written, I seem to be saying that I didn't mean it: I was just asking, or hoping. But is that what I really meant? Or did I mean

```
I was asking for just a small favor.
```
(The favor I asked for was small.)

The same sleight of hand can be performed with *only.* Consider the following sentence.

```
He said that he loved me.
```

Add the adverb *only* and see how the meaning changes.

```
Only he said that he loved me.
```

He only said that he loved me.

He said only that he loved me.

He said that only he loved me.

He said that he only loved me.

He said that he loved only me.

He said that he loved me only.

Each of these sentences conveys a different nuance, a variation on the theme. With that fact in mind, be careful where you put your adverbs.

EXERCISE 14: PROBLEM MODIFIERS

Instructions: Rewrite or edit the following sentences to eliminate the dangling, squinting, and misplaced modifiers. Without a context, it's hard to know exactly which noun or pronoun to use; simply remember that many variations are possible, depending on the rest of the paragraph.

1. ~~Watching~~ *as I watched* from the wings, the orchestra played the overture.

2. After ~~reading the~~ *she read* book, the train arrived at its destination.

3. While ~~taking a~~ *Julie took* nap, the cat jumped up ~~on Julie~~ and began to purr.

4. ~~Thinking~~ *as she thought* about her mother, who struggled to feed and clothe them, her eyes filled with tears.

5. To test well on vocabulary, ~~good books~~ *one* must be read *good books*

6. Yesterday I saw a man *with one leg* skiing down the mountain ~~with one leg~~.

7. The semester passed very quickly, ~~studying for~~ ^while I was^ studying for

   comps and writing my dissertation.

8. Seen off the coast of southern Italy only once

   before, two Italian sailors reported a large

   UFO about two miles out to sea.

9. When only a child, Mozart's father presented

   him at the Austrian court.

10. Short on hope, our patience wears thin;

    lacking in faith, our courage wanes.

11. Being new in the production department (7

    months), ~~it was~~ ^she^ assumed that this was a more

    technical class.

12. To be in fashion, ~~your colors should be kept~~

    ^wear colors^ ~~bold~~ and ^long^ ~~skirts should be kept long.~~

13. ^it is^ Described as the most polluted river in the

    country; ~~you should~~ hold your breath as you

    drive along the banks.

14. ^assailed^ Jogg~~ing~~ ^ed^ ~~in~~ the hot sun, her energy began to flag.

15. Cute and playful, ~~you will find that~~ this

    puppy will entertain you for hours.

ANSWERS

1. *As she* ~~Watching~~ *ed* from the wings, the orchestra played

   the overture.

   As she watched from the wings, the orchestra

   played the overture.

   Someone or something other than the orchestra is watching; it could
   be a soprano or a murderer.

2. After *I finished* reading the book, the train arrived at its

   destination.

   After I finished reading the book, the train

   arrived at its destination.

   Whether to put the corrected clause at the beginning or the end of a
   sentence depends on the flow of the paragraph, as well as on your personal preference. Note that what comes first in the sentence does,
   however, receive the greater emphasis.

3. *As Julie was* ~~While~~ taking a nap, the cat jumped up on ~~Julie~~ *her*

   and began to purr.

   As Julie was taking a nap, the cat jumped up

   on her and began to purr.

   Alternative:

   The cat jumped up on Julie, who was taking a

   nap, and began to purr.

   The second solution turns the dangling modifier into a nonrestrictive
   clause.

When she thought

4. ~~Thinking~~ about her mother, who struggled to feed
   and clothe them, her eyes filled with tears.

   When she thought about her mother, who struggled to feed and clothe them, her eyes filled
   with tears.

   The context should tell you whether she often thought about her
   mother or whether this was a particular instance. If you wish to emphasize that she often thought of her mother, you could replace the
   word *filled* with *would fill*. Note how the meaning shifts.

   When she thought about her mother, who struggled to feed and clothe them, her eyes would
   fill with tears.

   If the writer is describing an isolated incident, use *as* to begin the introductory clause.

   As she thought about her mother, who struggled to
   feed and clothe them, her eyes filled with tears.

   If you want,   *you must read*
5. To test well on vocabulary, good books ~~must~~
   ~~be read.~~

   If you want to test well on vocabulary, you
   must read good books.

   In this instance, it's probably best to cast the sentence into the second
   person. Of course, any number of other versions are possible, as long
   as you eliminate the dangling modifier.

6. Yesterday I saw a *one-legged* man skiing down the mountain~~with one leg.~~

   Yesterday I saw a one-legged man skiing down

   the mountain.

   The misplaced modifier consists of a phrase that needs to be moved closer to the noun it modifies. Here the phrase becomes an adjective or unit modifier (i.e., both parts of the hyphenated word modify the noun).

7. The semester passed very quickly *as I* stud~~ying~~ *ied* for comps and ~~writing~~ *wrote* my dissertation.

   The semester passed very quickly as I studied

   for comps and wrote my dissertation.

8. *a UFO had been,* ~~Seen~~ off the coast of southern Italy only once before, two Italian sailors reported a large UFO about two miles out to sea.

   Two Italian sailors reported a large UFO about

   two miles out to sea; a UFO had been seen off

   the coast of southern Italy only once before.

   The best way to edit this sentence is to create two independent clauses. Watch the antecedents.

9. When *Mozart was* only a child, ~~Mozart's~~ *his* father presented

   him at the Austrian court.

   When Mozart was only a child, his father pre-

   sented him at the Austrian court.

   As originally written, *him* refers to *father*, because *Mozart's* is an adjective and can't be an antecedent.

10. *If we are,*
Short on hope, our patience wears thin;
if we lacking ~~in~~ faith, our courage wanes.

If we are short on hope, our patience wears
thin; if we lack faith, our courage wanes.

11. Being new in the production department (7
months), ~~it was~~ *I* assumed that this *class* was ~~a~~ more
technical ~~class.~~

Being new in the production department (7
months), I assumed that this class was more
technical.

In the absence of context, you can use any number of nouns or pronouns.

12. To be in fashion, *keep* your colors ~~should be kept~~
bold, and *your* skirts ~~should be kept~~ long.

To be in fashion, keep your colors bold and
your skirts long.

We used the imperative to revise this example. The subject, then, is *you* (understood); the construction of the sentence is now parallel as well.

As you drive along the banks of that river,
13. ~~Described as the most polluted~~ ~~river~~ in the
country, you should hold your breath ~~as you~~
~~drive along the banks.~~

As you drive along the banks of that river, described as the most polluted in the country,
you should hold your breath.

The independent clause could go at either end.

14. ~~Jogging~~ *As she* in the hot sun, her energy began to flag.
~~Jogg~~*ed*

As she jogged in the hot sun, her energy began to flag.

Alternative:

Her energy began to flag as she jogged in the
hot sun.

The emphasis you want to convey determines the version you choose.

15. Cute, and playful, you will find that this
puppy will entertain you for hours.

You will find that this cute, playful puppy
will entertain you for hours.

This example reminds us that a dangling modifier needn't translate
into a complete clause.

If you want more practice with problem modifiers, turn to appendix A, exercise 7.

Spoken and written English diverge in the placement of modifiers. A sentence that's perfectly comprehensible may still be incorrect. Placement of
modifiers can convey nuance; there's often no right or wrong answer. Some
versions are simply better than others—they read or sound better, or they
suit the context better.

Modifiers add enormously to the richness of the language, but they must be
judiciously placed. Not all misplaced modifiers are funny; some are simply
clumsy. In either case, careful editing is necessary.

There's not much to be said about the period except that most writers don't reach it soon enough.

—William Zinsser

PUNCTUATION: The Pause That Clarifies

10

When you speak, your voice and your body language punctuate for you. On paper, however, you must depend on punctuation to give emphasis and meaning to your words. Rules of grammar govern most aspects of punctuation. This chapter discusses each mark of punctuation and presents some exercises to test your skill.

1. A period traditionally marks the end of a sentence.

Period

```
The operation went well.   The patient was awake.
```

2. Periods are also used with abbreviations.

```
Ave.    Dr.    Ms.    etc.
```

The trend today is to omit periods in abbreviations and acronyms such as IRA, NATO, IRS, ACTION, and PTA. Using these periods is therefore a style decision; consult your style manual.

3. Periods form an ellipsis (...), indicating that a word or words in a quotation have been omitted. If the part of the quotation that's omitted is in the middle of a sentence, use three dots.

```
"One nation...with liberty and justice for all."
```

If the citation contains punctuation at the point where you're stopping the citation, include the punctuation.

```
"Four score and seven years ago,..."
```

If the omission is at the end of the sentence, use four dots.

```
"To thine own self be true...."
```

The tendency today is to omit the ellipsis at the beginning of a sentence and replace it with a capital letter. Some styles use brackets to tell the reader that what's inside the brackets wasn't in the original quotation, but most styles simply substitute the capital for the lowercase letter.

```
"And justice for all."

"[A]nd justice for all."
```

Parentheses

Parentheses, which come in pairs, are often used to enclose asides or additional information.

```
The results of the survey (see appendix A) dem-
onstrate this dichotomy clearly.
```

In a list format, a single parenthesis is sometimes used.

```
The flow sheet should include
  a) the name of the project,
  b) the name of the manager,
  c) the deadline for the deliverable, and
  d) the specifications.
```

Such a list presented within a sentence, however, requires two parentheses.

```
The flow sheet should include (a) the name of
the project, (b) the name of the manager, (c)
the deadline for the deliverable, and (d) the
specifications.
```

Many style guides don't permit the single parenthesis in any list format and some prefer the use of bullets to numbers or letters when no ranking among the elements is intended or desired.

Brackets

Brackets (in pairs) are used to enclose words in a quotation that weren't in the original or to give stage directions in a play, among other things.

```
He said, "Once upon a midnight dreary [and here
he paused for effect]
While I pondered weak and weary,"

The Ghost:   [fading away] Remember what I
             told you.
```

Brackets are also used as parentheses within parentheses.

```
(The author also notes [pages 3-6] that Lincoln
suffered from depression.)
```

Authors often use the bracketed word [*sic*], which means *thus* in Latin, to indicate that they're reproducing the speaker's words exactly, grammatical mistakes, misspellings, and all. Essentially, to use [*sic*] is to insert a disclaimer.

The trend today is to do away with all unnecessary marks of punctuation, especially commas. Because commas clarify the meaning of sentences and help the reader understand the relationship of the parts, their omission can result in an unclear sentence.

Commas

```
I went riding with my father and my mother and
my sister stayed at home.
```

Who went riding?

```
I went riding with my father, and my mother and
my sister stayed at home.

I went riding with my father and my mother, and
my sister stayed at home.
```

If the context doesn't tell you which version is correct, you have to either query the author or leave the sentence alone. In editing, as in life, sins of commission are more serious than sins of omission.

Use a comma in the following constructions.

Compound sentences. Unless the sentence is extremely short, use a comma between two independent or main clauses (those that express a complete thought) joined by *and*.

```
She was angry and so was I.

She left to go shopping at the mall, and I
began to weed the garden.
```

Items in a series. Use a comma to separate items in a series.

```
He ate three hamburgers, three ears of corn,
and a banana split.
```

Some styles, notably journalistic ones, omit the comma before the final item except when one element in the series contains a conjunction.

```
Three cheers for the red, white and blue.

The funds were allocated for equipment,
salaries, and research and development.
```

Direct address. When the form of address is in the middle of the sentence, the address must be set off by two commas—one before and one after.

```
The truth is, Matt, that the company is bank-
rupt.
```

```
Remember, children, to clean your rooms.
```

Appositives. Appositives are nouns that explain, repeat, or stand in the same position as other nouns; appositives are also set off by two commas. Consider these two sentences.

```
David, our accountant, is on vacation.
```

```
David, our accountant is on vacation.
```

In the first example, David and the accountant are the same person; *our accountant* is an appositive. In the second, you're telling David that the accountant is on vacation. *David* is a noun of direct address.

Because they define or limit the meaning of the noun, restrictive appositives don't use commas.

```
The poet Longfellow was born in Maine.
```

```
Henry the Eighth had six wives.
```

```
Oscar the Grouch is a character on Sesame
Street.
```

Parenthetical words, phrases, or clauses. These items simply add information. You can remove them without changing the essential meaning of a sentence.

```
His strategy, however, backfired.
```

```
In fact, he asked his father for a loan.
```

```
To my chagrin, the professor read my paper to
the class.
```

```
Time management techniques, as we have said,
are based on a clear understanding of
priorities.
```

```
There are six persons, if you count the project
manager, working on the proposal.
```

Similar or identical verbs and nouns. Use a comma between identical words to prevent misunderstanding.

```
What it was, was football.

Who she is, is not your concern.
```

Missing words. Sometimes words can be replaced by a comma.

```
To err is human; to forgive, divine.

James is in charge of personnel; Mark, of
advertising.
```

Dates and locations. A comma is usually placed between a day and a year, but this issue shades over into style. In the following examples, note the two commas; both are necessary because the year or the location is really in apposition. Omitting the second comma in either sentence is incorrect.

```
I flew to Tokyo on January 4, 1995, and
returned 10 days later.

She lives in the Fairfax, Virginia, area.
```

No comma is used in international or military dates.

```
The fleet held maneuvers in the
Mediterranean from 17 October 1942
to 2 November 1942.
```

No comma is necessary when the day of the month isn't specified.

```
The references cite the September 1993 and
January 1992 issues of the journal.
```

After introductory (adverbial) clauses and phrases. Unless the introductory phrase is very short, a comma is necessary to indicate the pause in thought.

The comma in the following example provides the necessary break between the dependent and independent clauses.

```
Although he had been running competitively for
many years, he had never entered the Boston
Marathon.
```

According to many style guides, the comma can be omitted in the following sentence because the introductory phrase is short, it contains no verb, and the sentence is easily understood without the extra mark.

```
As part of its marketing strategy, FGH has in-
creased its advertising budget.
```

Between words or phrases linked by a coordinate or subordinate conjunction, if ambiguity could result from omission. Conjunctions are used to join words, phrases, or clauses. Coordinating conjunctions (*and, but, or, nor,* or *for*) join parts of equal grammatical weight; subordinating conjunctions (*because, if, since, where,* and *when*) join dependent clauses to main clauses.

```
The bridesmaid wore a dress trimmed with lace,
and pearls.
```

```
The bridesmaid wore a dress trimmed with lace
and pearls.
```

In the first sentence, she wore a lace-trimmed dress and a string of pearls. In the second, her dress was trimmed with both lace and pearls.

Between adjectives of equal weight not linked by *and*.

```
The cage was filled with angry, snarling lions.
```

Both *angry* and *snarling* independently modify *lions,* so a comma is necessary.

```
She wore a pale pink dress to the
graduation.
```

Pale modifies *pink,* not *dress,* and these two words shouldn't be separated by a comma.

Before and after nonrestrictive clauses.

```
Persons with disabilities, who still face dis-
crimination, must have an equal chance to suc-
ceed in the working world.
```

```
The cover, which was designed by our staff, is
riveting.
```

Remember that restrictive clauses don't use commas (see chapter 9).

```
Children who have talents should be allowed to
develop them.
```

Miscellaneous. Use commas in the following situations.

1. After exclamations such as *Oh* or *Yes.*

   ```
   Oh, dear, what can the matter be?

   Yes, I will go right away.
   ```

2. Before *of* when it denotes a place of residence.

   ```
   The speaker was Patrick Henry, of
   Virginia.
   ```

3. After digits that denote thousands, millions, billions....

   ```
   1,500    33,000
   ```

For five-digit numbers, most style guides advocate a comma; for four-digit ones, some styles omit it.

As you edit, watch for comma splices, characterized by the separation of two main clauses by a comma alone, with no coordinating conjunction such as *but* or *and.*

   ```
   I went down to the Lincoln Memorial, it was
   beautiful at night.
   ```

This is also called a run-on sentence, and it requires a conjunction or a semicolon.

   ```
   I went down to the Lincoln Memorial, and it was
   beautiful at night.
   ```

   ```
   I went down to the Lincoln Memorial; it was
   beautiful at night.
   ```

Apostrophes

Apostrophes show the possessive case of nouns or the omission of a letter or letters. Apostrophes are also sometimes used to denote plural letters, figures, and symbols.

Possessive case of nouns. Singular nouns that don't end in *s* almost always add *'s* to form the possessive.

   ```
   Mary's dog                the cat's paw
   ```

Singular nouns ending in *s* or an *s* sound sometimes add *'s* and sometimes just an apostrophe, according to the style guide being used. However you form the possessive, do it consistently throughout the manuscript.

```
hostess's, hostess'      Dickens's, Dickens'

Charles's, Charles'      Davis's, Davis'

Congress's, Congress'    Berlioz's, Berlioz'
```

Plural nouns not ending in *s* or an *s* sound form the possessive by adding *'s*.

```
children's

men's

women's
```

The possessive case of plural nouns ending in *s* is formed by adding an apostrophe after the final *s*.

```
the Adamses' house

the kittens' claws
```

Plural letters, figures, and symbols. Check your style manual for specified usage. Most agree on the need for apostrophes in the following examples.

```
P's and Q's        x's and y's

a's and b's        N's and n's

M.A.'s and Ph.D.'s
```

Style guides disagree on the following:

```
1960s, 1960's

HMOs, HMO's

three Rs, three R's
```

Contractions. The apostrophe replaces a missing letter in words such as *she's*, *don't*, and *o'er*.

Note that possessive personal pronouns (*its, hers, theirs, whose*) never take apostrophes.

The use of the apostrophe is a complicated issue. Every good style guide contains instructions on how to handle particular problems; dictionaries also contain solutions to issues such as *traveler's checks, user's manual, writer's cramp, teachers college, Teamsters Union,* and the *Court of St. James's.*

A colon is used to introduce, supplement, explain, or add something to a sentence. What precedes the colon should be a complete sentence.

Colon

```
Only one course was open to the president:  to
fire the secretary.

Everything was ready:  The audience was in
place, the lights were dimmed, and the orches-
tra began.
```

Some style guides capitalize the word following a colon if it introduces a complete sentence, but capitalization here is a style decision.

A colon is often used after an introductory statement containing the words *as follows* or *the following.*

```
We will discuss the following types of problems:
```

- Poor planning
- Sporadic communication
- Defective parts

A colon is used in formal salutations and before long quotations or formal resolutions.

```
Dear Madam:

The Declaration of Independence begins with
these words:  "When, in the course of human
events,..."

Resolved:  That this nation shall have a new
birth of freedom.
```

Semicolon

Because the semicolon shows a more definite break in thought than a comma does, the semicolon is "stronger." Use a semicolon when a comma doesn't seem to indicate enough of a pause.

1. Use a semicolon between independent clauses when the conjunction is omitted.

```
I'm going to the pool; I'll be back at
6 o'clock.

Claire is president of the company; Robin and
Andrea, vice presidents.
```

2. Use a semicolon to separate independent clauses joined by conjunctive adverbs (those used to connect main clauses).

```
Being a volunteer at the hospital isn't easy;
however, it's challenging and rewarding.

That child refuses to do any work for the
class; therefore, he's failing.
```

The most common conjunctive adverbs are the following: *accordingly, also, consequently, furthermore, hence, however, moreover, nevertheless, otherwise, still, therefore,* and *thus.*

3. Use a semicolon to separate items in a series when at least one of them already contains a comma.

```
This plane will stop in Denver, Colorado; Kan-
sas City, Kansas; Atlanta, Georgia; and Or-
lando, Florida.
```

This sentence already has commas within the elements of the series, between *Denver* and *Colorado,* for instance. Using commas alone would make the sentence very confusing; semicolons set each unit apart.

Also use a semicolon to separate elements of a series that are too long or complex for commas.

```
Parking spaces reserved for persons with dis-
abilities should be as close as possible to
building entrances; curbs in the route of
travel should have curb cuts or ramps; and all
walks should be level.
```

Quotation marks come in pairs. If a mark is missing, query the author and don't touch the passage in question until you know the extent of the citation. Editors should hesitate to tamper with direct quotations; legal and ethical ramifications are involved, and people don't take kindly to being misquoted.

Now look at quotation marks in relation to other kinds of punctuation.

1. Put a comma or period inside the closing quotation mark.

```
"I'm leaving now," she said.

He replied, "See you later."
```

2. Put a colon or a semicolon outside the closing quotation mark, unless it's part of the quotation.

```
The first topic was "Financing a College Educa-
tion"; the second was "How to Choose a College."
```

Those are the rules; at first glance, they don't seem very logical. According to an apocryphal tale, in the old days of movable type, periods and commas would break off, and so they were put inside the quotation marks to protect them. Colons and semicolons didn't break off and so were put outside. That explanation is as good as any other.

Note that some style guides—and British English—distinguish between quoted words and whole sentences or clauses. For example, look at the following.

```
She decided to avoid these "friends".
```

Logically, such a distinction is defensible; grammatically, it isn't, at least in the United States. One of the few hard-and-fast rules of American English is that commas and periods go inside closing quotation marks; semicolons and colons don't.

For question marks and exclamation points, the rules are more complicated. An exclamation point or a question mark goes inside the closing quotation marks if the punctuation was part of the original quotation; otherwise, it goes outside.

```
He asked, "Are you afraid?"

Did you reply, "Yes, I am"?
```

In the first example, the quotation is indeed a question, so the question mark goes inside the marks. In the second, however, the quotation is a declarative sentence that's part of a question. The question mark isn't part of the original quotation and goes outside the marks.

As for exclamation points, consider these sentences.

```
She screamed, "No, never!"

Some "friend"!
```

In the second example, the whole sentence is exclamatory, not just the word inside the quotation marks. The exclamation point therefore goes outside the marks.

1. Our plans, unfortunately, suffered a setback.

2. Unfortunately, our plans suffered a setback

3. I'd like a Greek salad with extra feta cheese, and coffee.

4. If you want to argue, with your father, not me.

5. Thomas Jefferson's home, Monticello, is located near the town of Charlottesville, Virginia.

6. Children, don't fight like that, said Mother.

7. On July 4, 1776, the members of the Continental Congress signed the Declaration of Independence in Philadelphia.

8. We grow eight vegetables in our garden: tomatoes, peppers, lettuce, beans, cucumbers, spinach, radishes and carrots

9. You're free to do as you like; however, what you propose will cost more money.

10. She said, "I refuse."

11. My niece, who's visiting from Boston, is a vegetarian.

12. After the soccer game is over, the team is going to Marty's to celebrate.

13. She slept late on Sunday morning; therefore she was late for church.

14. My son, who refuses to take music lessons, plays by ear.

15. The secretaries' desks were all unoccupied because of the strike.

16. He said (and I agreed with him) that there was no time to lose.

17. I didn't feel comfortable calling her "Peanuts."

18. Fortunately, Lee, this project won't be due for weeks.

19. Did he say, "I will not go"?

20. My father always said, "There's no fool like an old fool."

ANSWERS _____

1. Our plans, unfortunately, suffered a setback.

   The word *unfortunately* is traditionally set off by commas. If your style follows current trends and you omit the commas, be sure to omit both of them.

2. Unfortunately, our plans suffered a setback.

   If you choose (or your style dictates) the omission of the comma after *unfortunately*, delete the comma consistently throughout the manuscript whenever there is an introductory adverb.

3. I'd like a Greek salad with extra feta cheese,

   and coffee.

   The apostrophe, of course, belongs with the contraction *I'd*. The comma after *cheese* can't be omitted; otherwise, you'll have coffee in your Greek salad.

4. If you want to argue with your father, not me.

   Depending on the context, this clause could be a sentence fragment, but it does make sense if you punctuate it as shown here. Both commas are necessary for clarity.

5. Thomas Jefferson's home, Monticello, is located

   near the town of Charlottesville, Virginia.

   Monticello must be set off by commas because it's in apposition. The apostrophe in *Jefferson's* indicates possession, and the comma after *Charlottesville* shows that *Virginia* is also in apposition.

6. "Children don't fight like that, said Mother.

   This sentence is ambiguous. As a simple declarative sentence, the punctuation shown above is correct. The apostrophe marks the contraction, and the comma goes inside the quotation marks.

   But you could read the sentence as an admonition.

   "Children, don't fight like that!" said Mother.

   Children is set off by a comma because it's a form of direct address; the statement ends with an exclamation point inside the quotation mark because it goes with what was quoted. If the context doesn't tell you which interpretation is meant, query the author.

7. On July 4, 1776, the members of the Continental

   Congress signed the Declaration of Independence

   in Philadelphia.

   Again, the commas come in pairs. Although the second one is often left out, the omission is incorrect.

8. We grow eight vegetables in our garden: tomatoes, peppers, lettuce, beans, cucumbers, spinach, radishes, and carrots.

The colon is correct here; what precedes it is a complete sentence, and what follows it explains or adds to the statement. Commas are sufficient to separate the items in the series. Remember that the last comma—the one that precedes *and*—can be omitted according to some style guides. And did you count and make sure that eight vegetables were listed?

9. You're free to do as you like; however, what you propose will cost more money.

The apostrophe marks the contraction, and the semicolon precedes the conjunctive adverb *however*, which is also set off by a comma.

10. She said, "I refuse!"

The exclamation point is part of the quotation, so it goes inside the marks. A comma, not a colon, precedes the quotation.

11. My niece, who's visiting from Boston, is a vegetarian.

The apostrophe marks the contraction for *who is*. If two nieces were visiting at the same time—one from Boston and one from New York—the clause would be restrictive and wouldn't be set off by any punctuation at all.

My niece who's visiting from Boston is a vegetarian.

12. After the soccer game is over, the team is going to Marty's to celebrate.

The comma after *over* helps clarify a sentence that has an introductory adverbial clause longer than a few words. The apostrophe is necessary to indicate the possessive, whatever sort of place Marty's might be (house, restaurant).

13. She slept late on Sunday morning; therefore, she

    was late for church.

The conjunctive adverb *therefore* is preceded by a semicolon and followed by a comma.

14. My son, who refuses to take music lessons, plays

    by ear.

Putting commas around the clause (as shown here) makes it nonrestrictive; the information inside the commas becomes almost parenthetical. The implication is that the writer has only one son and that his refusal is not needed to distinguish him from other sons.

    My son who refuses to take music lessons plays
    by ear.

Without commas, the clause is restrictive. The refusal identifies a particular son, the one who refuses to take music lessons, as opposed to the one who doesn't refuse.

15. The secretaries' desks were all unoccupied

    because of the strike.

Indicate the plural possessive with an apostrophe following the *s*.

16. He said, and I agreed with him, that there was

    no time to lose.

The parenthetical clause *and I agreed with him* needs to be set off by commas. Dashes could be used instead if you prefer. (See the following section.)

17. I didn't feel comfortable calling her "Peanuts".

Be sure you add the apostrophe and that your closing quotation mark is outside the period.

18. Fortunately, Lee, this project won't be due for

    weeks.

Lee is a form of direct address, set off by commas, both of which are necessary, and the apostrophe marks the contraction.

19. Did he say, "I will not go"?

> Here, the question mark goes outside, because it applies to the whole sentence. The quotation itself is a simple assertion.

20. My father always said, "There's no fool like an old fool."

Hyphens

Although hyphens and dashes are marks of punctuation, their use is governed by style. The hyphen (-) has two important functions: At the end of a line, it divides a word between syllables; and it's also used to form compound words. The first function is self-evident; the second isn't. Many compound words are found in the dictionary: *coat-of-arms, make-believe, great-aunt,* and so on. Moreover, numbers between *twenty-one* and *ninety-nine* are hyphenated. (There's no simple rule for fractions that are spelled out.) Within these rules, however, is an enormous gray area.

Unit modifiers are hyphenated when they precede a noun, but not when they follow the verb as a predicate adjective.

    Garfield is a well-fed cat.

    Garfield is well fed.

In the second example, no noun follows for *well fed* to modify, so it isn't hyphenated. For compounding, it's always wise to check your dictionary. If a word is hyphenated there, it should be hyphenated wherever it's used in a sentence.

Style rules govern hyphens used with prefixes and suffixes. Most such compound words aren't hyphenated, except for those with prefixes such as *ex* and *self* (*ex-husband, self-worth*). For a prefix or suffix added to a proper noun (*post-World War II, Army-wide*), however, most style guides call for a hyphen to maintain the capitalization. When in doubt, check your style sheet or manual.

Dashes

Dashes come in two sizes—em-dashes (as in this sentence) and en-dashes. Em-dashes in a sentence show that there's an abrupt change in thought.

    He said—and I think he was wrong—that history
    would vindicate him.

    Everyone in the class—students and teachers—
    appreciated the joke.

In the second example, you might be tempted to use commas, because the phrase *students and teachers* is in apposition (explains what precedes it).

```
Everyone in the class, students and teachers,
appreciated the joke.
```

Here, however, the commas can be misread as serial commas, so dashes make the meaning clearer.

En-dashes (–) are longer than hyphens (-) and shorter than em-dashes (—). Their main use is in ranges of dates and pages to indicate *to* or *through*. En-dashes often appear in tables, references, bibliographies, and indexes, but not usually in text except in parenthetical references. En-dashes didn't appear in typewritten text because there's no such character on the keyboard. Moreover, the en-dash isn't usually appropriate as a substitute for *to* or *through* in text.

Although style guides vary extensively, they specify the use of en-dashes in some, if not all, of the following cases.

1. Use en-dashes when all elements are figures (numerals).

   $15–$20 (note that the $ sign must be repeated; in running text, use *from $15 to $20)*

   Public Law 85–1

   pp. 38–45

   chapters 6–12

   John 4:3–6

   1939–45 (in text, *from 1939 to 1945,* unless used as a unit modifier: *the 1939–45 war*)

2. Use en-dashes when all elements are letters (but not words).

   WXYZ–AM–FM–TV

   AFL–CIO

3. Use en-dashes when one element is a figure and another is a letter (or letters), but no element is a word.

   exhibit 6–A

   appendix B–2

   DC–10

Apply what you've learned in the following exercise. Some of the hyphens shown there should remain as hyphens, and some should appear as em- or en-dashes.

EXERCISE 16: HYPHENS AND DASHES

Instructions: According to the preceding rules, should the hyphens in the following sentences be hyphens, em-dashes, or en-dashes? Mark them all as follows.

If the hyphen should remain a hyphen, use ⹀ .
If the hyphen should be an em-dash, use ⹀ .
If the hyphen should be an en-dash, use ⹀ .

1. The vice-presidency, he said, and no one contradicted him, is up for grabs in the next election.

2. The entire staff worked on the AFL-CIO report (chapters 6-12).

3. Long-term loans, although in small amounts ($10,000-$20,000), have provided working capital for the small businesses of the area.

4. For a free copy of Questionnaire 3-C, write to 987-A North Main Street.

5. Is the web-footed, gray-billed platypus olive-green?

1. The vice-presidency, he said—and no one
    contradicted him—is up for grabs in the next
    election.

2. The entire staff worked on the AFL-CIO report
    (chapters 6–12).

3. Long-term loans—although in small amounts
    ($10,000–$20,000)—have provided working
    capital for the small businesses of the area.

4. For a free copy of Questionnaire 3-C, write to
    987-A North Main Street.

5. Is the web-footed, gray-billed platypus
    olive-green?

Punctuation consists of both grammatical rules and style issues, but most marks are governed by the rules found in any grammar book. As an editor, you must know these rules so well that placing punctuation marks is second nature to you. When you have so many other things to think about, proper punctuation must be automatic.

You must know not only what to do, but also why. If you can't give a reason, you won't be able to defend your choices.

The style issues alluded to in this chapter, especially those relating to apostrophes, commas, and hyphens, are further discussed in chapter 11, which follows.

The best style is the style you don't
notice.

—Somerset Maugham

EDITORIAL STYLE: Manuals and Word Lists

11

In the largest sense, style consists of those issues not governed by grammar—decisions about which editors may have a choice. Editors must first know the difference between style questions and rules of grammar and then use a manual to resolve style questions: No editor is ever expected to function without a style manual and dictionary.

Many organizations have developed their own formal or informal style guides to answer questions particular to their situations. The most widely used general style manuals are the *United States Government Printing Office Style Manual (GPO)* and *The Chicago Manual of Style (Chicago)*. In 1994, the *New York Public Library Writer's Guide to Style and Usage* (HarperCollins), written by EEI staff, was published with the intent of offering a guide for business and technical writers and editors. Newspapers have style manuals as well: *The Associated Press Stylebook and Libel Manual (AP)*, *The New York Times Style Manual*, and *The Washington Post Deskbook on Style*. Finally, organizations often develop their own style guides, some of which move into general use. Among these are the *Publication Manual of the American Psychological Association (APA)*, which now sets the standard for many social science journals.

Remember that the *GPO Style Manual* evolved as a guide for printers, so many of the questions it treats in detail may seem irrelevant to editors. The focus of the manual has shifted over the years, but it has never lost sight of its origins. A helpful spelling and compounding guide is *Word Division, Supplement to GPO Style Manual*, which was developed to aid printers in breaking words at the ends of lines.

The hallmark of a good copyeditor is consistency in the treatment of these basic elements of style.

abbreviations and acronyms	*U.S.* or *US*; *V.I.S.T.A.* or *VISTA*
alphabetization	*McBride, Malone* or *Malone, McBride*
capitalization	*Federal* or *federal*

citations	*Smith, Jones, and Scott 1988* or *Smith, Jones, & Scott, 1988* or *Smith et al. 1988*
compounding	*vice-president* or *vice president*
italics	*au secours* *Light in August*
numbers	*eight* or *8*
punctuation	*apples, oranges, and* *bananas* or *apples, oranges and* *bananas*
spelling	*judgment* or *judgement*

Abbreviations and acronyms can appear with periods (*M.I.T.*) or without (*NASA*); uppercase (*AM*), small caps (*AM*), or lowercase (*pm*); long (*Calif.*) or short (*CA*). No one can possibly remember all the rules from every style guide.

Alphabetization appears to be straightforward, but do you alphabetize word by word or letter by letter (ignoring word breaks)? Does *McBride* precede *Malone*? If no method is specified, you can ask your client or your supervisor, or you can look to see how the index in your style manual is alphabetized and follow its pattern.

Capitalization also appears relatively straightforward, but it isn't. Proper names should always be capitalized. GPO capitalizes any term referring to the federal government, the planets, and celestial bodies. But what about terms such as *french-fried potatoes* and *roman numerals*? (Most dictionaries lowercase common foreign words that have been anglicized.)

Citations are governed by style. The APA and Chicago manuals, which are the more academic guides, list extensive rules for notes and references, while GPO has no specific style for citations other than an admonition to be consistent.

Compounding refers to the presence or absence of hyphens in compound words such as *decision maker, fire tested, vice president,* and *well known.* Each style guide gives detailed (often quite complex) rules on compounding. Note that a word may be compounded differently, depending on its use as a noun, verb, predicate adjective, or unit modifier—for example, *run-down* as a noun and unit modifier, but *run down* as a verb and predicate adjective.

Italics is used for titles of books and magazines, as well as for foreign words. The rules differ from manual to manual.

Numbers may be the most complex subject of all. When do you use figures and when do you use words? The only general rule is that a number as the first word in a sentence is nearly always spelled out. Special rules govern usage when several numbers appear in the same sentence or paragraph, and style guides diverge widely.

Punctuation rules, especially those dealing with serial commas and introductory colons, also vary among guides. And the appearance of diacritical marks in foreign words (tilde in *mañana*, umlaut in *fräulein*) varies extensively as well.

Spelling refers to the choices you make among correct alternatives (*gray* or *grey*). *Merriam-Webster's Collegiate*, the abridgment of *Webster's Third New International Dictionary*, is the authority for most style guides. Other guides may specify other dictionaries, such as *Webster's New World Dictionary*, favored by several of the journalistic style manuals. If no dictionary is specified, ask your client or supervisor.

GPO contains extensive lists showing how words should be treated; the latest edition of the manual, published in 1984, eliminated many of the odd spellings that used to set GPO style apart. *Align, gauge, subpoena,* and *marijuana* have replaced *aline, gage, subpena,* and *marihuana*. Nevertheless, some unusual spellings remain; when in doubt, look up the word.

Style manuals exist to eliminate inconsistencies that can detract from the quality of a publication and distract the reader. Choices are often arbitrary or seem so, but they must nevertheless be followed. If no style guide is specified, compile your own style sheet or word list to help you remember the choices you made and to note those choices for others who may work on the manuscript. As you see items that can be treated in more than one way, write down your choice. Also note each acronym with its equivalent and the page number on which it first appears. That way you can tell at a glance whether a full name has been spelled out before (and how far back in the manuscript). By the time you get to page 222, you won't remember how you decided to handle a word on page 17.

The search-and-replace function of word processing software is no substitute for a style sheet; to be able to search, you have to know what to search for. It's very difficult to remember every word or issue about which you made a choice while editing a long manuscript.

There's no one way to compile a style sheet. Some editors prefer to list their choices alphabetically, while others use categories (abbreviations, capitalization, punctuation, and so on). Do whatever works best for you or for the particular manuscript.

A sample style sheet follows.

SAMPLE STYLE SHEET

Abbreviations

    FHA   Federal Housing
Administration (p. 7)

    HHS   Department of Health and
Human Services (p. 23)

    HEW   Department of Health, Education, and Welfare (p. 23)

    OJJDP   Office of Juvenile Justice and Delinquency Prevention (p. 109)

    R&D (p. 50)

    S&Ls (p. 23)

Capitalization

    Capitol Hill (the Hill)

    committee

    chair

    board

    president

Numbers

    one to nine (except for measurements of time, money, distance, etc.)

    10 and up

    5 percent

    20 million

    December 7, 1941

    4,000

Compounds

    action-oriented (unit modifier)

    build-up (noun), to build up

    follow-up (noun), to follow up

    fund-raising

    2-year term

    in-depth

    on-line

Spelling

    curricula

    memorandums

    ongoing

Punctuation

    Congress's

    U.S. Supreme Court (as a noun, United States)

Also, except in very informal circumstances, you should submit a cover
memo with each edited manuscript and keep a copy of the memo yourself.
It should explain in both general and specific terms what you've done to the
manuscript—the tasks performed (edited for grammar, consistency, and
style), the problems encountered, and the major changes made. A query
sheet, listing any specific questions, should accompany the cover memo.
Questions should be tactfully phrased, both in the memo and in the text (if
they appear there as well). A sample memo follows.

SAMPLE COVER MEMO

May 31, 1995

TO: Author
FROM: Editor
RE: Status of AFL-CIO Manuscript

I enjoyed working on your book. Per instructions, I have edited
for spelling, punctuation, grammar, and conformity to the style
sheet I was given.

Here are my queries:

Page	Paragraph	Query
3	2	Where does the direct quotation end?
20	1	What is the antecedent of _it_?
25	1	This book is not cited in the references.
40	3	Another example would be helpful here.

Please call me at 123-4567 if you have any questions or problems
with what I have done.

Sometimes the list of queries will be extensive, especially if there are many discrepancies in the citations. The manuscript may return to you after the author has answered the queries. Then you plug the holes, fill in the missing information, and check the changes to see that the author has approved them. In many cases, however, you'll never see the manuscript again; it moves on to the next stage in the production process.

Style guides vary enormously; to help pinpoint the differences among style guides, the matrix starting on page 162 shows how different guides treat several subjects. This matrix is by no means exhaustive; some of these subjects are extremely complex and don't lend themselves to distillation. Study the matrix and then use it to work exercise 17.

Instructions: *First pick a particular style—Chicago, GPO, APA, or AP. Working with the matrix in this chapter, copyedit the paragraph. Don't reword. Finally, check your version against the appropriate key.*

EXERCISE 17: STYLE

Bridge from Town to Suburbs

Samuel Smith, the well-known republican senator from the state of New Illiana, announced today the allocation of $152 MILLION in federal funds to build the long-planned Smith bridge at the confluence of the Illiana and Westering. The bridge will link the city of Inverness with the communities of Robinwood, Georgeville, and Five Corners and will route a badly-needed work force to Inverness's booming shale oil industry.

<table>
<tr>
<td>

The Chicago Manual of Style (Chicago) (14th Edition, 1994)

</td>
<td>

United States Government Printing Office Style Manual (GPO) (1984)

</td>
</tr>
</table>

Abbreviations

Gives extensive listing of rules and examples; recommends omission of most abbreviations in running text (except technical matter); uses periods with standard abbreviations like *St.* and *U.S.* and *E.* before a street name (but doesn't abbreviate in running text); prefers traditional abbreviations for state names (*Va.*).	Gives extensive listing of rules and examples; uses abbreviations to save space and eliminate repetition; uses periods with standard word abbreviations like *St.*, *E.*, and *U.S.*; doesn't use periods with units of measure or State abbreviations; prefers Postal Service abbreviations (*VA*) for State names.

Acronyms

Set in all caps without periods.	Uses acronyms with no periods; extensive list in chapter on capitalization.

Alphabetization

Prefers letter-by-letter method for most books (alphabetize up to the first mark of punctuation), but accepts word-by-word system (alphabetize up to the end of the first word).	Not covered.

Capitalization

Capitalizes proper nouns and trademarks and trade names, titles (except when used alone or in apposition, as in *Seward, the secretary of state*), and some cultural movements, awards, and so on; except in titles of works, doesn't capitalize after a colon if the second clause illustrates or amplifies the first; lowercases all forms of government (federal, state, and local); capitalizes proper (not descriptive) geographic and structural names, including *Capitol* and *Washington Monument*; in titles of works, capitalizes the first and last words and all nouns, pronouns, adjectives, verbs, adverbs, and subordinating conjunctions (e.g., *if, as, that*) but lowercases articles, coordinating conjunctions, and all prepositions unless they are the first or last words; lowercases the *to* in infinitives in titles; doesn't capitalize chapter references in text.	Capitalizes proper nouns and trade and brand names, titles of persons before (and sometimes after) the name; capitalizes the first word of a main clause following a colon; capitalizes words relating to the Federal Government and governments of the 50 States (but not localities); capitalizes geographic and structural names, including *Capitol* and *Washington Monument*; capitalizes first and important words in titles; doesn't capitalize chapter references if no title follows.

Publication Manual of the American Psychological Association (APA) (Fourth Edition, 1994)	The Associated Press Stylebook and Libel Manual (AP) (1994)
Restricts use of abbreviations to those that are conventional, familiar, and helpful; prefers few in text; spells out abbreviated terms on first appearance, immediately followed by the abbreviation in parentheses, which is used exclusively thereafter; abbreviations accepted as words by *Merriam-Webster's Collegiate Dictionary* can be used without spelling out; Latin abbreviations (*i.e.*) may be used only parenthetically; uses English translations (*that is*) in text; uses periods with abbreviations for geographic names (except states) and Latin abbreviations; doesn't use periods for measures (except *in.*) or capital-letter abbreviations (*APA*); prefers Postal Service abbreviations (*VA*) for states.	Provides most entries under individual listings; uses familiar abbreviations or acronyms that should not be placed in parentheses immediately after their full names; recognized groups (*FBI*) may be identified fully at first reference or not at all; follows manual or first-listed abbreviation in *Webster's New World Dictionary* for use of caps and periods, and for abbreviations not listed, uses caps and omits periods; uses "a.m." and "p.m."; prefers traditional abbreviations (*Va.*) for state names, except for eight states that are never abbreviated.
Uses acronyms with no periods.	Usually omits periods; see individual listings.
Alphabetizes letter by letter.	Not covered.
Capitalizes proper nouns and trade and brand names, but not names of laws, theories, or hypotheses; capitalizes the first word following a colon in a title and the first word of an independent clause; capitalizes Day 2, Trial 5, Figure 2, but not chapter 3 or page 72; capitalizes the first word, all major words, and all words of four letters or more in titles; capitalizes both words of a hyphenated compound in titles; doesn't address items such as government or geography.	Prefers lowercase in general; capitalizes proper nouns and trade and brand names; capitalizes formal titles used immediately before a name; lowercases those that are job descriptions; lowercases words derived from proper nouns that don't depend on the original for meaning (*roman numerals*); lowercases all forms of government (federal, state, and local); capitalizes geographic and structural names, including *Capitol* and *Washington Monument*; in titles of works, capitalizes the first, last, and all major words and prepositions and conjunctions of four or more letters; capitalizes the first word after a colon only if an independent clause follows; if no individual listing, check *Webster's New World Dictionary* and use the lowercase form if given.

The Chicago Manual of Style (Chicago) (14th Edition, 1994)	United States Government Printing Office Style Manual (GPO) (1984)

Citations

Sets forth two basic systems in two chapters: author-date and humanities, which uses documentary notes. Recommends author-date citations in text for all natural science and most social science manuscripts; presents extensive discussions and examples.

Says only that many styles are acceptable; lists some examples.

Compounding

States that most questions are answered by an unabridged dictionary; offers general principles and an expanded table of examples; hyphenates most unit modifiers; doesn't hyphenate most common prefixes (such as *mini, non, pre, post*), except for compounds in which the second element is a capitalized word or numeral, those that must be distinguished from similar words (*re-cover*), and those in which the second element has more than one word.

Doesn't use hyphens in most words with combining forms, suffixes, and prefixes, including those beginning with *anti, multi, non,* and *pre*; exceptions include unit modifiers, some prefixes and suffixes (*ex, quasi, self*), compounds with proper nouns or adjectives, duplicated prefixes, compound numbers, chemical elements, and improvised compounds.

Italic Type

Recommends limited use for emphasis; uses italics for foreign words, except those that have passed into English; technical or key terms at first mention; letters (in some cases); legal case names; genera, varieties, species, and mathematical symbols; theorems and proofs; and titles of literary works, periodicals, newspapers, movies, television shows, some musical compositions, and works of art.

Decries overuse of italics and doesn't use for emphasis, foreign words, technical or key terms, or titles of publications (unless specifically requested). Does use italics for letters; indexes (*See*); legal case names (except the *v.*); genera, species, and varieties; and mathematical symbols, theorems, and proofs.

164

Publication Manual of the American Psychological Association (APA) (Fourth Edition, 1994)	The Associated Press Stylebook and Libel Manual (AP) (1994)
Offers a style; presents an extensive discussion similar to *Chicago*.	Not covered.
Asserts that most questions are answered by the dictionary (*Merriam-Webster's Collegiate* preferred); for those that aren't, hyphenates "purposefully" for clarity, especially unit modifiers; most common prefixes aren't followed by hyphens; doesn't hyphenate compounds that aren't misleading (e.g., *grade point average*).	Uses hyphens to avoid ambiguity; hyphenates unit modifiers, two-thought compounds (like *socio-economic*), some prefixes and suffixes (especially to avoid duplicated vowels and tripled consonants—consult individual entries), compound proper nouns and adjectives; hyphenates modifiers that occur after the verb *to be* (He is *well-known*) and some numbers and fractions.
Recommends infrequent use; uses italics for [*sic*] and to introduce new technical and key terms; letters; legal case names; genera, species, and varieties; mathematical symbols and algebraic variables; volume numbers in reference lists; words used as examples; and titles of books and periodicals. Doesn't use italics for Greek letters, nonstatistical subscripts, commonly used foreign words, or trigonometric terms.	Italics, emphasis, etc., not listed in the manual; "composition titles" entry recommends quotation marks to set off names of books (except the Bible and reference books, catalogs, and directories), movies, television shows, works of art, poetry, and speeches. Doesn't use quotation marks with names of newspapers and magazines.

The Chicago Manual of Style (Chicago) (14th Edition, 1994)	United States Government Printing Office Style Manual (GPO) (1984)

Numbers

Spells out whole numbers under 100; treats numbers that are part of the same category the same way within the same paragraph—consistency should rule; expresses fractions less than one in words (*two-thirds*) and sometimes uses figures and words for large numbers starting with *million*; in scientific and other technical text only, uses figures for physical quantities, decimals, percentages, and (often) money; advises applying the same general rules to ordinal numbers; doesn't allow a sentence to begin with a figure; if the first word of a sentence must be a number, the words must be written out.

Spells out whole numbers under 10; if two or more numbers, one of which is more than nine, appear in a sentence, all numbers in that sentence should be figures, unless the number over nine is a unit of time, money, or measurement; always uses figures for time, distance, money, measures, decimals, and percentages (even those under 10); advises applying the same general rules to ordinal numbers; expresses fractions less than one in words and uses figures and words for large numbers (*3 million*); doesn't allow a sentence to begin with a figure; if the first word of a sentence must be a number, the words must be written out.

Punctuation

Uses the serial comma and the en-dash; gives rules and examples for each mark of punctuation; doesn't use apostrophes with plurals of numbers or letters (*three Rs*), but does with abbreviations (*Ph.D.'s*); adds *'s* to all singular possessives (*Charles's*) except *Jesus'*, *Moses'*, and names with more than one syllable with an unaccented ending pronounced *eez* (*Euripides' plays*).

Uses the serial comma and the en-dash; gives rules and examples for each mark of punctuation; uses apostrophes with plurals of letters and numbers (*10 A's* and *6 B's, 3 R's*); to form the possessive of singular or plural nouns ending in an *s* or *s* sound, adds only an apostrophe (*Moses'*).

Spelling

Recommends *Merriam-Webster's Collegiate Dictionary* and *Webster's Third New International*; uses the first spelling; gives general rules for plurals, proper names, compounds, word divisions, special terminology, and foreign words.

Recommends *Webster's Third New International* for words not listed in the manual; contains an extensive spelling list; treats plurals, diacritical marks, geographic names, and transliterations.

Publication Manual of the American Psychological Association (APA) (Fourth Edition, 1994)	The Associated Press Stylebook and Libel Manual (AP) (1994)
Spells out whole numbers under 10; treats numbers that are part of the same category the same way within the same paragraph—consistency should rule; always uses figures for statistical or mathematical functions (*1st quartile*), time, distance, money, measures, decimals, and percentages (even those under 10); applies the same general rules to ordinal numbers; expresses fractions less than one in words (*one fifth*, but *two-thirds* majority) and uses figures and words for large numbers starting with *million*; doesn't allow a sentence to begin with a figure; if the first word of a sentence must be a number, the words must be written out.	Spells out whole numbers under 10 and follows that general rule even for two or more numbers in the same sentence; always uses figures for time, money, decimals, and percentages (even those under 10); advises applying the same general rules to ordinal numbers; expresses fractions less than one in words (*two-thirds*) and uses figures and words for large numbers (*3 million*); doesn't allow a sentence to begin with a figure; if the first word of a sentence must be a number, the words must be written out; the one exception is in the case of a year: *1066 was the year....*
Uses the serial comma; doesn't use an apostrophe with plurals of letters or numbers (*three Rs*); briefly discusses punctuation marks.	Doesn't use the serial comma; uses the apostrophe with plurals of a single letter (*three R's*), but not with plurals of numerals or multiple letters; to show possession, adds *'s* to singular common nouns ending in *s* unless the next word begins with an *s* (*the hostess's invitation, the hostess' seat*); adds only an apostrophe to singular proper names ending in *s*; doesn't add an apostrophe to words ending in *s* that are descriptive (*teachers college*); check the listing for each mark.
Recommends *Merriam-Webster's Collegiate Dictionary*—if the word isn't there, use *Webster's Third New International*; uses the first spelling; for compounds, see the dictionary and the manual's table of hyphenation for compound psychological terms (page 72).	Organized like a dictionary; for spelling, style, and usage questions not covered in the manual, consult *Webster's New World Dictionary*; uses the first spelling, unless a specific exception is noted in the manual.

CHICAGO STYLE

Bridge from Town to Suburbs

Samuel Smith, the well known republican
senator from the state of New Illiana, announced today the allocation of
$152,000,000.00 in federal funds to build the
long planned Smith bridge at the confluence of
the Illiana and Westering. The bridge will
link the city of Inverness with the com-
munities of Robinwood, Georgeville and Five
Corners and will route a badly needed work
force to Inverness's booming shale oil
industry.

GPO STYLE

Bridge from Town to Suburbs

Samuel Smith, the well-known republican
senator from the state of New Illiana, announced today the allocation of
$152,~~000,000.00~~ *million* in federal funds to build the
long planned Smith bridge at the confluence of
the Illiana and Westering. The bridge will
link the city of Inverness with the com-
munities of Robinwood, Georgeville, and Five
Corners and will route a badly needed work
force to Inverness's booming shale oil
industry.

APA STYLE

Bridge from Town to Suburbs

Samuel Smith, the well-known republican senator from the state of New Illiana, announced today the allocation of $152 million in federal funds to build the long-planned Smith bridge at the confluence of the Illiana and Westering. The bridge will link the city of Inverness with the communities of Robinwood, Georgeville, and Five Corners and will route a badly needed work force to Inverness's booming shale oil industry.

ANSWERS

AP STYLE

Bridge from Town to Suburbs

Samuel Smith, the well-known republican
senator from the state of New Illiana, announced today the allocation of
                                        million
$152~~,000,000.00~~ in federal funds to build the
long-planned Smith bridge at the confluence of
the Illiana and Westering. The bridge will
link the city of Inverness with the com-
munities of Robinwood, Georgeville and Five
Corners and will route a badly needed work
force to Inverness' booming shale oil
industry.

For a while, you'll have to look everything up, but as you become familiar
with a particular guide, you'll make many of the correct choices instinctively. If you've been using one style guide for one manuscript and then
have to use a different guide for another, you'll need some time to shift
gears mentally.

The adjective that exists solely as decoration is a self-indulgence for the writer and an obstacle for the reader.

—William Zinsser

CONCISE LANGUAGE: Or, A Rose by Any Other Name

12

Prose need not be pedestrian, but it must always be clear. Today, government offices, businesses, and consumer advocates are increasingly emphasizing the use of plain English instead of bureaucratese. Anyone who has ever waded through an insurance form or the instructions for preparing a tax return can only cheer.

This isn't to say that editors should vigorously excise all uncommon or erudite words from manuscripts. As an editor, you must watch nuances in the changes you're proposing. If an unusual word expresses the author's meaning and its everyday variant doesn't, you should respect the author's choice. If the text is awash in jargon and redundancy, however, you must help clarify meaning. Remember that each profession has its favorite words, its particular vocabulary, and its sacred cows. You can edit many of these words to enhance readability or to reach a larger audience and offend no one. But if there is the slightest ambiguity or doubt, either query or leave the words alone.

As an editor, you'll make many judgment calls in the course of working on a manuscript, but you must always respect the integrity of the author's style. You must also consider the intended audience: A specialist writing for other specialists can use expressions that someone writing for a lay audience can't.

What's familiarly called jargon often falls into the category of a noun string, a combination of nouns grouped together as if they were adjectives. Many phrases that began as noun strings have passed into common usage: *health maintenance organization* and *sample selection bias*, for example. Other strings, however, defy understanding.

Noun strings

```
Oklahoma Natural Gas Company Employee Counsel-
ing Program Evaluation Model

community banking funds transfer risk management
```

Sometimes nouns and adjectives are strung together.

```
Urban American Indian Adolescent Alcohol and
Drug Abuse Research Center

Spanish-speaking mental health resource center
```

Such strings create problems because you don't know until you get to the end of the string exactly what you're talking about. Even then, you may not be sure. Consider the following example.

```
paperwork reduction plan implementation meeting
preparation
```

What seems to be the subject? The very last word? Preparation for what? A meeting.... What's the meeting for? Implementation of a paperwork reduction plan..., but even that phrase can be broken down further. Untie the noun string.

```
preparation for a meeting to implement a plan
to reduce paperwork
```

One way to attack noun strings is to start from the end and break them into manageable chunks. Wherever possible, turn nouns into verbs and insert prepositions and articles to make the meaning clearer and to define the relationship among the elements. Consider this string.

```
computer spreadsheet program advance information
```

Again, go to the end; the last word is usually the subject of the phrase or clause. So the subject is *information* or rather *advance information*. Then deciphering the noun string becomes easy.

```
advance information on spreadsheet programs for
the computer
```

As you can see, noun strings are taxing and often frustrating for both the reader and the editor. Left uncorrected, noun strings obscure meaning and bog the reader down. Remember, too, that your interpretation of an ambiguous phrase may not conform to the author's. Unless you're absolutely certain of the meaning, query the author to be sure that you've correctly interpreted the thought.

Instructions: Try to make sense out of the sentences by turning nouns into verbs, adding prepositions, and breaking strings apart. For more practice, turn to appendix A, exercise 8.

1. Rapid operational equipment distribution is a
    strength of the new plan.

2. The plant safety standards committee discussed
    recent air quality regulation announcements.

3. This paper is an investigation into
    information processing behavior involved in
    computer human cognition simulation games.

4. Based on our extensive training needs
    assessment reviews and on selected office site
    visits, there was an identification of
    concepts and issues to constitute an initial
    staff questionnaire instrument.

5. Pancreatic gland motor phenomena are regulated
    chiefly by parasympathetic nervous system
    cells.

6. Diabetic patient blood pressure reduction may
    be a consequence of renal extract depressor
    agent application.

7. Corporation organization under state law supervision has resulted in federal government inability as to effective implementation of pollution reduction measures.

8. The end results of the evaluation will be furnished to the automotive parts item manager in the inventory control department.

ANSWERS

1. Rapid *of* operational equipment (distribution) is a strength of the new plan.

   Rapid distribution of operational equipment is a strength of the new plan.

   Adding a preposition and rearranging the words clarify the sentence enormously.

2. The plant safety standards committee discussed recent *on* air quality regulation announcements *about*

   The plant safety standards committee discussed recent announcements about regulations on air quality.

   You now have a sentence that clearly delineates the relationship among the various elements.

3. This paper ~~is an~~ investigat~~ion into~~ es how
information processing ~~behavior involved in~~ is ed in games where
computer~~ ~~ human cognition~~, simulation games.~~ is simulate

This paper investigates how information is

processed in games where computers simulate

human cognition.

The sentence now flows better and is comprehensible.

4. ~~Based on our~~ extensive training needs After an of

~~assessment~~ reviews ~~and on~~ selected office site~~s~~ to

visits, ~~there was an~~ identifi~~cation of~~ we ed the

~~concepts and~~ issues to ~~constitute~~ an initial include in

staff questionnaire ~~instrument~~.

After an extensive review of training needs

and visits to selected office sites, we identi-

fied the issues to include in an initial staff

questionnaire.

Some redundancies are gone now, and the sentence is in the active
voice.

5. Pancreatic gland, ~~motor phenomena~~ are regulated chiefly by parasympathetic nervous system ~~cells.~~

(handwritten edits: "the chief", "ors of the", "cells of the")

Cells of the parasympathetic nervous system

are the chief regulators of the pancreatic

gland.

Remove both the passive voice and the noun strings. If, for some reason, you want to leave the sentence in the passive voice, you can still remove the noun strings as shown above.

6. Diabetic patient, blood pressure, ~~reduction~~ may ~~be a consequence of~~ renal extract depressor ~~agent application.~~

(handwritten edits: "'s", "reduce a", "Applying a")

Applying a renal extract depressor may reduce

a diabetic patient's blood pressure.

This solution eliminates many unnecessary words and pares the sentence down to a simpler, more understandable form.

7. ~~Corporation organization under~~ state law ~~supervision has resulted in~~ federal government ~~inability as to~~ effective~~ly~~ implementation ~~of~~ pollution reduction measures.

(handwritten edits: "Because", "regulates", "the incorporation procedure, the", "Cannot", "by")

Because state law regulates the incorporation

procedure, the federal government cannot effec-

tively implement pollution reduction measures.

8. The ~~end~~ results of the evaluation ~~will be~~ ~~furnished to~~ the automotive parts item manager for in the inventory control department. *will receive*

The item manager for automotive parts in the inventory control department will receive the results of the evaluation.

Wherever possible, prefer the simple word. Many writers, especially those whose milieu is highly technical, are afraid to use simple words. Perhaps they fear that, in some readers' minds, simple words mean simple ideas; but simple prose can be lucid and elegant. Delete or replace jargon if you can do so with no loss of meaning. Avoid buzzwords like *to liaise, to interface,* and *to impact.* Eliminate redundancy: Phrases such as *final product, serious crisis,* and *end result* are redundant.

Replaceable words and phrases

Instructions: Find a shorter, simpler way to express the ideas shown below. Try to put the idea into one word. For many of the words, there are several equivalents, and context may dictate the choice of one variant over another. Appendix B contains a list of complex words and phrases and their simpler equivalents.

EXERCISE 19: CONCISE WRITING

Example: afford an opportunity   give a chance, or better, *let*

are desirous of *desire*
are in receipt of *have*
as a result of *because*
at an early date *earlier (soon)*
at a later date *later*
at the present time *currently / now*
at this point in time   "   "
at this time *now*
beneficial aspects *benefits*
by means of *by*

comes into conflict *conflicts with*
despite the fact that *despite*
during the course of *during*
effect an improvement *change (improve)*
for the purpose of *to ~~do this~~ / for*
for the reason that *because / for*
give consideration to *consider*
have a need for *need*
in agreement with *agree with*
in a timely manner *quickly / appropriately*
in close proximity to *close to*
in large measure *(largely)*
in order to *to*
in the absence of *without*
in the course of *during*
in the event that *if*
in the very near future *soon*
in view of the fact that *since*
make a determination of *determine*
make an adjustment in *adjust*
make provision for *provide / provide for*
make the assumption that *assume*
not in a position to *not able to / unable*
take action *acted / moved*
take appropriate measures *acted app.*
take into consideration *consider*
the extent to which *how*
to a large extent *largely*
until such time as *until*
with the exception of *except*
with the knowledge that *knowing that*
without further delay *quickly, soon, now*

are desirous of	*want*
are in receipt of	*have*
as a result of	*because*
at an early date	*soon*
at a later date	*later*
at the present time	*now*
at this point in time	*now*
at this time	*now*
beneficial aspects	*benefits*
by means of	*by*
comes into conflict	*conflicts*
despite the fact that	*despite*
during the course of	*during*
effect an improvement	*improve*
for the purpose of	*to*
for the reason that	*because*
give consideration to	*consider*
have a need for	*need*
in agreement with	*agree*
in a timely manner	*soon*
in close proximity to	*near*
in large measure	*largely*
in order to	*to* or *for*
in the absence of	*without*
in the course of	*during*
in the event that	*if*
in the very near future	*soon*
in view of the fact that	*because*
make a determination of	*determine*
make an adjustment in	*adjust*
make provision for	*provide*
make the assumption that	*assume*

not in a position to	*cannot*
take action	*act* or *do*
take appropriate measures	*act accordingly*
take into consideration	*consider*
the extent to which	*how much*
to a large extent	*largely*
until such time as	*until*
with the exception of	*except for*
with the knowledge that	*knowing*
without further delay	*now*

Smothered verbs

Smothered verbs are action words buried in a group of words: *have a need for* instead of *need*. Adverbs also get buried: *in large measure* or *to a great extent* for *largely*.

Exercise 20 will help you focus on smothered verbs in context. Many of these phrases are so common that we accept them without thinking. Remember that verbs carry the force of the language; eliminating excess words produces a tighter, more forceful sentence. So, usually, does removing the passive voice.

Instructions: Clarify these sentences by changing nouns into verbs. Decide which action the sentence is relating; try to use active verbs to indicate that action. Another exercise on smothered verbs appears in appendix A, exercise 9.

1. ~~A~~ modified ~~modification of~~ the original plan ~~was made~~ ~~by the staff assistant.~~

2. ~~The elimination of~~ wordy constructions ~~by~~ writers *should* ~~is a desirable feature.~~

3. ~~The~~ locat*ed* ~~location of~~ the missing memorandums ~~was~~ ~~discovered by~~ Mr. Prince.

4. The defendant ~~made a~~ confessed ~~confession~~ that he had been in town on Tuesday.

5. Upon court appearance by the defendant, courtroom legal proceedings will ~~be effected~~ ~~by the presiding judge.~~

6. The finalization of the plan was brought about by the committee, but only after 10 hours of discussion had been conducted.

7. The regulation makes it specific that analysis of the data must be conducted by technically qualified personnel.

8. Delivery of all the material must be achieved by the distributor within five working days of receipt of the order.

9. Compilation of the statistical data must reach completion by resource personnel no later than 15 June.

10. The accusation was leveled at the Nuclear Regulatory Commission by the GAO that it succumbed to failure in its attempt to force compliance to the ruling by local power plants.

ANSWERS

1. A modified ~~modification of~~ the original plan ~~was made~~ by the staff assistant.

The staff assistant modified the original plan.

The passive served no useful purpose in the original version; the corrected sentence is clearer.

2. The should ~~elimination of~~ eliminate wordy constructions ~~by~~ writers ~~is a desirable feature.~~

Writers should eliminate wordy constructions.

Cutting through wordy constructions isn't always as easy as it was here, but, as a maxim, the sentence is certainly valid.

3. The located ~~location of~~ the missing memorandums ~~was discovered by~~ Mr. Prince.

Mr. Prince located the missing memorandums.

4. The defendant ~~made a~~ confession^{ed} that he had

   been in town on Tuesday.

   The defendant confessed that he had been in

   town on Tuesday.

5. ~~Upon court appearance by~~ ^{When} the defendant[,] ^{appears in court}

   ~~courtroom legal~~ proceedings will ~~be effected~~ ^{begin}

   ~~by~~ (the presiding judge).

   When the defendant appears in court, the pre-

   siding judge will begin proceedings.

6. The ~~finalization of~~ ^{Committee approved} the plan, ~~was brought about~~

   ~~by the committee,~~ but only after 10 hours of

   discussion ~~had been conducted.~~

   The committee approved the plan, but only af-

   ter 10 hours of discussion.

7. The regulation ~~makes it~~ specifie^{es} that ~~analysis~~ ^{must ze}

   ~~of~~ the data ~~must be conducted by~~ technically

   qualified personnel.

   The regulation specifies that technically

   qualified personnel must analyze the data.

8. Delivery of all the material ~~must be achieved~~ *must* by the distributor within five working days of receipt of the order.

The distributor must deliver all the material within five working days of receipt of the order.

The last part of the sentence could still be reworked, but this version uncovers the verb and removes the passive voice.

9. Compilation of the statistical data ~~must reach completion by~~ resource personnel *must* no later than 15 June.

Resource personnel must compile the statistical data no later than 15 June.

10. The *GAO* accusa~~tion~~ *ed* ~~was leveled at~~ the Nuclear Regulatory Commission ~~by the GAO that it~~ ~~succumbed to~~ failure *of* ~~in its attempt~~ *ing* to force compl~~iance to~~ the ruling ~~by~~ *with* local power plants.

The GAO accused the Nuclear Regulatory Commission of failing to force local power plants to comply with the ruling.

Editors should watch for redundancies (tautologies, needless repetitions of an idea) and eliminate them. Many of the catchwords and phrases with which we are so familiar are actually redundant. For example, consider phrases such as these.

serious crisis	future plans
untimely death	important essentials
basic fundamentals	true facts
unconfirmed rumor	final outcome
past history	

By definition, a crisis is serious. Can facts be other than true? Has there ever been a timely death, except perhaps Attila the Hun's?

Each sentence in exercise 21 contains needless words; deleting them should become almost automatic. Many of the redundancies in this exercise seem commonplace, but they're still repetitious. Some are tautologies, like *new innovations;* some (such as *in order to*) are just superfluous. For more practice, see appendix A, exercise 10.

Instructions: Edit the sentences as needed. Delete redundant words and phrases; uncover smothered verbs and adverbs.

EXERCISE 21: REDUNDANCY

1. The agency seeks ~~new~~ innovations for

   disseminating standards.

2. We are accumulating the data ~~items~~ that ~~are~~

   needed to ~~carry out an~~ evaluation of the

   situation.

3. We must extend the deadline ~~in order~~ to

   guarantee delivery.

4. The chairman is ~~currently~~ reviewing the

   regulation.

5. A question contained on the form concerned the past history of the agency.

6. For the purpose of implementing your request, we need to know the nature of your future prospects.

7. The Department recognizes the general consensus of opinion.

8. The end result of the conference was satisfactory.

9. Headquarters is now in the process of preparing statements regarding policy.

10. The car you want can be obtained for the price of $15,000.

11. The requirements with respect to recruitment are similar to those used during the previous year.

12. Policy questions frequently arise during the course of complaint investigations.

13. Additional resources are required only in those instances when the data indicate the need to add them.

14. We might lighten the paperwork burden imposed
    on employees.

15. Emphasis is ~~placed~~ on voluntary compliance.

16. I was asked to review the decision ~~that was~~
    reached by the local units.

17. We must focus ~~our attention~~ on clear writing.

18. The litigant has 60 days ~~in which~~ to file an
    appeal.

19. Members ~~tended to choose~~ *chose* the location ~~which~~
    ~~was~~ nearest ~~to~~ their home.

20. You may prereserve your seat ~~by~~ calling in *ahead*
    ahead ~~advance~~.

1. The agency seeks ~~new~~ innovations for disseminating standards.

   The agency seeks innovations for disseminating standards.

   Innovations are by definition new.

2. We are accumulating the data ~~items that are~~ needed to ~~carry out an~~ evaluat~~ion~~ ~~of~~ the situation.

   We are accumulating the data needed to evaluate the situation.

   This sentence contains a smothered verb as well as extraneous words. Why say *carry out an evaluation* when *evaluate* alone is much stronger?

3. We must extend the deadline ~~in order~~ to guarantee delivery.

   We must extend the deadline to guarantee delivery.

4. The chairman is ~~currently~~ reviewing the regulation.

   The chairman is reviewing the regulation.

   The *-ing* form of the verb tells you that the action is in progress, so *currently* is redundant.

5. A question ~~contained~~ on the form concerned the

   ~~past~~ history of the agency.

   A question on the form concerned the history

   of the agency.

   Here, two words are unnecessary; if a question is on a form, it is contained there, and all history is past.

6. ~~For the purpose of~~ To implement~~ing~~ your request,

   we need to know ~~the nature of~~ your ~~future~~

   prospects.

   To implement your request, we need to know

   your prospects.

   The verb is buried, *the nature of* is unnecessary, and *prospects* are always future.

7. The Department recognizes the ~~general~~

   consensus ~~of opinion.~~

   The Department recognizes the consensus.

   This sentence contains a tautology: *Consensus* includes opinion and is general.

8. The ~~end~~ result of the conference was

   satisfactory.

   The result of the conference was satisfactory.

9. Headquarters is ~~now in the process of~~ preparing (statements ~~regarding~~ policy).

   Headquarters is preparing policy statements.

   The progressive form of the verb (*is preparing*) makes the phrase *now in the process* redundant. So is *regarding*.

10. The car you want ~~can be obtained for the price~~
    costs
    ~~of~~ $15,000.

    The car you want costs $15,000.

    You can shorten this sentence in several ways without losing any information.

11. The (requirements) ~~with respect to~~ recruitment
    are similar to ~~those used during the previous~~
    last
    year~~.~~ '*s*

    Recruitment requirements are similar to last year's.

    If you cut out the redundancy, the meaning is much clearer.

12. Policy questions frequently arise during ~~the course of~~ complaint investigations.

    Policy questions frequently arise during complaint investigations.

13. Additional resources are required only ~~in~~
    ~~those instances~~ when the data ~~indicate the~~ [Support]
    ~~need to add~~ them.

    Additional resources are required only when

    the data support them.

14. We might lighten ~~the~~ paperwork burden ~~imposed~~
    ~~on~~ employees.

    We might lighten employees' paperwork burden.

    As a sentence, this version leaves something to be desired; in context,
    it would be easier to fix. Avoid a discussion of whether paperwork is
    by definition a burden. The solution presented here assumes that it is.

15. ~~Emphasis is placed on~~ voluntary compliance. [is emphasized]

    Voluntary compliance is emphasized.

    Compliance could be grudging, so *voluntary* is necessary. Without
    more information it's difficult for an editor to eliminate the passive
    construction.

16. I was asked to review the decision ~~that was~~
    ~~reached by the~~ local units.

    I was asked to review the local units' decision.

    The passive should remain, unless you know who asked.

17. We must ~~focus our attention~~ on clear writing. [Concentrate]

    We must concentrate on clear writing.

    Focus our attention has a simpler equivalent.

18. The litigant has 60 days ~~in which~~ to file an

    appeal.

    The litigant has 60 days to file an appeal.

    The litigant has 60 days to appeal reflects a change in meaning. Filing an appeal is a legal process; appealing is not.

19. Members tended to choose the location ~~which~~

    ~~was~~ nearest to their homes.

    Members tended to choose the location nearest

    to their homes.

    This conservative edit retains the concept of a tendency. A heavier edit results in the following.

    Most members chose the location nearest their

    homes.

    There's a slight shift in meaning, and only the context will tell you whether this version is acceptable.

20. You may ~~pre~~reserve your seat by ~~calling in~~ telephone.

    ~~advance.~~

    You may reserve your seat by telephone.

In summary, when you can do so with no loss of meaning, use simple words. Your goal is not to impoverish the language, but rather to free it and allow it to communicate. The so-called plain English movement has clarified the language and even generated insurance policies that are readable. As an editor, keep your audience in mind, while heeding nuances in meaning.

Instructions: This article on a subject of interest to editors and publishers appeared a few years ago in The Editorial Eye. *The article has been extensively reworked to introduce errors. The main problems in the text are punctuation, spelling, grammar, and redundancy, but some style decisions have to be made as well. Use a dictionary to verify any unfamiliar spellings.*

Read through the exercise before you mark anything. Then concentrate on making the manuscript internally consistent. Be sure to note any general instructions or queries to the author. Also mark heads.

Note how long it takes you to edit the manuscript to your satisfaction. You'll need to make several passes through the text.

The answer key largely reflects the Eye's *version, followed by a detailed analysis of what needed to be fixed. (The paragraphs have been numbered to help you compare your corrections with the answer key.)*

FAIR USE AND COPYRIGHT: AN UNANSWERED QUESTIONS

1. What is copyright? Who owns it? How does

    an author or publisher obtain copy right?

    What is eligable for copyright protection?

    How much of a piece of work can be quoted or

    produced again without being considered as an

    infringement on the copyright laws? What

    affects has new technology had upon copyright?

    Of all these questions, fair use is the

    largest source of constraint for authors and

    editors.

    Fair Use

2.   Fair use is the one biggest exception to

    the copy-right law. That is, whatever the

    copyright owner decides is a fair quotation or

    use of the protected material does not create

copyright infringement. The current copyright law of recent years recognizes that the printing press is no longer the primary media of communication and fair use now includes phonorecords and reproduction copies, as well as printed material. The law specifies also the legitiment boundaries of fair use "criticism, comment, news reporting, teaching (including multiple copies for use in the classroom, scholarship, or research.

3.   It is this phase of the copyright law that is being so troublesome to authors, editors and publishers who get very confused with the details of the law. Exactly just what constitutes fair use? The law is unclear on this point and this point ultimately leaves the problem of its definition up to the owner of the copyright.

4.   For those people who wish to quote the material written by others than themselves, the lack of definition are most definite sources of worry and frustration. The law says that many factors could be considered in determining fair use, including:

• The purpose and characteristics of the use,
including whether such use is of a commercial
nature or that it is being used for nonprofit
purposes in an educational situation.

• what is the nature or topic of the work that
has been copyrighted.

- how much and how substantial a portion
used with respect to the ...whole piece is
important, too, and last but not least,

- How effective the use is upon the
potential market for the work that has been
copy righted

5. This means that the use an author besides
the original author makes of some copyrighted
material is not allowed in any way, shape, or
form to compete or diminish the existing
market value of the original work. Many
publishers believe 250 words to be fair use of
copyrighted material-that is material that
anyone can use and quote without first
obtaining permission from whomever they should
have obtained it from. But now think for a
minute, just suppose an author quoted 250
words from a 500 word article. Clearly, this

kind of quotation would diminish the value of the original work.

6.   Sometimes an author will object to having too little quoted. The chief book reviewer of the Washington Post took recently exception to a publishers' use, in promoting a trashy novel, of just two words from his review of the book, quoted, but not quoted in context. The general unfavorable review had been made to appear like an unqualified rave because of the purpose and character of the publisher's use of the quoted words obviously commercial in its use.

7.   A sample of a crosssection of publishers turned up a general consensus for a general policy of a request and requiring permission for anything and everything that is quotable. Most publishers want to know the use of the quoted material will be used, whether the person who wants permission will be charging a fee for the publication that the quoted material will appear in, and whether such use might be in direct competition with the original work. If you want to always be on

the safe side, ask permission in writing in advance of your publication date for anything you want to print again in a work you are publishing.

NEW TECHNOLOGY AND COPYRIGHT

8.   A very important recently new amendment to the law, closely related to fair use, has to due with reproduction, xerographic or otherwise, of a copyrighted work. The Copyright Act provide that libraries and Archives may make one copy or phonorecord of a work, and diseminate such single copies under certain particular stringent conditions. The reproduction must be made without any single purpose of commercial advantage, the collections of the library or Archive must be open and available to the public cummunity or available to all persons who are doing research in a specialized field, not just to those who are affiliated with the institution, and the reproduction must include the copyright notice. These rules only apply to unpublished works such as letter, dairies, journals, thesis, and disertations.

9.   The Newsletter Association of America contends, in its newsletter Hotline (vol. 6, no. 17) that libraries are abusing this section of the Act. Siting a report done for the Copyright office, Hotline says that the majority of users making library photocopies are either unaware of copyright notices or presume that duplication of copyright materials is permitted for educational or research purposes." In particular, NAA says that data-bases "use [copyright] materials without permission, under the guise of abstracts."

10.   To fight this abuse of the law, at least one computer based permissions system has appeared—the Copyright Clearance Center in Salem Massachusettes. The center is setup, according to its promotional material, to protect copyright holders from both deliberate and inadvertant infringment. The center used coded publication registartion forms, quite like those for copyright registration, to collect royalty fees, and convey permissions on behalf of it's participating publishers.

11.   Another instant of the affect of
communication technology are the provisions in
the now current law for paying, under a system
of compulsory liscencing, of certain royalties
for the secondary transmission of copyrighted
works vie cable tv.

Background on Copyright

12.   The first legislation on copyright was an
Act of Parliament passed in Britain in 1907,
aimed at preventing scrupulous book-sellers
from publishing works without the conscent of
the authors. It provided that the author of a
book had the soul right of publication for a
term of twentyone years, and the penalty for
infringement was a penny a sheet. The British
Copyright Law was amended and changed in 1801
(the fine went up to three-pence a sheet), and
again in 1842. In 1887 a group of Nations,
which was not including the US, ratified the
Berne Union copyright convention, which
required members of said group to have minimum
standards of copyright protection, and
applying them equally to all citizens of all
the nations that are all represented.

13. In the U.S.A., copyright found its protection in the constitution, Article One, section 1, Clause eight, ratified in 1879. In 1790, seperate legislation on copyright was enacted. The copyright Law was revised and altered again in 1831, 1870, 1909, 1976 and 1978, and the 1978 Law was amended in 1890.

14. According to The Nuts and Bolts of Copyright a pity booklet published by the copyright Office of the library of congress:

> Copyright is a form of protection given by the laws of the United States...to the authors of original works of authorship" such as literary, dramatic, musical, artistic, and certain other intellectual works.

"Copyright ownership"

15. Only the author or only the persons whom the author has given or assigned the rights to the work may have the opportunity to claim the copyright for that material. Between those other than the author, who may legitimatly claim copyright is an employer who's employees have created a copyrightable work as a result

of his or her employment (work for hire); a publisher to whom the author has relinquished the copyright or who has paid the author to create the work; someone who has comissioned a work, such as a sculptor, painting or piece of music, or someone who has asked the author to contribute their work to a collective endeaver such as a motion picture, a translation, or a anthology or as a test or instructional materials. It is extremely, extremely important to note that the owner of a manuscript, or original sheet music, or a painting, for example is not necessarily the owner of the copyright to those particular works that are copyrightable.

16.   To get and obtain copyright protection that protects copyrightable material, the orignator of the original work needs only to attach to it a notice of copyright, the form of which is specified in absolute detail in the copyright law. The notice must contain the symbol or the word "copyright" or the abbrev. "Copr;" the year of publication; and the name of the copyright owner; for example

" John Doe 1980". The notice of copyright must appear in a prominant place in the work that is to be protected. This element is something that again is extremely, extremely important in light of the 1978 revision of the revised copyright law wich specifies that any work published after January 1, 1987 without such notice permanently forfiets any and all copyright protection in the U.S. of A. This notice is all that is required to obtain and get the necessary copyright protection. Registration of copyright means filling out a series of forms and to send them with the correct amount of the fee, and with two copies of the work to the Copyright Office at its correct location. The copyright owner need not register the copyright with the library of Congress, however, if a law suit should ever araise over the work, the registration is very necessary to prove that ownership belongs to the owner.

The Final Summary In Brief

17.   On fair use and reproduction of copyrighted material, the copyright law undoubtedly

without a doubt rises more questions that they

answer. It does not try or make an attempt to

adress sophisticated electronic methods of

infringing on copyright and it spells out in

more detail than ever before the boundaries of

fair use. But it still is not descriptive in

the area of fair use, and that section of the

Act will continue to confuse and addle authers

and publishers and provide fertil ground for

legal and impartial, judicial debatable items.

ANSWERS

Remember to check your marks for correctness.

Format: First, you had to indicate the head level of the title. If this text were part of a larger manuscript, you would ensure that the format of the head levels corresponded to what went before and after. In this exercise, however, only one A-level head appears.

Find the first B-head, *Fair Use,* following the first paragraph. The head is shown flush left, caps and lowercase. Make the other B-heads (*New Technology and Copyright, Background on Copyright, Copyright Ownership,* and *The Final Summary in Brief*) match this one.

Note that the first paragraph was flush left, but others were indented. You should have marked the paragraph style for consistency. (Sometimes the first paragraph in an article is not indented, however, although the rest of the paragraphs are.) Did you notice that the other indents were inconsistent? Some paragraphs were indented three spaces; others, four. Such format errors may not seem like editorial problems, but they are.

(A) FAIR USE AND COPYRIGHT: AN UNANSWERED QUESTIONS

Paragraph 1: The first paragraph contains style questions, redundancies, and misspellings. According to the dictionary, *copyright* is one word. To achieve parallel construction in the third question, substitute *it*. Correct the spelling of *affects* and *eligable*. Note the redundancies: *produced again, being considered as,* and *upon.* You might have substituted *confusion* for *constraint,* although the change does affect the meaning slightly.

(margin, circled) # indents vary - make consistent

1.   What is copyright? Who owns it? How does
an author or publisher obtain copy right? *(it)*
What is eligable for copyright protection? *(i)*
How much of a piece of work can be quoted or
produced again without being considered as an *(re)*
infringement on the copyright laws? What *(ing)*
affects has new technology had upon copyright? *(e)*
Of all these questions, fair use is the
largest source of constraint for authors and *(confusion)*
editors.

(B) Fair Use

Paragraph 2: The first two sentences are relatively straightforward, but the third contains not only a redundancy (*of recent years*); it also lacks a comma (after *communication*). Note the plural *media* instead of the singular that is meant. The last sentence lacks an end quotation mark, about which you must query the author. You're also missing a closing parenthesis, but you can fix that yourself. For the sentence to make sense, you have to do something after *fair use;* add *as* or a colon. Finally, *legitimate* was misspelled and the sentence flows better if *also* precedes *specifies.*

(margin, circled) word OK?

(margin, circled) check quote - where does quote end?

2.   Fair use is the one biggest exception to *(R)*
the copyright law. That is, whatever the *(T)*
copyright owner decides is a fair quotation or *(of the)*
use of the protected material does not create
copyright infringement. The current copyright *(R)*
law of recent years recognizes that the
printing press is no longer the primary media *(um)*
of communication and fair use now includes
phonorecords and reproduction copies, as well
as printed material. The law specifies also
the legitiment boundaries of fair use *(ate)* *(as)*
"criticism, comment, news reporting, teaching

(including multiple copies for use in the

classroom), scholarship, or research.

3.   It is this ~~phase~~ *aspect* of the copyright law that

is ~~being~~ so troublesome to authors, editors,

and publishers ~~who get very confused with the~~

~~details of the law.~~ Exactly ~~just~~ what

constitutes fair use? The law is unclear on

this point and ~~this point~~ ultimately leaves

the problem of its definition up to the owner

of the copyright.

Paragraph 3: Deletions improve the first sentence. Also, add a serial comma after *editors* and change *phase* to *aspect* to clarify the meaning. The last sentence contains repetition of *this point*.

4.   For those ~~people~~ who wish to quote ~~the~~

material written by *persons* others than themselves,

the lack of definition ~~are~~ *is* most definite~~ly~~

a sources of worry and frustration. The law

says that many factors could be considered in

determining fair use, including: *the following*

• *What are* The purpose and characteristics of the use~~,~~?

~~including~~ *Is the quotation for* ~~whether such use is of a~~ commercial *use or*

~~nature or that it is being used~~ for nonprofit

purposes in an educational situation~~.~~?

• what is the nature or topic of the work? ~~that~~

~~has been~~ copyrighted~~.~~?

bullet • ~~how much and~~ how substantial *is the* ~~a~~ portion

used with ~~respect~~ *regard* to the whole piece? ~~is~~

Paragraph 4: Rewriting is necessary to make the first sentence flow better; moreover, the subject of the second clause disagrees with its verb. Both issues are easily resolved. The colon introducing the list, however, needs some support. (A colon must be preceded by a complete sentence.) Did you make the elements of the list consistent? Whether you chose bullets or dashes is immaterial, as long as you don't have both. Also, did you eliminate the redundancy?

Paragraph 5: This paragraph begins with a pronoun for which there is no antecedent. *Concept* works, although there are certainly other choices. The rest of the sentence needs tightening. You also need to add *with* after *compete* and then delete extraneous words and clarify meaning by adding a few words. To finish the paragraph, you need to mark the em-dash (*material—that*) and to add a hyphen to the unit modifier *500-word*.

Paragraph 6: The title of the newspaper (*The Washington Post*) needs to be marked for italics. The two transpositions (*recently took exception* and *publisher's*) are self-explanatory. The rest of the paragraph needs careful reading and editing.

~~important, too, and last but not least,~~

[bullet] ~~How~~ [What] effective [will] the use ~~is~~ [have] upon the potential market for the work? ~~that has been copyrighted~~

5. This [concept] means that the use ~~an author besides the original author makes~~ of ~~some~~ copyrighted material is not allowed ~~in any way, shape, or form~~ to compete [with] or diminish the existing market value of the original work. Many publishers believe [that] 250 words ~~to be~~ [constitute] fair use of copyrighted material—that is, ~~material that~~ anyone can ~~use and~~ quote [250 words] without first obtaining permission ~~from whomever they should have obtained it from.~~ ~~But now think for a minute, just~~ suppose an author quoted 250 words from a 500-word article. Clearly, this kind of quotation would diminish the value of the original work.

6. Sometimes an author will object to having too little quoted. The chief book reviewer of [*ital*] the Washington Post [took] ~~took~~ recently exception to a publisher's use, in promoting a trashy novel, of just two words from his review of the book, quoted [out of] ~~but not quoted in~~ context.

The general~~ly~~ unfavorable review had been made

to appear ~~like~~ an unqualified rave because of

the purpose and character of the publisher's

use of the quoted words obviously commercial for ~~purposes.~~

~~in its use.~~

7. (word OK?) A sampl~~e~~ing of a cross§section of publishers

~~turned up~~ showed a ~~general~~ consensus for a general

policy of ~~a request and~~ requiring permission

for anything ~~and everything~~ that is quotable.

Most publishers want to know how ~~the use of~~ the

quoted material will be used, whether the

person who wants permission will be charging a

fee for the publication in which ~~that~~ the quoted

material will appear in, and whether such use

might be in direct competition with the

original work. Editors and publishers who ~~If you~~ want to ~~always~~ be on

the safe side, should request ~~ask~~ permission, in writing, ~~in~~

before the ~~advance of your~~ publication date for anything

they ~~you~~ want to re§print ~~again in a work you are~~

~~publishing.~~

Paragraph 7: You can replace *sample* with *sampling,* but query the author. *Sampling* seems to make better sense, although it carries the connotation of a formal poll. If *crosssection* is left (it is redundant), it needs to be separated into two words as shown. The next sentence contains nonparallel elements in a series (use *how* to make the first phrase parallel with *whether* in the other two). In the last sentence the person changed for no apparent reason; edit into the third person and recast the sentence.

New Technology: Mark and correct the head.

Paragraph 8: Correct the redundancies, misspellings, and punctuation errors in this paragraph. Note the transposition: It fixes a misplaced modifier (*apply only*).

Ⓑ

NEW TECHNOLOGY AND COPYRIGHT

8.　　A very important recently new amendment to the law, closely related to fair use, has to deals due with reproduction, xerographic or otherwise, of a copyrighted work. The Copyright Act provides that libraries and [word OK?] Archives may make one copy or phonorecord of a work, and disseminate such this single copies copy under certain particular stringent conditions. The reproduction must be made without any single purpose of commercial advantage intent, the collections of the library or Archive must be open and available to the public cummunity or available to all persons who are anyone doing research in a specialized field, not just to those who are affiliated with the institution, and the reproduction must include the copyright notice. These rules only apply to unpublished works such as letters, dairies, journals, theses, and disertations.

9.   The Newsletter Association of America (NAA) contends, in its newsletter _Hotline_ (vol. 6, no. 17) that libraries are abusing this section of the Act. Citing a report done for the Copyright office, _Hotline_ says that "most majority of users making library photocopies are either unaware of copyright notices or presume that duplication of copyrighted materials is permitted for educational or research purposes." In particular, NAA says that data bases "use [copyright] materials without permission, under the guise of abstracts."

10.   To fight this abuse of the law, at least one computer-based permissions system has appeared—the Copyright Clearance Center in Salem, Massachusetts. The center is set up, according to its promotional material, to protect copyright holders from both deliberate and inadvertent infringement. The center used coded publication registration forms, quite like those used for copyright registration, to collect royalty fees, and convey permissions on behalf of its participating publishers.

Paragraph 9: Add the abbreviation _NAA_ to the first sentence, so that its later use in the paragraph is clear. The comma after _contends_ is wrong, unless you add another comma after the closing parenthesis. The name of the newsletter needs to be marked for italics both times it appears. _Most_ seems stronger here than _majority_. Query the lack of a beginning quote, and delete the hyphen in _data bases_. This term is sometimes found as one word and sometimes two, but it's not usually hyphenated.

Paragraph 10: _Computer-based_ is a unit modifier and needs a hyphen. Be sure to mark the em-dash also. The next sentence had two misspellings and a misplaced modifier; edit to read _According to its promotional material, the center...._ The rest of the paragraph has only straightforward corrections.

Paragraph 11: Edit this paragraph for spelling, punctuation, and redundancy.

11. Another instance of the effect of communication technology is the provisions in the current law for paying, under a system of compulsory licensing, certain royalties for the secondary transmission of copyrighted works via cable tv.

(B) Background on Copyright

Background on Copyright: Although the subhead is correctly formatted, you should mark the head anyway. (Marking even correct ones in this manner makes it easy to make global format changes later.)

Paragraph 12: The misplaced modifier (*passed in Britain in 1907*) needs to be corrected, and the date *1907* must be queried. If the rest of the dates in the paragraph are correct, this one isn't. How to treat *twenty-one* constitutes a style decision; if you're using GPO, the answer is *21*; Chicago specifies *twenty-one*. The rest of the errors in the paragraph are fairly mechanical. Remember, though, that most styles require you to spell out *United States* when it's used as a noun.

12. The first legislation on copyright was an Act of Parliament passed in Britain in 1907, [1709?] aimed at preventing unscrupulous booksellers from publishing works without the consent of the authors. It provided that the author of a book had the sole right of publication for a term of twenty-one years; and the penalty for infringement was a penny a sheet. The British Copyright Law was amended in 1801 (the fine went up to three-pence a sheet), and again in 1842. In 1887, a group of Nations, not including the US, ratified the Berne Union copyright convention, which required members of the group to have minimum

standards of copyright protection, and

applying them equally to all their citizens ~~of all~~

~~the nations that are all represented.~~

13. In the ~~U.S.A.~~ United States, copyright ~~found its~~

protection ed by ~~in~~ the constitution, (Article ~~One~~ I,

section 1, Clause eight), ratified in 1879. In

1790, seperate a legislation on copyright was

enacted. The copyright Law was revised ~~and~~

~~altered~~ again in 1831, 1870, 1909, 1976, ~~and~~

1978, and ~~the 1978~~ Law was amended in 1890. *[circled: 1980 ok? correct as edited?]*

14. According to The Nuts and Bolts of *[circled: ital]*

Copyright, a pithy booklet published by the

copyright Office of the library of congress,

Copyright is a form of protection given by

the laws of the United States...to the

[circled: open quote ok?] authors of "original works of authorship"

such as literary, dramatic, musical, artis-

tic, and certain other intellectual works.

Paragraph 13: This paragraph contains many problems. Articles of the Constitution are roman (*Article I*). There's a smothered verb (*found its protection*), which is replaced in the edited version with a present passive (present tense because the protection is continuing, passive because the focus is on copyright). Finally, query the dates. Without clarification, it's hard to know whether the edited version changed the meaning.

Paragraph 14: The corrections to this paragraph are fairly mechanical (adjusting spelling, capitalization, and punctuation).

Copyright Ownership: Of course, you deleted the quotation marks on the subhead.

Paragraph 15: Fix the subject-verb disagreement in the second sentence, and delete the auxiliary verbs (redundant in this case). The nonparallel constructions need correction, and errors in punctuation and spelling abound.

(B) "Copyright ownership"

15.   Only the author or ~~only~~ the persons to whom the author has given or assigned the rights to the work may ~~have the opportunity to~~ claim the copyright for that material. ~~Between~~ those other than the author who may legitimately claim copyright are an employer whose ~~who's~~ employees have created a ~~copyrightable~~ work as a result of ~~his or her~~ their employment (work for hire); a publisher to whom the author ~~has~~ relinquished the copyright or who ~~has~~ paid the author to create the work; someone who ~~has~~ commissioned a work, such as a sculpture ~~sculptor~~, painting, or piece of music, or someone who ~~has~~ asked ~~the~~ an author to contribute ~~their~~ work to a collective endeavor, such as a motion picture, a translation, or an anthology, or as a test or instructional materials. It is ~~extremely, extremely~~ important to note that the owner of a manuscript, ~~or~~ original sheet music, or a painting, for example, is not necessarily the owner of the copyright to ~~those~~ at ~~particular~~ works ~~that are copyrightable.~~

16.   To ~~get and~~ obtain copyright protection, ~~that protects copyrightable material,~~ the originator of the ~~original~~ work needs only ~~to~~ attach to it a notice of copyright, the form of which is specified in ~~absolute detail in~~ the ~~copyright~~ law. The notice must contain the symbol, or the word "copyright" *[ital]*, or the abbreviation *[ital]* "Copr"; the year of publication; and the name of the copyright owner; for example "© John Doe 1980". The notice of copyright must appear in a prominent place in the work. ~~that is to be protected.~~ This element is ~~something that again is extremely, extremely~~ important in light of the 1978 revision of the ~~revised~~ copyright law, which specifies that any work published after January 1, 1987, without such notice permanently forfeits any and all copyright protection in the U.S. ~~of A.~~ This notice is all that is required to ~~obtain and~~ get ~~the necessary~~ copyright protection. Registration of copyright means filling out a series of forms and ~~to~~ sending them with ~~the~~ a ~~correct amount of the~~ fee, and ~~with~~ two copies of the work to the Copyright Office. ~~at its~~

[margin annotations: "abbreviation correct? citation ital"; "ok? language of the law?"]

Paragraph 16: The second sentence contains many punctuation problems (the placement of commas and quotation marks) and needs a copyright symbol. Reference to words used as words should be italicized (*copyright*, *Copr*). Query the abbreviation, as well as the *any and all* phrase that appears later. Note the addition of the commas and the semicolon, all of which are grammatically necessary. The other corrections are self-explanatory.

correct location. The copyright owner need

not register the copyright with the library of

Congress; however, if a law suit should ever

arise over the work, the registration is very

necessary to prove that ownership belongs to

the owner.

(B) The Final Summary In Brief

The Final Summary In Brief: You can call it a *Summary* or *In Brief*, but not both.

Paragraph 17: There are antecedent problems (*they* can't refer to *law*, and *It* needs to be explained). Eliminate redundancies and make the other necessary corrections.

17.   On fair use and reproduction of copyrighted

material, the copyright law undoubtedly

without a doubt rises more questions than it

answers. It does not try or make an attempt to

adress sophisticated electronic methods of

infringing on copyright and it spells out in

more detail than ever before the boundaries of

fair use. But it still is not descriptive in precise enough about

the area of fair use, and that section of the the law

that deals with this subject

Act will continue to confuse and addle authers

and publishers and provide fertil ground for

legal and impartial, judicial debatable items.

How well did you do? Did your second and third passes through the material uncover more problems? Remember that even experienced editors don't find every error the first time. An experienced editor would need about 90 minutes for a manuscript of this length. If the text had been single spaced, editing would have taken longer, because the pages would then have been harder to read and mark.

Read the exercise again carefully and check your work against the key. The original article appears in appendix D; you may want to refer to it as well. If you still don't understand the corrections or the notations, refer to the appropriate sections in this book. If you believe that the work is especially difficult or that you worked too slowly, remember that speed and accuracy come with practice.

N obody goes broke in America now; we have money problem areas. It no longer rains; we have precipitation activity. Choose one noun, preferably one that is short and specific. Choose it carefully and it will do the job.

—William Zinsser

CITATIONS AND TABLES: The Supporting Documentation

13

Citations and tables are full of editorial style elements: colons, capitals, commas, page numbers, and other things. Attention to these details is the test of a good copyeditor. Editing citations and tables isn't easy, and there's no substitute for practice. Sloppy citations reflect poorly on their authors; readers look at such work with a jaundiced eye, no matter how sound the research or electrifying the results.

The descriptions in this chapter aren't meant to be exhaustive; they merely serve to point out the kinds of information in citations and the sorts of things you must make consistent. To edit references successfully, you must cultivate methodical work habits and attention to detail. It also helps to have a sample format for each type of citation you might encounter.

As a copyeditor, you'll rely heavily on a style guide or style sheet to work on references. When you edit them, be alert for missing information or inconsistencies; you can't edit references mechanically and simply impose the proper format.

As intimidating as references seem to a beginning editor (and even to experienced ones), you learn the patterns of the different formats eventually, and the job does get easier. This is not to say that you won't need to use a style guide; rather, you'll know where to look when you have a question, and you'll know what questions to ask.

The form of the in-text references (footnotes, endnotes, or in-text citations) and the format of the citations themselves (capitalization, punctuation, and word order) are style questions. *The Chicago Manual of Style* and the *Publication Manual of the American Psychological Association* devote entire chapters to citations. The *GPO Style Manual* devotes only one page to citations, saying merely that many styles are acceptable.

Many journals or publishers have their own preferred style for citations. A style sheet or manual with examples of each sort of citation—journal, book, chapter, report, single author, multiple author, corporate author, and so on—is indispensable.

Citations must contain certain kinds of information, although each style presents the information differently. Facts that must be included are the name of the author or authors, the title, the year of publication, and the publishing data (i.e., the city of publication, publisher, or title of the journal or book in which the work appeared). The purpose of such detailed citation is to allow readers to verify or obtain information. Authors often write extensively on a particular subject, and each publishing fact is important to distinguish one citation from another.

References

Although traditional footnotes haven't disappeared altogether (see the Chicago manual), most trade books and nonscientific journals now put the notes at the end of each chapter or together at the end of the book (hence the term *endnotes*). Moreover, many style guides have adopted the author-date style of citation exclusively.

When the author-date system is used, the details of publication are relegated to a reference list at the end of the book or article, which contains only works mentioned in the text; additional sources are listed in a bibliography.

As an alternative to this author-date citation method, some scientific journals list all cited sources in a numbered, alphabetized reference list and then insert the number of the reference in parentheses in the text whenever the source is to be cited.

Here are some examples of these more concise, in-text citation systems:

```
Before proceeding with a discussion of our find-
ings, it is helpful to examine the conclusions
of previous researchers in the field (Adams and
Taylor 1986; Cormier 1987; and Mickle 1985).
```
[Chicago]

```
Before proceeding...in the field (Adams & Tay-
lor, 1986; Cormier, 1987; and Mickle, 1985).
```
 [APA style]

```
Before proceeding...in the field (1, 3, 6).
```
[Council of Biology Editors Style Manual]

Note that Chicago uses no punctuation between the author's name and the date in text, whereas the APA style manual does.

Each of these examples uses an abbreviated mention in text to correspond to the full citation in the references.

No matter which system (author-date or numbers) is used, as a copyeditor you're expected both to put the references in the proper format according to the manual used and to check the citations in text against the references to see that the list matches the text. For instance, if the text says that the Mickle reference dates from 1985 and the reference list says 1986, you should try to verify the date and make the appropriate change or call the discrepancy to the author's attention.

As a manuscript goes through various revisions, references invariably suffer. Text gets shifted and references get misnumbered, misplaced, or even dropped. A copyeditor should check references at the end of every revision cycle, even if they've been checked before. Such a review is a form of insurance—and it's essential for heavily referenced material that has been extensively edited.

Checking in-text citations against the references should be the last step in the editing cycle. It's too hard to edit and cross-check references at the same time. As you encounter each reference, put a check mark next to it or highlight it. If you're dealing with sequential numbers, note any that are missing and query the author. If an author-date citation lacks a date, query the author also.

Here are two generic formats for books cited in a reference list or bibliography.

```
Tuchman, B. 1962.   The guns of August.   New
York: Dell.
```

```
Tuchman, Barbara.   The Guns of August.   New
York: Dell Publishing Co., 1962.
```

The most obvious difference in these two citations is the placement of the date. Also, in the first case, the author's first name and the publisher's name are abbreviated. In both examples, each segment of information is followed by a period and the title is italicized. The capitalization style differs; some styles always use initial caps, and some prefer sentence-style capitalization—in which only the first word of a title or subtitle is capped (unless it contains proper nouns). Some styles separate parts of the reference with commas, some use only initials of authors, some use no space between initials, some use two spaces after a colon, and so on.

A citation to a chapter in a book or to a revised or subsequent edition of a book must reflect the chapter or edition. The format might then be as follows.

```
Adams, Mara.   "In Defense of the Passive."   In
Bruce Boston, ed., Stet! Tricks of the Trade
for Writers and Editors.   Alexandria, VA:  Edi-
torial Experts, Inc., 1986.
```

```
Tuchman, Barbara.  The Guns of August (2d ed.).
New York:  Dell Publishing Co., 1962.

Tuchman, B. 1962. The guns of August (rev.
ed.). New York: Dell.
```

Capitalization or abbreviation of information also varies from style to style (2d ed., 2nd ed., rev. ed.). If the work is a compilation of articles, the author's name is given first and the title and editor of the work follow (In J. Smith, *Here We Are*). Any other aberrations (two locations for the publisher, translation of a foreign work, report number for technical documentation, treatment of unpublished material, and so on) must also be dealt with. It's easy to see why you need a standard style manual or a style sheet from your own organization.

Here are some typical formats for a reference to a journal article.

```
Chomsky, Noam, and Morris Halle. "Some Contro-
versial Questions in Phonological Theory." Jour-
nal of Linguistics 1(1965): 97-138.

Chomsky, N., & Halle, M. 1965. Some controver-
sial questions in phonological theory. Journal
of Linguistics 1(2): 97-138.
```

Look at the differences again. In the first case, the date follows the volume number of the journal; in the second, it follows the authors' names. Some styles use ampersands to connect multiple authors; some put the title of the article in quotation marks; some cite the issue number as well as the volume [(2) above]; some use initial caps.

The order of unnumbered references at the end of a section or a manuscript is also a style question. The general rule is that works are arranged alphabetically (but even the system of alphabetization is a style question); works by an individual author precede works by that author and others; and entries by the same author or authors are arranged chronologically. Works by the same author or authors in the same year are alphabetized according to the title.

Footnotes or endnotes contain the same information as references, in a slightly different format. Usually the author's name is given in normal (not reverse) order, and the elements are separated by commas rather than periods. Also different is the practice of abbreviating information, using such terms as ibid. (in the same place), op. cit. (the work cited), loc. cit. (in the place cited), and id. (the same). Ibid. refers to the work mentioned in the preceding note. No author or title is used with ibid., but a page number or volume can be cited if the information differs from the earlier mention. (All these common terms that were previously set in italics because they were Latin have now entered the dictionary as English words; hence they are no longer italicized.)

Many organizations require that op. cit. and loc. cit. be replaced with references giving the last name of the author, a shortened title, and a page number. In a heavily referenced book, you could search endlessly for that earlier citation (*Adams, op. cit., p. 12*), only to discover that Adams was deleted in an earlier revision. It's also easy to confuse two works by the same author and cite the wrong one.

Tables illustrate material in a form that makes the text easier to grasp. The reader must draw inferences from or interpret the tables, and the copyeditor should make that task easy. As a copyeditor, you won't normally set up tables or decide on the specifications for table makeup; the author or substantive editor has presumably already made those decisions. Rather, you'll examine the tables in relation to the text and in relation to one another, suggest a subhead here or a footnote there, and make sure the tables are consistent in format. Both the Chicago and GPO style manuals devote whole chapters to handling tabular material.

Different copyeditors approach tables differently; as you work, you'll develop your own approach and decide which practices serve you best. As a general rule, however, look first at each table in relation to its description in the text. Does the table match its description? Does it prove or illustrate what the author says it does? Next, mark its callout in the margin (*T. 1*, in a circle) or highlight it so that the keyboarder can insert the table in the proper place. Then edit the table for format and obvious inconsistencies. Always check simple math and query any discrepancies. If percentages don't total 100 percent, you'll need a disclaimer on rounding. (*Note: numbers may not total exactly because of rounding.*) Without such disclaimers, readers will assume that math is correct; obvious errors leave the audience suspicious and less disposed to accept the author's premises and assertions.

As a final step, pull all the tables out of the text and look at them together; this step brings inconsistencies to light. For example, the absence of a column head will be more glaring when one table is seen alongside others that do have such heads. Other format errors will be easier to see as well.

Notes

Tables

Traditionally, tables are considered artwork, as are figures, exhibits, schematics, and so on. Because materials of this kind are often prepared and stored separately from the text, the margin for error increases. Figure and exhibit captions must be checked against their descriptions in text and against the figures themselves. Most style sheets specify the format for captions; if your particular style sheet doesn't, ask your supervisor or client.

Tables are often set off from text by rules above and below. A few years ago, vertical rules (down rules) had somewhat gone out of fashion both because they tend to make a table look cluttered and because they often had to be drawn in by hand (and thus added to publication expense). Software, however, makes such rules easier and less expensive to include than in the past.

Each entry or item in a table has a correct name, as indicated on the following table. Note the following definitions.

Table: The term used to designate the entire tabular presentation.

Body: The "tabular" part of the table; excludes the title, headnote, and footnotes.

Field: The area within the body of the table in which the figures are entered (excludes the stub and boxhead).

A few of the terms merit some additional explanation. *Cell* refers to any entry in a table; *footnotes* usually appear in the text of the table as superscript letters, although (especially in a table with dense text) numbers or asterisks are also used. At the bottom of the table, the footnote numbers may be either superscript or level with the text of the note and followed by a period (1.). The presence or absence of commas in groups of figures is a style question, as are the format and order of the notes at the end. You must always follow the style guide and ensure consistency among the tables themselves.

TERMS USED IN DISCUSSING TABULAR PRESENTATIONS

Main Title

Subtitle

Headnote

TENTH ARMY FY 19XX ANNUAL FUNDING PROGRAM
AND OBLIGATIONS, BY INSTALLATION
As of 31 December 19XX
(Thousands of dollars)

Stub

Spanner Heading

Stub Heading

Boxhead

Group Caption

Line Caption

Leaders

Reference Symbol

Column Heading

Cell

Ruling

General Note

Source Note

Reference Note

Footnotes

Installation[a]	Annual Funding Program[b]	Obligations			
		Actual Jul - Dec 19XX		Estimated Jan - June 19XX	
		Amount	Percentage of Program	Jan - March	Apr - Jun
TENTH ARMY TOTAL .	107,785	55,018	51.0	28,937	23,830
CLASS I	95,843	48,797	50.9	25,812	21,234
Fort Allen	20,612	10,265	49.8	6,519	3,828
Fort Gates	10,942	5,526	50.5	2,702	2,714
Fort Montgomery	44,939	23,413	52.1	111,123	10,403
Fort Schuyler.	5,148	2,502	48.6	1,320	1,326
Fort Sullivan	4,765	2,425	50.9	1,405	935
Camp Clark	2,375	1,181	47.6	719	525
Camp Greene	967[c]	493	51.0	253	221
Camp Putnam	4,406	2,040	46.3	1,321	1,045
Camp Stark	1,125	623	55.4	265	237
Camp Ward	564	379	67.2	185	[d]
CLASS II.	11,942	6,221	52.1	3,125	2,596
Buchanan Army Depot . . .	661	364	55.1	161	136
Dearborn Arsenal	1,534	822	53.6	375	337
Funston Army Terminal . .	1,221	600	49.1	354	267
Hull Missile Plant	2,242	1,258	56.1	502	482
Pierce General Hospital . .	1,262	557	44.1	417	288
Shafter Proving Ground . .	1,196	636	53.2	296	264
Taylor Armory	1,715	885	51.6	475	355
Warren Ordnance Works .	1,291	611	47.3	361	319
Other[e]	820	488	59.5	134	148

NOTE: This table presents for the first time the status of funds for each installation for all appropriations for which funds are allocated to Tenth Army.

SOURCE: Status of Allotments and Operating Accounts, RCS ARACO-14.

a. Data for each installation include funds for subinstallations.
b. Funds increased $11 million from 30 November 19XX.
c. An increase of $700,000 has been requested of higher headquarters for activation of two infantry battalions.
d. Less than $500. Installation to be inactivated.
e. Includes three District Engineer offices and Wheeler Army Depot.

EXERCISE 23: TABLES

Instructions: *Assume that the following three tables belong to the same document and need to be made consistent. Figure out how to approach the tables; look at each part alone and in relation to the whole; then make a list of the discrepancies and inconsistencies you see here. Don't edit the tables yet. Compare your list with the answer key on page 230.*

TABLE 1

STATEMENT OF OPERATING AND NET WORTH
(DEFICIT) FOR 1994 AND 1995

	YEAR ENDED DECEMBER 31	
	1995	1994
REVENUES:		
Member Dues and Fees (Net of Journal Credit) . .	$ 1,098,335	$ 1,033,794
Journal Subscriptions	2,750,551	2,131,036
Advertising	254,907	200,816
Other Journal Revenue	216,623	223,304
Sales of Other Publications, Goods, and Services	835,815	415,257
Registration Fees	126,587	64,975
Exhibit Space Rental	58,650	33,718
Accreditation Fees	90,025	69,300
Investments	106,816	89,441
Building Revenue	286,637	299,552
Grants and Contracts	314,791	717,743
[a]Other Revenue	135,253	108,955
TOTAL REVENUES	$ 6,274,990	$ 5,387,891
EXPENSES		
Personnel	$ 2,415,982	$ 2,068,591
Printing and Mailing of Publications	1,646,075	1,454,925
Editor's Stipends and Office Expenses	233,536	216,044
Professional, Consulting and Contractual Services	356,549	334,125
Travel (Other Than Boards and Committees) . . .	96,882	142,998
Boards and Committees	216,048	193,779
Convention and Local Site Expenses	69,760	43,246
Supplies, Postage, Telephone, Other Common Office Expenses	535,635	340,307
Building Expenses	561,391	552,779
[b]Other Expenses	216,072	162,435
TOTAL EXPENSES	$ 6,347,930	$ 5,508,229
NET SURPLUS (DEFICIT)	$ (272,940)	$ (120,338)

[a]Includes line items of revenue such as mailing list rentals and royalties.

[b]Includes line items of expense such as offsite data processing, allotments to
  divisions, office equipment purchase and rental.

(Exercise 23 continued)

TABLE 2

REVENUES, EXPENSES AND NET BY MAJOR PROGRAM:

JANUARY 1 - DECEMBER 31, 1995

MAJOR PROGRAM	REVENUES	EXPENSES	NET SURPLUS (DEFICIT)
SERVICES AND ACTIVITIES (NON-PUBLISHING). . .	$1,720,364	1,967,046	$(246,682)
COMMUNICATIONS. . . . (PUBLICATIONS AND BIOGRAPHICAL SERVICES)	3,752,605	3,623,014	129,591
BUILDING OPERATIONS .	286,637	286,637	0
GRANTS AND CONTRACTS	314,791		0
OTHER (INVESTMENTS, MAILING LABELS, AND OTHER).	200,593	156,442	44,151
TOTAL	$6,274,990	6,347,930	$(72,940)

Table 3. REVENUES, EXPENSES, AND SURPLUS (DEFICITS) FOR 1982 - 1994

YEAR	REVENUES	EXPENSES	SURPLUS (DEFICIT)	SURPLUS (DEFICIT) AS % OF EXPENSES
1982[A]	1,275	1,165	110	9.4
1983	1,603	1,582	21	1.3
1984[B]	1,615	1,668	(53)	(3.2)
1985	1,642	1,602	40	2.5
1986	2,406	2,271	135	6.0
1987	2,850	2,661	189	7.1
1988	2,983	2,836	147	5.2
1989	3,528	3,485	43	1.2
1990	4,235	4,197	38	.9
1991	5,053	5,041	12	.2
1992	5,286	5,308	(22)	(.4)
1993	5,388	5,508	(120)	(2.2)
1994	6,275	6,348	(73)	(1.1)

NOTE: IN THOUSANDS
    A   DOES NOT REFLECT GRANT ACTIVITY
    B   DOES NOT REFLECT CAPITAL GAIN OF $148,858 ON SALE OF
        PROPERTY LOCATED IN WASHINGTON, DC

The most glaring difference among the three tables is that two have boxes and one doesn't. Also look at the format of the table titles—caps and score; caps, colon, and partial score; caps. You should be able to resolve these discrepancies by working with the specifications for the job or the style guide. Next, table 1 has caps only in the heads; all table 2 entries are in caps. In addition, table 1 group captions (REVENUES, EXPENSES) have inconsistent ending punctuation—one has a colon and one doesn't. It seems logical to make table 2 entries caps and lowercase, but check the style sheet.

You should have found inconsistencies in the following areas. (Text discussion follows.)

Rules

No box on table 1

Boxes on tables 2 and 3

Table notation

TABLE 1 (all caps)

TABLE 2 (caps and score)

Table 3. (clc with period)

Title

STATEMENT OF OPERATING AND NET WORTH (DEFICIT) FOR 1994 AND 1995 (caps and score)

REVENUES, EXPENSES AND NET BY MAJOR PROGRAM:

JANUARY 1 - DECEMBER 31, 1995 (caps, colon, partial score)

REVENUES, EXPENSES, AND SURPLUS (DEFICITS) FOR 1982 - 1994 (caps, no score)

Spacing

Around the titles

Around the notes

Within the tables, between entries and under column heads

Text

Caps and lower case (table 1)

All caps (table 2)

Notes

Superscript reference notes (table 1)

Reference notes on the line (table 3)

Notes in sentence style (table 1)

Notes all caps (table 3)

Notes flush left (table 1)

Notes indented (table 3)

No serial comma in title (table 2) and inconsistent serial comma in text (table 1)

Serial comma in title (table 3) and in text (table 2)

Colon after group caption (table 1); no colon after group caption (table 1)

Period after reference notes (table 1)

No period after reference notes (table 3)

Now, go back and edit the tables. Compare your answers against the following keys. There's no style sheet, so you'll have to make up your own specifications. Just be consistent.

Remember that if you, the editor, find the text of tables too dense or hard to read or understand, your reader is likely to do the same. Sometimes a little more space will make all the difference; occasionally you may have to work with the author to revise the presentation.

TABLE 1.

STATEMENT OF OPERATING AND NET WORTH
(DEFICIT) FOR 1994 AND 1995

[handwritten: delete scores under title]
[handwritten: add rules]
[handwritten: needs stub]
[handwritten: center cols]

	YEAR ENDED DECEMBER 31	
	1995	1994
REVENUES:		
Member Dues and Fees (Net of Journal Credit) . .	$ 1,098,335	$ 1,033,794
Journal Subscriptions	2,750,551	2,131,036
Advertising	254,907	200,816
Other Journal Revenue	216,623	223,304
Sales of Other Publications, Goods, and Services	835,815	415,257
Registration Fees	126,587	64,975
Exhibit Space Rental	58,650	33,718
Accreditation Fees	90,025	69,300
Investments	106,816	89,441
Building Revenue	286,637	299,552
Grants and Contracts	314,791	717,743
[a]Other Revenue	135,253	108,955
TOTAL REVENUES	$ 6,274,990	$ 5,387,891
EXPENSES		
Personnel	$ 2,415,982	$ 2,068,591
Printing and Mailing of Publications	1,646,075	1,454,925
Editor's Stipends and Office Expenses	233,536	216,044
Professional, Consulting and Contractual Services	356,549	334,125
Travel (Other Than Boards and Committees) . . .	96,882	142,998
Boards and Committees	216,048	193,779
Convention and Local Site Expenses	69,760	43,246
Supplies, Postage, Telephone, Other Common Office Expenses	535,635	340,307
Building Expenses	561,391	552,779
[b]Other Expenses	216,072	162,435
TOTAL EXPENSES	$ 6,347,930	$ 5,508,229
NET SURPLUS (DEFICIT)	$ (272,940)	$ (120,338)

[a]Includes line items of revenue, such as mailing list rentals and royalties.

[b]Includes line items of expense, such as offsite data processing, allotments to divisions, and office equipment purchase and rental.

In table 1, each entry has leaders, and runover lines are indented. Note that the <u>TOTAL</u> cells are indented. Such a format is typical, but the presence of reference notations before the entries ([a]<u>Other Revenue...</u>) is not. These notes should be moved to follow their entries. Also, check that reference notes appear both in the table and at the end. A callout in the table must have a matching note and vice versa.

The right-hand columns of table 1 follow accounting style; that is, 1995 precedes 1994. (Ordinarily tables should read left to right chronologically.) See whether the columns are aligned consistently (they are), and check that dollar signs appear at the first entry and at the total entries in each column. Finally, check the math; there is indeed a discrepancy in table 1. Total revenues should equal total expenses, plus surpluses or deficits: The 1995 net deficit in table 1 appears to be off by some $200,000.

TABLE 2

REVENUES, EXPENSES, AND NET BY MAJOR PROGRAM for

JANUARY 1 DECEMBER 31, 1995

MAJOR PROGRAM	REVENUES	EXPENSES	NET SURPLUS (DEFICIT)
SERVICES AND ACTIVITIES (NON-PUBLISHING) . . .	$1,720,364	1,967,046	$(246,682)
COMMUNICATIONS. . . . (PUBLICATIONS AND BIOGRAPHICAL SERVICES)	3,752,605	3,623,014	129,591
BUILDING OPERATIONS .	286,637	286,637	0
GRANTS AND CONTRACTS	314,791	314,791	0
OTHER (INVESTMENTS, MAILING LABELS, AND OTHER)	200,593	156,442	44,151
TOTAL	$6,274,990	6,347,930	$(72,940)

add leaders (handwritten)

missing number added = ok? (handwritten)

In table 2, the title and the format of the entries must conform to your style guide and the format of table 1. Furthermore, the EXPENSES column is missing one entry; checking the math shows that zero isn't the answer. You can readily conclude what the correct figure is; insert it and query the author to make sure it's correct. This column is also missing dollar signs. These figures relate to those in the previous table: REVENUES, EXPENSES, and NET DEFICIT figures (corrected) are the same. One further correction needs to be made to the second entry in the left-hand column: The leaders should follow the runover line, not the first one. You then need to move the figures in the next three columns down three lines to follow their leaders; mark with brackets (⌊⌋) or with one long bracket to include all three (⌊_____⌋). While you're looking at spacing, note that the first two column heads are centered over the figures, while the third is aligned right.

(Exercise 23 continued)

Table 3. REVENUES, EXPENSES, AND SURPLUS (DEFICITS) FOR 1982 - 1994

YEAR	REVENUES	EXPENSES	SURPLUS (DEFICIT)	SURPLUS (DEFICIT) AS % OF EXPENSES
1982	1,275	1,165	110	9.4
1983	1,603	1,582	21	1.3
1984	1,615	1,668	(53)	(3.2)
1985	1,642	1,602	40	2.5
1986	2,406	2,271	135	6.0
1987	2,850	2,661	189	7.1
1988	2,983	2,836	147	5.2
1989	3,528	3,485	43	1.2
1990	4,235	4,197	38	.9
1991	5,053	5,041	12	.2
1992	5,286	5,308	(22)	(.4)
1993	5,388	5,508	(120)	(2.2)
1994	6,275	6,348	(73)	(1.1)

NOTE: (IN THOUSANDS)
A DOES NOT REFLECT GRANT ACTIVITY
B DOES NOT REFLECT CAPITAL GAIN OF $148,858 ON SALE OF PROPERTY LOCATED IN WASHINGTON, DC

For table 3, you must make the title consistent with the others. The placement of the column heads is erratic—the stub and far-right column heads align to the right; the other three are centered. As an editor, you need to determine the style and make a circled notation in the margin (e.g., *center cols under heads*, or *align on the right*). Use close-up hooks on the parentheses in the fourth and fifth columns. Finally, check to see that no years are missing from the series in the stub (always a good idea with any list or series) and that the reference notes correspond to those in the text. At this point, it becomes apparent that the format of the notes here differs from that of table 1. You'd have to check your style guide or the specifications to edit and space one of the sets of notes. Other problems are simple inconsistencies in spacing and punctuation.

Good editors are not obsessed with
commas, spacing around headings,
or parallelism. We are obsessed with readers
and their ability to understand printed words
and thoughts as effortlessly as possible.

—*Mary J. Scroggins*

CONCLUSION: Editing in the Electronic Age

14

Today, no book about editing techniques is complete without a discussion of on-line editing—work performed at a computer terminal.

Just as word processing has revolutionized writing, so eventually will on-line editing change editors and editing. Computers allow text to be transmitted and stored electronically; they also check spelling and perform search-and-replace tasks. These functions all save time and money.

With computers, several reviewers can work on one document at the same time, each person making changes and incorporating comments. When the reviewers finish, they can send their document electronically to the author. No longer must pieces of paper change hands. Even when you're the sole editor, having the manuscript on disk allows you and the writer to work together. You can each look at a screen as you discuss matters over the telephone and make the appropriate changes. You can ask for data or clarification, and the author can transmit either one simply and easily.

There are certain disadvantages, however, as critics are quick to point out. Working at a terminal can be more fatiguing than working on paper, and visualizing a document is harder, because most screens don't display an entire page.

Until recently, no programs designed specifically for editing were available; this presents no problem for people who simply edit a text and pass it on to the next stage of production. In other words, if a clean, edited copy is all that is required, an editor who is conversant with the word processing system being used can start with the electronic file (which has been duplicated for safety's sake) and make the necessary changes. The original version can also be printed out in hard-copy (manuscript) form, in case the editor needs to refer to it.

A problem arises when the author or editor must see both the original and the edited versions on screen at once. Some programs save the original in a window; others use a feature called "hidden text," which allows the user to place comments or changes in the text and print them out or hide them at will. Hidden text allows an editor to embed questions or proposed changes in the text and determine later whether the changes should be seen or done. Another feature is redlining, which uses strikeout and shadowing to mark additions or deletions to the text. This feature is particularly useful to the legal profession, which scrutinizes every change for possible repercussions. These features are a boon to writers, who can sprinkle their work with reminders visible only to themselves and track changes as well.

What are now called "editing programs" or "grammar checkers," however, work on the same principle as spelling checkers: That is, they compare the text with a dictionary of rules and practices, advise the user on the status of the document (readability level, jargon index, complexity, and so on), and suggest possible changes.

Machine editing is mechanical; the computer doesn't think or make judgments. Each time it recognizes *occur*, for example, it may suggest that *occur* be replaced by *happen*. Sometimes this substitution is advisable and sometimes it isn't. Or the software may be programmed to avoid the use of the word *very* and seek to replace *very* whenever it appears. Aggravation is inevitable.

Editing programs certainly have their place; they point out punctuation problems (they look for pairs of quotation marks and parentheses, for example) and glaring grammatical errors. But they're no substitute for a person who can weigh alternatives and make judgments.

Furthermore, any system is only as good as the person who uses it. A keyboarder with an editing program isn't an editor, any more than a clerical worker with a desktop publishing program is a graphic artist. In editing there are often no right or wrong answers; choices depend on contexts and intangibles such as flow, euphony, and audience.

True editing software is still in its infancy, but, like other offspring of the information revolution, it will grow up fast. Editors need to understand the advantages computers offer while being aware of the limitations and changes technology imposes.

Editors also need to understand that they will likely find themselves doing more keyboarding, not less. In the publications workplace, roles are shifting. Companies are increasingly doing more with less, and for editors that means being expected to key their changes and sometimes even produce camera-ready pages. Many journals are now edited exclusively on-line because companies have discovered that it's more cost-effective that way. The whole production cycle is streamlined if editing is done electronically. It's perhaps unrealistic to think that paper can be completely eliminated, but it's certainly a goal to strive for.

We all need to remember that using a pencil instead of a keyboard doesn't make a person an editor; it's the function that a person performs, rather than the tools used or the number of passes through a manuscript. Editors strive for the perfect sentence—the sentence that sounds as if it could have been written no other way. It's the striving that characterizes editors as professionals—the passion for the perfect word.

Glossary

absolute—descriptive word that can't be qualified with *more* or *most* (*unique, perfect, complete*)

active voice—*see* **voice, active**

actor—doer of the action inherent in a verb

agreement—grammatically, having the same number, case, gender, or person (subjects and verbs agree in person and number; pronouns and their antecedents agree in number, person, and gender)

alignment—position of a line of type, word, or individual type character in relation to another line, word, or character
flush left—beginning at the left margin
flush right—ending at the right margin
justified—all lines even at the right margin (usually accomplished by varying the spacing between words in the lines and by hyphenating)
ragged right—uneven right margin (spacing between words in the lines is the same throughout)

alphabetization—act of ordering a list according to the alphabet
letter by letter—order by letters, ignoring word spaces and stopping only at punctuation or at the end of an entry
word by word—order by letters in the word, stopping at word spaces

antecedent—word, phrase, or clause to which a pronoun or other substitute refers
implied—antecedent is an idea rather than a single word
unclear—antecedent can't be determined by context

appositive—second noun placed immediately following another noun to identify it more fully (e.g., in "George Washington, the first president," *president* is in apposition)
restrictive—appositive that provides essential information and therefore isn't set off by commas (e.g., "My sister Nancy")

cadence—rhythm of the language

callout—first mention of a table, figure, footnote, or reference in the text of an article or chapter

case—form of nouns and pronouns determined by their usage in a sentence
nominative—case used for subjects and predicate nominatives (*I, he, she, they*)
objective—case used for direct and indirect objects and objects of prepositions (*me, him, her, them*)
possessive—case used to denote ownership (*my, your, his, her, its, their*)

citation—mention, usually in abbreviated form, of the source for information just presented in the text of an article or chapter; the full information for the source is usually found in a list of references at the end

clause—group of words that has a subject and a verb and is used as part of a sentence
    main or **independent**—clause that expresses a complete thought and could stand alone as a sentence
    subordinate or **dependent**—clause that requires a main clause to complete its meaning

collective noun—noun that is singular in form but can be plural in meaning (*staff, variety, herd, majority*)

comma splice or **comma fault**—incorrect use of a comma to separate two related main clauses in the absence of a coordinating conjunction; a run-on sentence is the result

compound sentence—sentence that has two or more main clauses

compound word—combination of two or more words that expresses a single idea; can be hyphenated (*blue-green*); closed, i.e., with no word space (*grandfather*); or open, i.e., retained as separate words (*follow up*)

conditional tense or **mood**—phrase or clause using the word *would* or *could*; conveys a feeling of uncertainty

conjunction—word used to join other words, phrases, or clauses
    coordinating—conjunction joining elements of equal rank (*and*)
    correlative—conjunction pairs joining elements of equal rank (*either...or, neither...nor*)
    subordinating—conjunction joining a subordinate clause to a main clause (*because, therefore*)

conjunctive adverb—adverb used to join main clauses by showing the relationship in meaning between them (*then, however*)

descriptive dictionary—dictionary that includes all words used in both written and spoken English, in contrast to one that prescribes correct usage

direct address—noun used to indicate the particular person to whom a sentence is directed ("*Bill*, please go.")

draft—version of a manuscript; also called an **iteration**

ellipsis—punctuation mark (three dots) that signals an omission from a direct quotation

endnotes—notes of explanation, emendation, or source placed at the end of a chapter or article

euphony—harmonious progression of words having a pleasing sound

extract—long quotation typeset in a block in which indention from the margins substitutes for quotation marks

format—appearance and arrangement of type elements on a page or in relation to each other; to check format is to ensure visual consistency

fragment—group of words presented as a sentence but not conveying a complete thought; fragments usually lack one element of a main clause, such as a subject or verb, or else are subordinate clauses

gender—feature of personal pronouns that differentiates between masculine, feminine, and neuter antecedents

gender-neutral—*see* **sexist language**

gerund—verb form that ends in *-ing* and is used as a noun ("*Driving* is difficult.")

heads/subheads—short titles at the beginning of sections in a piece of writing; also called **headings/subheadings**

infinitive—verb form preceded by *to* and used as a noun, adjective, or adverb

inverted sentence—sentence in other than the usual subject-verb order; e.g., most questions and all sentences beginning with *there*

iteration—*see* **draft**

jargon—terminology characteristic of a particular group, profession, or activity; also overuse of a discipline's vocabulary

layout—design or arrangement of elements on a printed page

modifier—word, phrase, or clause used as an adjective or adverb
    misplaced—modifier that can't grammatically or logically describe the word it appears to describe
    nonrestrictive—modifier that presents parenthetical information about the word it describes; also called **nonessential**
    restrictive—modifier that presents information needed to identify the word it describes; also called **essential**

modify—to describe or qualify the meaning of another word, phrase, or clause

mood—property of a verb that tells the manner in which the writer regards the action or state of being
    imperative—mood that gives a command (e.g., "*Give* him the book.")
    indicative—mood that makes a statement of fact (e.g., "The trees *are* very old.")
    subjunctive—mood that conveys a condition contrary to fact, improbable, or doubtful (e.g., "If I *were* a rich man, ...")

nonrestrictive—*see* **modifier, nonrestrictive**

noun—word that names a person, place, or thing

noun string—several nouns being used together as if they were adjectives and having no intervening prepositions or articles

parallel construction—idea that sentence elements in a series should have the same grammatical structure (e.g., "He likes *to run, to swim*, and *to ski.*")

passive voice—*see* **voice, passive**

person—point of view conveyed by personal pronouns
    first person—the one writing or speaking (*I, we*)
    second person—the one reading or spoken to (*you*)
    third person—the one written or spoken about (*he, she, it, they*)

predicate—part of a sentence containing the verb and all its modifiers

predicate adjective—adjective used in the predicate to refer to the subject (e.g., "She is *pretty.*")

predicate nominative—noun or pronoun that follows a linking verb (one that shows state of being) and renames or modifies the subject of the sentence (e.g., "Joe is the *manager.*")

prescriptive dictionary—dictionary that prescribes correct usage rather than including all words in use by writers and speakers of English

proofreading—checking the most recent version of a manuscript against the original

query—question an editor asks an author

redundancy—use in a sentence of several words or phrases with the same meaning (e.g., *new innovation, past experience*)

references—sources for information contained in a piece of writing; each reference consists of author, title, and publication data (place of publication, publisher's name, year for a book; periodical name, volume, page number, and year for a journal article); usually listed alphabetically by author's last name at the end of an article or book chapter

relative pronoun—pronouns *who, whom, whose, which,* or *that*; used to introduce an adjectival subordinate clause

restrictive—*see* **modifier, restrictive**

serial comma—comma used after the next-to-last element in a series; also called a **series comma** and a **terminal comma** (*red, white, and blue*)

sexist language—wording that includes masculine but not feminine nouns and pronouns; can be alleviated by using gender-neutral words (*journalist*, not *newsman*; *salesperson*, not *salesman*) or by pluralizing (*the authors/they* rather than *the author/he*)

smothered verb—verb that has been turned into a phrase based on its noun form (*make reference to*)

style—choice among acceptable alternatives in spelling, abbreviation, capitalization, punctuation, numbers; usage conforming to a particular publications manual; literary expression of a particular author
  house style—style choices of a particular organization, usually set down in a style guide or style sheet

subject—part of a sentence that names the person, place, or thing that the sentence is about
  compound—subject consisting of two or more elements of equal weight

tense—form of a verb that shows its time of action—past, present, or future

unit modifier—two or more adjectives that function as a single entity to modify a noun; individual words in the unit don't, by themselves, modify the noun (*well-fed* cat, but not a *well* cat or a *fed* cat)

verb—word conveying action or state of being
  compound—two or more such words having equal weight and serving as the action or state of being in the sentence (e.g., "The doll *walks* and *talks*.")

voice—property of a verb that shows whether the subject is the doer or receiver of the action of the verb
  active—verb form used when the doer of the action is the subject of the verb (e.g., "The dog *catches* the ball.")
  passive—verb form used when the subject of the verb is the receiver of the action (e.g., "The ball *is caught* by the dog.")

APPENDIX A: Additional Exercises

Instructions: In some of the following groups of words, one word is spelled incorrectly. Circle it. If all the words in the group are spelled correctly, circle "none of the above."

1. prejudice

    rhythm

    symmetry

    amateur

    none of the above

2. tragedy

    harrass

    analyze

    meanness

    none of the above

3. fierce

    preceed

    querulous

    accommodate

    none of the above

4. antecedent

    ukulele

    advantageous

    villain

    none of the above

5. skiing

    acquaintance

    conscientious

    occurred

    none of the above

6. paraphernalia

    mesmerize

    prevalance

    prurient

    none of the above

7. correspondent

   adjudicate

   millionaire

   mispell

   none of the above

8. biscuit

   indispensible

   disillusion

   conqueror

   none of the above

9. kidnaped

   judicious

   irelevant

   hygiene

   none of the above

10. interrogate

    precedent

    inadmisible

    totaled

    none of the above

11. concensus

    noticeable

    auxiliary

    calendar

    none of the above

12. newsstand

    pidgeon

    judgment

    traveled

    none of the above

13. dietitian

    rheumatism

    exaggerate

    defendant

    none of the above

14. wholly

    geneology

    grievance

    quash

    none of the above

15. liaison

    copywright

    diphtheria

    occasion

    none of the above

16. alleviate

    respondant

    awkward

    coolly

    none of the above

17. athletics

    benifitted

    cemetery

    wherever

    none of the above

18. minature

    naive

    pavilion

    liable

    none of the above

19. controlled

    unnecessary

    personnel

    perogative

    none of the above

20. disappoint

    maneuver

    murmer

    quotable

    none of the above

21. plaintiff

    usable

    Portuguese

    existance

    none of the above

22. quell

    dessicate

    wintry

    believable

    none of the above

23. salable

    garrish

    affidavit

    fluorescent

    none of the above

24. connoisseur

    picnicking

    soliloquy

    anonymity

    none of the above

25. monotonous

    exhilerate

    allegiance

    truly

    none of the above

26. boundary

    insistence

    weird

    yield

    none of the above

27. achieve

    seize

    vengeance

    sizable

    none of the above

28. advertizing

    planetarium

    altruistic

    slough

    none of the above

29. satelite

    meander

    dilemma

    ecstasy

    none of the above

30. gayety

    inoculate

    barrel

    guerrilla

    none of the above

31. drudgery

    gist

    imposter

    relevant

    none of the above

32. supercede

    subpoena

    appellate

    pantomime

    none of the above

33. legionnaire

    indictment

    inflammation

    allot

    none of the above

34. publicly

    questionnaire

    intergrate

    canceled

    none of the above

35. niether

    Philippines

    Caribbean

    diarrhea

    none of the above

36. wiener

    allegedly

    credibility

    neccesary

    none of the above

37. crucial

    formost

    nucleus

    fiery

    none of the above

38. skied

    paralel

    realtor

    prejudicial

    none of the above

39. kahki

    sparse

    accelerator

    hemorrhage

    none of the above

40. acclaim

    desirable

    definate

    drunkenness

    none of the above

ANSWERS

1. prejudice

    rhythm

    symmetry

    amateur

    (none of the above)

2. tragedy

    (harrass)

    analyze

    meanness

    none of the above

3. fierce

    (preceed)

    querulous

    accommodate

    none of the above

4. antecedent

    ukulele

    advantageous

    villain

    (none of the above)

5. skiing

    acquaintance

    conscientious

    occurred

    (none of the above)

6. paraphernalia

    mesmerize

    (prevalance)

    prurient

    none of the above

7. correspondent

   adjudicate

   millionaire

   (mispell)

   none of the above

8. biscuit

   (indispensible)

   disillusion

   conqueror

   none of the above

9. kidnaped

   judicious

   (irelevant)

   hygiene

   none of the above

10. interrogate

    precedent

    (inadmisible)

    totaled

    none of the above

11. (concensus)

    noticeable

    auxiliary

    calendar

    none of the above

12. newsstand

    (pidgeon)

    judgment

    traveled

    none of the above

13. dietitian

    rheumatism

    exaggerate

    defendant

    (none of the above)

14. wholly

    (geneology)

    grievance

    quash

    none of the above

15. liaison

   (copywright)

   diphtheria

   occasion

   none of the above

16. alleviate

   (respondant)

   awkward

   coolly

   none of the above

17. athletics

   (benifitted)

   cemetery

   wherever

   none of the above

18. (minature)

   naive

   pavilion

   liable

   none of the above

19. controlled

   unnecessary

   personnel

   (perogative)

   none of the above

20. disappoint

   maneuver

   (murmer)

   quotable

   none of the above

21. plaintiff

   usable

   Portuguese

   (existance)

   none of the above

22. quell

   (dessicate)

   wintry

   believable

   none of the above

23. salable

    (garrish)

    affidavit

    fluorescent

    none of the above

24. connoisseur

    picnicking

    soliloquy

    anonymity

    (none of the above)

25. monotonous

    (exhilerate)

    allegiance

    truly

    none of the above

26. boundary

    insistence

    weird

    yield

    (none of the above)

27. achieve

    seize

    vengeance

    sizable

    (none of the above)

28. (advertizing)

    planetarium

    altruistic

    slough

    none of the above

29. (satelite)

    meander

    dilemma

    ecstasy

    none of the above

30. (gayety)

    inoculate

    barrel

    guerrilla

    none of the above

31. drudgery

    gist

    (imposter)

    relevant

    none of the above

32. (supercede)

    subpoena

    appellate

    pantomime

    none of the above

33. legionnaire

    indictment

    inflammation

    allot

    (none of the above)

34. publicly

    questionnaire

    (intergrate)

    canceled

    none of the above

35. (niether)

    Philippines

    Caribbean

    diarrhea

    none of the above

36. wiener

    allegedly

    credibility

    (neccesary)

    none of the above

37. crucial

    (formost)

    nucleus

    fiery

    none of the above

38. skied

    (paralel)

    realtor

    prejudicial

    none of the above

39. (kahki)

   sparse

   accelerator

   hemorrhage

   none of the above

40. acclaim

   desirable

   (definate)

   drunkenness

   none of the above

Instructions: Correct or improve the following sentences as necessary.

1. A arms limitation treaty was proposed by the Soviet Union.

2. Not only did she refuse to read the letter, but also burned it.

3. Courses in data processing are offered by many vocational schools.

4. Would Joe Jones have been smarter if he would have retired sooner?

5. Next month, Boris will be in exile 19 years.

6. Mr. Judge told the class that water boiled at 100 Centigrade.

7. I have entered the hospital last Tuesday.

8. If he hadn't have taken that trip, he would of been alive today.

9. Dickens wrote about the lives of the common people of 19th-century England, which was unusual at the time.

10. It says in the cookbook that onions must be sauteed in oil.

11. He was drinking and driving, which is illegal.

12. If you study the designs of these buildings, you will find that they reflect the architect's early training.

13. Politics fascinate me, but statistics bore me.

14. I will argue with whoever disagrees with me.

15. If he was willing to make a career change, he would not have delayed so long.

16. Look at that child holding the ice cream cone with the red balloon.

17. I only drove 100 feet before sliding into a snow bank.

18. He near jumped off the ledge before the police convinced him to climb down.

19. He made frequent illusion to his recently published autobiography.

20. When an editor discovers an error, they should correct it using the proper symbols.

21. Having heard that joke over and over again, it is sure driving me crazy.

22. Before his illness, the comic strip was written by Jack Wallace.

23. Either you or your brother have broken the window.

24. Neither of the stories were plausible.

25. Everybody is closing their windows.

26. Snow White and the Seven Dwarfs is coming.

27. The board accepts the report of the committee and sends it to the director with their recommendations.

28. The number of resumes we receive in any week vary from 20 to 50.

29. Each of the children are ready to perform.

30. Neither the manager nor the employees is going to the conference.

31. It is she who suffers from heart disease.

32. The childrens' poverty was appalling.

33. Neither black nor white are my favorite colors.

34. Here come the referee and the opposing team.

35. The remains of the settlement is being excavated by student archaeologists this summer.

36. Jim is one of the foremen that suggested the change.

37. Frequent commuters are a different kind of
    traveler; everybody hurries around running for
    their planes.

38. When a person learns to swim as a child, they
    enjoy it all their lives.

39. His father asked him to behave like an adult,
    and not running around like an ill-mannered
    fool.

ANSWERS

1. ~~A~~ *an* arms limitation treaty ~~was proposed by~~ the Soviet Union. *proposed*

2. Not only ~~did she~~ refuse *d* to read the letter, but *she*
   also burned it.

3. Courses in data processing ~~are offered by~~ many
   vocational schools. *offer*

4. Would Joe Jones have been smarter if he ~~would~~ *had*
   ~~have~~ retired sooner?

5. Next month, Boris will ~~be~~ *have been* in exile 19 years.

6. Mr. Judge told the class that water boiled *s* at
   100° Centigrade.

7. I ~~have~~ entered the hospital last Tuesday.

8. If he hadn't ~~have~~ taken that trip, he would ~~of~~ ^be^ ~~been~~ alive today.

9. Dickens wrote about the lives of the common people of 19th-century England; ^Such stories were^ ~~which was~~ unusual at the time.

10. ~~It says~~ in the cookbook ~~that~~ onions ~~must be~~ ^to sauté^ ~~sautéed~~ in oil.

11. He was drinking and driving; ^to do so^ ~~which~~ is illegal.

12. ~~If you study~~ the designs of these buildings, ~~you will find that they~~ reflect the architect's early training.

13. Politics fascinate^s^ me, but statistics bore me.

14. I will argue with whoever disagrees with me.

15. If he ^were^ ~~was~~ willing to make a career change, he would not have delayed so long.

16. Look at that child holding the ice cream cone ^and^ ~~with~~ the red balloon.

17. I only drove 100 feet before sliding into a snow bank.

18. He near^ly^ jumped off the ledge before the police ^persuaded^ ~~convinced~~ him to climb down.

19. He made frequent *a*llusion to his recently pub-

    lished autobiography.

20. ~~When~~ an editor who discovers an error, ~~they~~ should

    correct it using the proper symbols.

21. ~~Having~~ *I've* heard that joke over and over again, it

    ~~is~~ sure*ly* driving me crazy.

22. Before his illness, the comic strip ~~was written~~

    ~~by~~ Jack Wallace *wrote*.

23. Either you or your brother ~~have~~ *has* broken the

    window.

24. Neither of the stories ~~were~~ *was* plausible.

25. ~~Everybody is~~ *All of us are* closing ~~their~~ *our* windows.

26. <u>Snow White and the Seven Dwarfs</u> is coming. *ital*

27. The board accepts the report ~~of the~~ committee *vs*

    and sends it to the director with ~~their~~

    recommendations.

28. The number of résumés we receive ~~in any week~~ *weekly*

    vary *ies* from 20 to 50.

29. Each ~~of the~~ children ~~are~~ *is* ready to perform.

30. Neither the manager nor the employees ~~is~~ *are* going

    to the conference.

31. ~~It is~~ she ~~who~~ suffers from heart disease.

32. The children's poverty was appalling.

33. Neither black nor white ~~are~~ *is* my favorite colors.

34. Here come the referee and the opposing team.

35. The remains of the settlement ~~is~~ *are* being excavated by student archaeologists this summer.

36. Jim is one of the foremen ~~that~~ *who* suggested the change.

37. Frequent commuters are a different kind of traveler; ~~everybody hurries around~~ *they are always* running for their planes.

38. *People who* ~~When a person~~ learns to swim as a child, ~~they~~ *ran* enjoy ~~it~~ *the sport* all their lives.

39. His father asked him to behave like an adult, ~~and~~ not ~~running around~~ like an ill-mannered fool.

264

Instructions: Select the correct words to fill in the blanks. Fix anything else that's wrong.

1. One or the other of you _____ (is, are) lying.

2. When snow, rain, or sleet _____ (falls, fall), the traffic becomes unbearable.

3. When family or friends _____ (comes, come) to call, my cat always runs and hides.

4. Neither the fox nor the hounds _____ (was, were) in sight.

5. Neither the King nor the Parliament _____ (controls, control) the loyalties of the barons.

6. The Cardinals _____ (is, are) a team that _____ (is, are) coming on in this year's race for the pennant.

7. No one but you and two of my friends _____ (knows, know) what I've put in the will.

8. The schools in which the after-school care centers are located _____ (is, are) shown on this map of the county.

9. None of the elevators in the building _____ (is, are) accessible to persons in wheelchairs.

10. A majority of the voters in this area _____ (is, are) conservative.

11. She is one of those students who _____ (plays, play) too much, and _____ (works, work) too little.

12. Ask one of the parents who _____ (understands, understand) the system to help you.

13. One of my favorite meals _____ (is, are) ham and eggs.

14. Neither she nor her children _____ (has, have) ever forgiven her father.

15. A variety of solutions _____ (was, were) proposed at the meeting yesterday.

16. A directory of editorial resources, including publications firms and hotlines staffed by various English departments, _____ (was, were) produced on the laser printer.

17. One of the food service supervisors _____ (was, were) working on the floor for the first time in over ten years.

18. Someone had left _____ (her, a, their) research paper in my box in the department office.

19. Neither Bill nor Karen _____ (has, have) finished _____ (his, her, their, the) assignment.

20. Neither of the two teachers who _____ (was, were) on the board last year _____ (is, are) willing to continue.

ANSWERS

1. One or the other of you _is_ (is, are) lying.

2. When snow, rain, or sleet _falls_ (falls, fall), the traffic becomes unbearable.

3. When family or friends _come_ (comes, come) to call, my cat always runs and hides.

4. Neither the fox nor the hounds _were_ (was, were) in sight.

5. Neither the King nor the Parliament _controls_ (controls, control) the loyalties of the barons.

6. The Cardinals *is* (is, are) a team that *is* (is, are) coming on in this year's race for the pennant.

7. No one but you and two of my friends *knows* (knows, know) what I've put in the will.

8. The schools in which the after-school care centers are located *are* (is, are) shown on this map of the county.

9. None of the elevators in the building *are* (is, are) accessible to persons in wheelchairs.

10. ~~A majority~~ *Most* of the voters in this area *are* (is, are) conservative.

11. She is one of those students who *play* (plays, play) too much ˅ and *work* (works, work) too little.

12. Ask one of the parents who *understand* (understands, understand) the system to help you.

13. One of my favorite meals *is* (is, are) ham and eggs.

14. Neither she nor her children *have* (has, have) ever forgiven her father.

15. A variety of solutions _were_ (was, were) proposed at the meeting yesterday.

16. A directory of editorial resources, including publications firms and hotlines staffed by various English departments, _was_ (was, were) produced on the laser printer.

17. One of the food service supervisors _was_ (was, were) working on the floor for the first time in over ten years.

18. Someone had left _a_ (her, a, their) research paper in my box in the department office.

19. Neither Bill nor Karen _has_ (has, have) finished _the_ (his, her, their, the) assignment.

20. Neither of the two teachers who _were_ (was, were) on the board last year _is_ (is, are) willing to continue.

Instructions: Change passive voice to active. Fix anything else that's wrong.

1. Several unit funds may be centrally administered by one single fund manager.

2. A comprehensive survey will be conducted biennially by each branch of the corporation to identify staffing needs.

3. Operational usage standards for utility vehicles will be established by each office.

4. Locally fabricated training devices will be maintained by the user of the device.

5. All modifications that are proposed will be endorsed by the affected parties.

6. The condition will be validated by a needs assessment team.

7. Guidance and budget information is provided by the manager on each level.

8. Centralized purchasing is accomplished for the fund manager by procurement personnel.

9. The sale of alcoholic beverages by ABC stores is controlled by the state.

10. It is the opinion of this board of inquiry
that the equipment ~~was being~~ used in an unsafe
manner by the operators.

11. By using computers, much time can be saved by
editors.

12. The plan was approved by the committee, but
only after six hours of acrimonious debate had
~~been held.~~

13. The directive was sent down by company
headquarters, that All reports were to be done in
triplicate by the staff.

    Thank you for
14. ~~Reference is made to~~ your letter of May 24,
    yes
~~and~~ our answer is ~~in the affirmative.~~

1. Several unit funds may ~~be centrally~~ *administer* ~~administered by one~~ single fund manager.

   A single fund manager may administer several unit funds.

2. A *biennial* comprehensive survey will ~~be~~ conducted ~~biennially by~~ each branch of the corporation to identify staffing needs.

   Each branch of the corporation will conduct a biennial comprehensive survey to identify staffing needs.

3. Operational usage standards for utility vehicles will be established by each office.

   Each office will establish operational usage standards for utility vehicles.

4. *Users will maintain* Locally fabricated training devices ~~will be maintained by the user of the device~~.

   Users will maintain locally fabricated training devices.

5. *will endorse* All modifications that are proposed ~~will be endorsed by~~ the affected parties.

   The affected parties will endorse all proposed modifications.

6. The condition will be validated by a needs
assessment team.

A needs assessment team will validate the
condition.

7. Guidance and budget information is provided by
the manager on each level.

The manager on each level provides guidance and
budget information.

8. Centralized purchasing is accomplished for the
fund manager by procurement personnel.

Procurement personnel do centralized purchasing
for the fund manager.

9. The sale of alcoholic beverages by ABC stores
is controlled by the state.

The state controls the sale of alcoholic beverages by ABC stores.

10. It is the opinion of this board of inquiry
that the equipment was being used in an unsafe
manner by the operators.

This board of inquiry believes the operators
were using the equipment in an unsafe manner.

11. By using computers, much time can be saved by editors. *[handwritten edits: "Editors" inserted, text rearranged]*

Editors can save much time by using computers.

12. *The committee* The plan was approved by the committee, but only after six hours of acrimonious debate had been held.

The committee approved the plan, but only after six hours of acrimonious debate.

13. *Company headquarters* The directive was sent down by company headquarters. *a directive that required the staff to do* All reports were to be done in triplicate by the staff.

Company headquarters sent a directive that required the staff to do all reports in triplicate.

14. *Thank you for* Reference is made to your letter of May 24; and our answer is *yes* in the affirmative.

Thank you for your letter of May 24; our answer is yes.

1. The boss told him to do his work and not going about undermining morale.

2. Neither his disgrace nor whatever prison term he gets will make any difference to his loving family.

3. The chief road engineer discussed the causes as well as giving the ramifications of the drainage problem on the project.

4. No matter what he does or all the ways he tries, he still has trouble understanding math.

5. Jack is an intern who is bright, personable, and has potential.

6. Keep your feet flat on the ground, your eye on the ball, and don't swing too soon.

7. Visiting family can be pleasant, but to spend a whole vacation that way can be hard on everyone.

8. Children have to learn to ask nicely instead of going around making demands.

1. The boss told him to do his work and not go~~ings~~ *around* ~~about~~ undermining morale.

    The boss told him to do his work and not go around undermining morale.

2. Neither his disgrace nor ~~whatever~~ *his possible* prison term ~~he gets~~ will make any difference to his loving family.

    Neither his disgrace nor his possible prison term will make any difference to his loving family.

3. The chief road engineer discussed the causes as well as ~~givings~~ the ramifications of the drainage problem on the project.

    The chief road engineer discussed the causes as well as the ramifications of the drainage problem on the project.

4. No matter what he does or ~~all the ways~~ *how hard* he tries, he still has trouble understanding math.

    No matter what he does or how hard he tries, he still has trouble understanding math.

5. Jack is an intern who is bright, personable, and promising and has potential.

   Jack is a bright, personable, and promising intern.

6. Keep your feet flat on the ground, keep your eye on the ball, and don't swing too soon.

   Keep your feet flat on the ground, keep your eye on the ball, and don't swing too soon.

7. Visiting family can be pleasant, but to spending a whole vacation that way can be hard on everyone.

   Visiting family can be pleasant, but spending a whole vacation that way can be hard on everyone.

8. Children have to learn to ask nicely instead of going around making demanding.

   Children have to learn to ask nicely instead of demanding.

EXERCISE 6: RESTRICTIVE AND NON-RESTRICTIVE CLAUSES

Instructions: Decide whether the relative clauses in the following sentences are restrictive or nonrestrictive and correct if necessary.

1. The child who pulled the sword out of the stone was crowned king. *R*

2. People who live in glass houses shouldn't throw stones. *R*

3. David Harvey, who is my agent, is on vacation. *N*

4. The table which I found at the flea market is an antique. *that* *R*

5. The exposé which John wrote has been sent off to a publisher. *that* *R*

6. John's book, which has been accepted for publication, will probably go through several printings. *N*

7. My Bible, which burned in the fire, had been in the family for many years. *R N*

8. Foods which contain artificial sweetener may be a health hazard. *that* *R*

1. The child who pulled the sword out of the
    stone was crowned king.

2. People who live in glass houses shouldn't
    throw stones.

3. David Harvey, who is my agent, is on vacation.

4. The table ~~which~~ *that* I found at the flea market is
    an antique.

5. The exposé ~~which~~ *that* John wrote has been sent off
    to a publisher.

6. John's book, which has been accepted for
    publication, will probably go through several
    printings.

7. My Bible, which burned in the fire, had been in
    the family for many years.

8. Foods ~~which~~ *that* contain artificial sweetener may
    be a health hazard.

EXERCISE 7: PROBLEM MODIFIERS

Instructions: Eliminate the dangling and misplaced modifiers in the following sentences.

1. Having a large family, her house is always cluttered.

2. He found my wallet walking by the river.

3. The CEO spoke to the vice president with a stern voice.

4. These regulations were developed to adapt to new conditions last week.

5. Sale of alcoholic beverages is regulated by the state in public restaurants.

6. A transformer caught fire underground, exploding manhole covers over a radius of several blocks.

7. Puffing on his pipe, the article was attacked by the editor.

8. He found the ring exposed by the waves walking on the beach.

1. ~~Having~~ *Because she has* a large family, her house is always cluttered.

   Because she has a large family, her house is always cluttered.

2. He found my wallet *as he was* walking by the river.

   He found my wallet as he was walking by the river.

3. The CEO spoke to the vice president with a stern voice.

   With a stern voice, the CEO spoke to the vice president.

4. These regulations were developed *last week* to adapt to new conditions ~~last week.~~

   These regulations were developed last week to adapt to new conditions.

5. *the* Sale of alcoholic beverages *The state* is regulated by the state in public restaurants.

   The state regulates the sale of alcoholic beverages in public restaurants.

6. A transformer caught fire underground, *and* exploding*ed* manhole covers over a radius of several blocks.

   A transformer caught fire underground and exploded manhole covers over a radius of several blocks.

7. Puffing on his pipe, the *editor* ~~article~~ ~~was~~ attacked *article* by the ~~editor~~.

   Puffing on his pipe, the editor attacked the article.

8. *While* He found the ring exposed by the waves walking on the beach.

   While walking on the beach, he found the ring exposed by the waves.

Instructions: *Eliminate the noun strings from the following sentences. Also correct any other problems.*

1. The project will benefit from computer programs advance information.

2. Your manning-level authorizations reassessment suggestion should lead to major improvements.

3. The regulation offers an explanation of Communication Center operations personnel training.

4. Enforcement of guidelines for new car model tire durability is a Federal Trade Commission responsibility.

5. The main goal of this article is to formulate narrative information extraction rules.

6. Determination of support appropriateness for community organization assistance need was precluded by difficulty in the acquisition of data relevant to a committee activity review.

1. The project will benefit from computer programs advance information. *on*

    The project will benefit from advance information on computer programs.

2. *suggestion to reassess*

    Your manning-level authorizations ~~reassessment~~ ~~suggestion~~ should lead to major improvements.

    Your suggestion to reassess manning-level authorizations should lead to major improvements.

3. *ins the training*

    The regulation ~~offers an~~ explanation of Communication Center operations personnel ⊙ ~~training.~~

    The regulation explains the training of Communication Center operations personnel.

4. *ing* *on the durability of tires on*

    Enforcement of guidelines for new car models *The* ~~tire durability is a~~ Federal Trade Commission *is* *le for* ~~responsibility.~~

    The Federal Trade Commission is responsible for enforcing guidelines on the durability of tires on new cars.

5. ~~The main goal of~~ this article ~~is~~ to formulate [aims] [rules to] (narrative information) ~~extraction~~ ~~rules.~~

   This article aims to formulate rules to ex-

   tract narrative information.

6. Determin~~ation of support~~ [ing] appropriateness [an] [level of support] for

   community organization~~s~~ ~~assistance need~~ was

   [not possible because of] ~~precluded by~~ difficulty in ~~the~~ acquisition of [ring]

   (data) relevant ~~to a~~ committee ~~activity~~ review. [for the] [to]

   Determining an appropriate level of support

   for community organizations was not possible

   because of difficulty in acquiring relevant

   data for the committee to review.

Instructions: *Resuscitate the smothered verbs in the following sentences. Correct any other problems you may find.*

1. Additional authorization for the administration of the survey by the staff members has emanated from the director of the department.

2. The project manager is vested with the responsibility for the appointment of one individual office to serve as a central focal point to perform coordination functions and provide information to all regional offices about the company's activities.

3. A diagnosis of a recurrent disorder may be made by the patient, but a confirmation should also be made by the physician.

4. The aim of this article is a presentation of a summary overview of the drugs most commonly used in an effort to render treatment and achieve prevention of psychological disorders.

5. The expenditures made by organizations in the provision of services and the administration of programs resulted in a substantial increase in operating costs.

6. Managers got information about resource allocation by direct participation in daily operations, personal observation of the operations, or supervision of the operations.

7. The goal of this research program is the elucidation of the physiological and behavioral correlates of voluntary alcohol consumption by humans through conducting an analysis of animal models.

8. Apathy and withdrawal was a consequence of the dogs' inability as to shock alteration or prevention.

1. *The department director has issued,* ~~A~~dditional authorization for the

   ~~administration of the survey by the~~ staff

   members ~~has emanated from the director of the~~ *to administer the survey.*

   ~~department~~.

   The department director has issued additional

   authorization for the staff members to adminis-

   ter the survey.

2. The project manager is ~~vested with the~~

   responsib~~ility~~ *le* for the ~~appointment~~ *ing* ~~of~~ one

   ~~individual~~ office to ~~serve as a central focal~~

   ~~point to perform~~ coordinat~~ion~~ *e* functions and

   ~~provide~~ inform~~ation to~~ all regional offices

   about the company's activities.

   The project manager is responsible for

   appointing one office to coordinate functions

   and inform all regional offices about the com-

   pany's activities.

3. A diagnosis of a recurrent disorder, ~~may be~~
Although a
made by the patient, ~~but a confirmation should~~
~~also be made by~~ the physician. Should confirm the diagnosis.

Although a patient may diagnose a recurrent

disorder, the physician should confirm the di-

agnosis.

4. ~~The~~ aim ~~of~~ this article ~~is~~ to presentation ~~of~~ an

~~summary~~ overview of ~~the~~ drugs most commonly

used ~~in an effort~~ to render treatment and
Prevent

~~achieve prevention of~~ psychological disorders.
treat

This article aims to present an overview of

drugs most commonly used to prevent and treat

psychological disorders.

5. ~~The~~ expenditures ~~made by~~ organizations ~~in the~~
al) to

provision of services and the administration
de   er

~~of programs resulted in a~~ substantial increase
Caused operating costs to   -ly

~~in operating costs.~~

Organizational expenditures to provide ser-

vices and administer programs caused operating

costs to increase substantially.

6. Managers got information about resource allocation by direct participation in, daily operations, personal observation of the operations, or supervision of the operations.

    Managers got information about resource allocation by participating directly in, observing, or supervising daily operations.

7. The goal of this research program is the elucidation of the physiological and behavioral correlates of voluntary alcohol consumption by humans through conducting an analysis of animal models.

    The goal of this research is to clarify the physiological and behavioral bases of voluntary alcohol consumption in humans by analyzing animal models.

8. Apathy and withdrawal was a consequence of the dogs' inability as to shock alteration or prevention.

    Apathy and withdrawal were consequences of the dogs' inability to alter or prevent shock.

1. These various different agencies and offices that provide aid and assistance services to individual persons who participate in our program activities that we offer have reversed themselves back from the policy that they recently announced to return to the original policy they followed earlier.

2. The scientific endeavor in general depends on essentially true and fully accurate data if it is to offer any ideas and theories that will actually allow mankind to advance forward into the future in a safe and cautious way.

3. It is probably true that in spite of the fact that the educational environment is a very significant and important facet to each and every one of our children in terms of his or her own individual future development and growth, various different groups and people do not at all support certain tax assessments at a reasonable and fair rate that are required for the express purpose and intention of providing an educational context at a decent level of quality.

4. Most likely, a majority of all the patients who appear at the public clinic facility do not expect specialized medical attention and treatment, because their health problems and concerns often seem not to be of a major nature and can for the most part usually be adequately treated with enough proper understanding and attention by the clinic staff.

5. It is necessary to make special and particular mention of von Willebrand's disease as a consequence of the suggestion inferred from coagulation test results that the possibility exists that there might be a disorder of the platelet.

6. An additional question that was asked in the survey instrument centers around the problem of whether or not the extension of the roles of women to include roles that have been the traditional domain of men will have the effect of leading to an increase or reduction of problems that are related to abusive alcohol usage among women.

ANSWERS

1. These various ~~different~~ agencies ~~and offices~~
    that ~~provide aid and~~ assist~~ance services to~~
    ~~individual persons who~~ participate in our
    program ~~activities that we offer~~ have reversed
    ~~themselves back from the policy that~~ they
    recently announced to return to the original one.
    ~~policy they followed earlier.~~

    The various agencies that assist participants
    in our program have reversed the recently
    announced policy to return to the original one.

2. The scientific endeavor in general depends on
    ~~essentially true and fully~~ accurate data if it
    is to offer any ~~ideas and~~ theories that will
    ~~actually~~ allow mankind to advance safely ~~forward into~~
    ~~the future in a safe and cautious way.~~

    The scientific endeavor in general depends on
    accurate data if it is to offer any theories
    that will allow mankind to advance safely.

3. ~~It is probably true that in spite of the fact~~ *Although school*
   ~~that the educational environment~~ is a ~~very~~
   development factor for
   significant ~~and important facet to each and~~

   ~~every one of~~ our children, ~~in terms of his or~~

   ~~her own individual future development and~~

   ~~growth,~~ various ~~different~~ groups ~~and people~~ do
   the reasonable   *necessary to provide good schools.*
   not ~~at all~~ support ~~certain~~ tax ~~assessments at~~

   ~~a reasonable and fair rate that are required~~

   ~~for the express purpose and intention of~~

   ~~providing an educational context at a decent~~

   ~~level of quality.~~

   Although school is a significant development

   factor for our children, various groups do not

   support the reasonable taxes necessary to

   provide good schools.

4. Most ~~likely, a majority~~ of ~~all~~ the patients ~~who appear~~ at the public clinic ~~facility~~ do not expect specialized medical attention and treatment, because their health problems ~~and concerns~~ often seem ~~not to be of a major nature~~ minimal and can ~~for the most part~~ usually be ~~adequately~~ treated ~~with enough proper understanding and attention~~ by the clinic staff.

Most of the patients at the public clinic do not expect specialized medical attention and treatment because their health problems often seem minimal and can usually be treated by the clinic staff.

5. ~~It is necessary to make special and particular mention of~~ von Willebrand's disease ~~as a consequence of the suggestion inferred from~~ When coagulation test results ~~that the possibility~~ suggest ~~exists that there might~~ be a disorder of the platelet, be sure to consider ~~von Willebrand's disease~~.

When coagulation test results suggest a disorder of the platelet, be sure to consider von Willebrand's disease.

6. ~~An additional question that was asked in~~ the

survey *asked* ~~instrument centers~~ around the problem

~~of~~ whether ~~or not the~~ exten*ding* ~~sion~~ *of* the roles

of women to include *those* ~~roles that have been the~~

traditional *ly the* domain of men will ~~have the effect~~

~~of leading to an~~ increase or reduc*e*~~tion of~~

~~problems that are related to abusive~~ alcohol

abuse in ~~usage among~~ women.

The survey asked whether extending the roles

of women to include those traditionally the

domain of men will increase or reduce alcohol

abuse in women.

APPENDIX B:
Simpler Words
and Phrases

One-syllable words are the essence of English. Not only do they save keyboarding and reading time, but they make writing livelier and ideas clearer.

Instead of	Try	Instead of	Try
accompany	go with	benefit	help
accomplish	carry out, do	be responsible for	handle
accordingly	so	by means of	by, with
accrue	add, gain		
accurate	correct, exact, right	capability	ability, can
achieve	do, make	category	class, group
actual	real	caveat	warning
additional	added, more, other	close proximity	near
address	discuss	cognizant	aware, responsible
adjacent to	next to	combined	joint
advantageous	helpful	comply with	follow
advise	recommend, tell	component	part
afford an opportunity	allow, let	comprise	form, include, make up
aircraft	plane	concerning	about, on
anticipate	expect	conclude	close, end
a number of	some	concur	agree
apparent	clear, plain	confront	face, meet
appear	seem	consequently	so
appreciable	many	consolidate	combine, join, merge
appropriate	proper, right	constitutes	is, forms, makes up
approximately	about	construct	build
as a means of	to	contains	has
ascertain	find out, learn	continue	keep on
as prescribed by	under	contribute	give
assist, assistance	aid, help		
attempt	try		
at the present time	now		

Instead of	Try	Instead of	Try
deem	think	facilitate	ease, help
delete	cut, drop	factor	reason, cause
demonstrate	prove, show	failed to	did not
depart	leave	feasible	can be done, workable
designate	appoint, choose, name	females	women
		final	last
desire	wish	finalize	complete, finish
determine	decide, figure, find	for a period of	for
develop	grow, make, take place	for example	such as
		forfeit	give up, lose
disclose	show	for the purpose of	for, to
discontinue	drop, stop	forward	send
disseminate	issue, send out	function	act, role, work
due to the fact that	due to, since, because		
		herein	here
echelons	levels	however	but
effect	make		
elect	choose, pick	identical	same
eliminate	cut, drop, end	identify	find, name, show
employ	use	immediately	at once
encounter	meet	impacted	affected, changed, hit
encourage	urge	implement	carry out, do, follow
endeavor	try	in accordance with	by, following, under
ensure	make sure	in addition	also, besides, too
enumerate	count	in an effort to	to
equitable	fair	inasmuch as	because
equivalent	equal	in a timely manner	on time, promptly
establish	set up, prove, show	inception	beginning
evaluate	check, rate, test	in conjunction with	with
evidenced	showed	in consonance with	agree with
evident	clear	incorporate	blend, join, merge
examine	check, look at	incumbent upon	must
exhibit	show	indicate	show, write down
expedite	hurry, rush, speed up	indication	sign
expeditious	fast, quick	initial	first
expend	pay out, spend	initiate	start
expense	cost, fee, price	in lieu of	instead of
expertise	ability, skill	in order that	to
explain	show, tell		

300

Instead of	Try	Instead of	Try
in regard to	about, concerning, on	objective	aim, goal
interface with	deal with, work with, meet	obligate	bind, compel
		observe	see
interpose no objection	do not object	obtain	get
in the course of	during, in	on a regular basis	regularly
in the event that	if	on a timely basis	immediately
in the near future	soon	operate	run, work
in view of	because	operational	working
it is essential	must	optimum	best, greatest, most
it is recommended	we recommend	option	choice, way
it is requested	please, we request		
		parameters	limits, dimensions
justify	prove	participate	take part
		perform	do
legislation	law	permit	let
liaise with	coordinate, talk with	personnel	people, staff
		pertaining to	about, of, on
limitations	limits	point in time	point, time
limited number	few	portion	part
locate	find	position	place, put
location	place, scene, site	possess	have, own
		practicable	practical
magnitude	size	preclude	prevent
maintain	keep, support	prepared	ready
majority	greatest, longest, most	previous	earlier, past
methodology	method	previously	before
minimize	decrease, lessen, reduce	prioritize	rank
		probability	chance
modify	change	procedures	rules, ways
monitor	check, watch	proceed	do, go on, try
		proficiency	skill
nebulous	vague	programmed	planned
necessitate	cause, need	promulgate	announce, issue
non-concur	disagree	provide	give, say, supply
notify	let know, tell	provided that	if
not later than	by	provides guidance for	guides
numerous	many, most	purchase	buy
		pursuant to	by, following, under

Instead of	*Try*	*Instead of*	*Try*
reason for	why	take action to	act, do
recapitulate	sum up	task	ask
reduce	cut	terminate	end, stop
reflect	say, show	therefore	so
regarding	about, of, on	therein	there
relating to	about, on	this command	us, we
relocation	move	timely	prompt
remain	stay	time period	time, period
remainder	rest	transmit	send
remuneration	pay, payment	transpire	happen, occur
render	give, make		
request	ask	until such time as	until
require	must, need	utilize, utilization	use
requirement	need		
reside	live	validate	confirm
retain	keep	value	cost, worth
review	check, go over	verbatim	word for word, exact
		viable	practical, workable
selection	choice		
shall	will	warrant	call for, permit
shortfall	shortage	whenever	when
similar to	like	whereas	since
solicit	ask for	with reference to	about
state	say	with the exception of	except for
state-of-the-art	latest, advanced	witnessed	saw
subject	the, this, your		
submit	give, send	your office	you
subsequent	later, next		
subsequently	after, later, then	/ (slash)	and, or
substantial	large, real, strong		
sufficient	enough		

APPENDIX C:
Reference Books

Information is the most recent available at the time of publication.

American Heritage Dictionary. 3rd ed. Boston: Houghton Mifflin, 1992. **(Prescriptive)**

Merriam-Webster's Collegiate Dictionary. 10th ed. Frederick C. Mish, ed. Springfield, MA: Merriam-Webster, 1993. **(Descriptive)**

Random House Dictionary of the English Language. 2d ed.; unabridged. Stuart B. Flexner, ed. New York: Random House, 1987. **(Prescriptive)**

Webster's New World Dictionary of American English. 3rd college ed. Victoria Neufeldt, ed. New York: Prentice-Hall Trade, 1988. **(Prescriptive)**

Word Division: Supplement to Government Printing Office Style Manual. Washington, DC: U.S. Government Printing Office, 1984.

DICTIONARIES AND WORD GUIDES

H. Ramsey Fowler, Jane E. Aaron, and Jo Koster Travers. *Little, Brown Handbook.* 6th ed. New York: HarperCollins, 1995.

John C. Hodges, Mary E. Whitten, Winifred B. Homer, and Suzanne S. Webb. *Harbrace College Handbook.* 12th ed. San Diego: Harcourt Brace, 1995.

William A. Sabin. *The Gregg Reference Manual.* 7th ed. Lake Forest, IL: Glencoe, 1992.

Harry Shaw. *Punctuate It Right!* 2d ed. New York: HarperPerennial, 1993.

Harry Shaw. *Spell It Right!* 4th ed. New York: HarperPerennial, 1993.

BOOKS ON GRAMMAR, SPELLING, AND PUNCTUATION

The ACS Style Guide: A Manual for Authors and Editors. Janet Dodd, ed. American Chemical Society, 1986.

American Medical Association Manual of Style. 8th ed. Cheryl Iverson et al., authors and editors. Baltimore: Williams & Wilkins, 1989.

The Associated Press Stylebook and Libel Manual. Norm Goldstein, ed. New York: The Associated Press, 1994.

The Chicago Manual of Style. 14th ed. Chicago: University of Chicago Press, 1993.

The New York Public Library Writer's Guide to Style and Usage. Andrea J. Sutcliffe, ed. New York: HarperCollins, 1994.

STYLE AND USAGE MANUALS

Publication Manual of the American Psychological Association. 4th ed. Washington, DC: American Psychological Association, 1994.

Scientific Style and Format: The CBE Manual for Authors and Editors. Council of Biology Editors. New York: Oxford University Press, 1994.

U.S. Government Printing Office Style Manual. Washington, DC: U.S. Government Printing Office, 1984.

The Washington Post Deskbook on Style. 2d ed. Thomas W. Lippman, ed. New York: McGraw-Hill, 1989.

Words Into Type. 3rd rev. ed. Marjorie E. Skillin and Robert M. Gay. Englewood Cliffs, NJ: Prentice-Hall, 1974.

BOOKS ON USAGE, STYLE, AND WRITING

Theodore M. Bernstein. *The Careful Writer: A Modern Guide to English Usage.* New York: Atheneum, 1965.

Theodore M. Bernstein. *Dos, Don'ts & Maybes of English Usage.* New York: Times Books, 1977.

Roy H. Copperud. *American Usage and Style: The Consensus.* New York: Van Nostrand Reinhold, 1980.

Robin A. Cormier. *Error-Free Writing: A Lifetime Guide to Flawless Business Writing.* Englewood Cliffs, NJ: Prentice-Hall, 1995.

Wilson Follett. *Modern American Usage: A Guide.* Jacques Barzun, ed. New York: Avenel Books, 1980.

H.W. Fowler. *A Dictionary of Modern English Usage.* 2d rev. ed. New York: Greenwich House, 1983.

William and Mary Morris. *Harper Dictionary of Contemporary Usage.* 2d ed. New York: Harper & Row, 1985.

Arthur Plotnik. *The Elements of Editing.* New York: Macmillan, 1986.

Judith Tarutz. *Technical Editing: The Practical Guide for Editors and Writers.* New York: Addison-Wesley, 1992.

Webster's Dictionary of English Usage. Springfield, MA: Merriam-Webster, 1989.

William Strunk, Jr., and E.B. White. *The Elements of Style.* 3rd ed. New York: Macmillan, 1979.

William Zinsser. *On Writing Well.* 4th rev. ed. New York: HarperCollins, 1990.

APPENDIX D:
Selected Readings

All the articles that appear in this appendix were printed in *The Editorial Eye,*
EEI's monthly newsletter for publications professionals.

Lessons from 50 Years' Editorial Experience

by Lola M. Zook

"I have not made any novel discoveries or found any magical remedies. What I have done is to survive 50-plus years of trying to be a communicator—and still like what I'm doing."

With these words, Lola Zook introduced a talk on "Lessons Learned," delivered at the International Technical Communications Conference.... Here is the essence of her talk:

Lessons I Wish I Hadn't Had to Learn

1. There is absolutely no limit to the number of times authors or clients will change their minds.

2. The more firmly an author or client says that all the copy will be ready for you by a certain time, the later the material will be.

3. The rule on the innate perversity of inanimate objects applies. When I am in no hurry, the copying machine works perfectly. But if I need 20 copies for a meeting that starts in 3 minutes, a demon takes over.

   Likewise, all machines for putting words on paper—from linotype to photocomp—are, on occasion, possessed by demons. Surely, in a proposal, no human mind could take the phrase "government duplication" and change it into "government duplicity."

4. You can't have everything. What is essential is to recognize this fact—to be aware that you must choose, but that this gives you the opportunity to take control.

   With a tight budget, you balance the advantages and the costs of color work, quality paper stock, and so forth. You can't have everything, but you can have a satisfactory product.

   With a tight deadline, you decide where the limited time can be used to best effect. You can't do everything, but you can make your time count.

Lessons I Wish I Had Learned Sooner

1. It is impossible to overestimate the infinite capacity of things to go wrong.

2. It is impossible to overestimate the capacity of people to do something you don't expect.

3. When you are trying to tell graphics people how you want something done, one layout is worth ten thousand words.

4. There is one absolutely universal shortcoming that afflicts everyone in the publications business: Everyone underestimates the amount of time a job will take.

Lessons I Never Did Learn

1. I never did learn to spell *supersede*.

2. I never did solve the problem of *he/she* usage.

3. I never did learn to abhor the passive voice. I prefer the active voice; I know it is more vigorous and all those good, strong things. But still, there are times when what-was-done is more important than who-did-it. So I confess: Now and then, I put a sentence in the passive voice—deliberately!

4. I never did convince myself that shortest is best. I do indeed believe that good technical prose should not slop around with extra words and meandering sentences. But I have wasted many an editorial hour struggling to make sense of a passage where the author was determined to obey the rules and Be Concise, Brief, and To the Point. Unfortunately, in so doing, the author forgot the reader—and omitted the transitions, the explanatory phrases, or the line of reasoning that provided the base for an assumption or conclusion.

   So, when someone sings the glories of conciseness, I still tend to say, "Well-l-l, yes, but it's not that simple."

Lessons I Am Still Trying to Learn

1. For one who works with words, the ultimate goal is to produce a sentence that sounds as if it could have been written no other way.

2. One of the best ways to judge whether prose is effective is to use your ear. Listen to the rhythm of the sentence, the sound of the words, the cadence of the paragraph. If the words are awkward neighbors, if the breaks are too close, the flow is interrupted. That may be just what you want—but do it on purpose and not by accident! Hear rhythm and flow and contrast; use them as tools to make the language harmonize with the meaning.

3. A good way to improve editorial skills is to teach someone else in a one-to-one, tutorial relationship. With a bright, assertive apprentice who questions and challenges every aspect of the work, you'll find yourself reviewing rules you've grown careless about, looking up items you've taken for granted, sharpening style—all because you had to take a fresh look at things that had become so familiar you didn't even see them any more.

4. Borrow the first step of the Scientific Method: Define the problem.

   If you are having trouble, back off and consider: What really is the problem? If you can't focus the writing, is the problem in the writing, the reasoning, or the organization? If the author has specified one audience but written for a different one, is the problem in the perception of the audience or in the writing? If there is too much work and not enough time to produce a big job, should you sound the alarm for emergency help or try to get someone to take a hatchet to the size of the job?

And be sure that problem definition moves in two directions: You must know management's problems in a project, and you must inform management about problems you face that could endanger success. A problem is not likely to be solved unless the right people know it exists.

5. As an editor, you must be aware of what you do not know about a technical subject but not let yourself be intimidated.

   Poor organization is poor organization whatever the subject matter. Bad grammar or careless documentation has to be corrected in any discipline. Preparing a manuscript for publication is the same process whether it deals with maintaining tanks or projecting energy demands.

   What you must do is keep sharply aware of technical danger points. Of course the subject matter specialist is afraid of what an untested editor might do to technical statements. When you show that you are sensitive to these hazards, you are likely to get more freedom.

6. Remember: You, the editor, are a bridge between two people, the person who has written and the person who will (or may) read. Everything else in the process is simply a means to that end.

   There is a corollary to this lesson. Every editor must like working with words, but to be fully effective an editor must also like working with people.

7. Keep a sense of perspective. The editor who sets a goal of perfection is in for a lifetime of disappointment. Set a goal that is reasonable, and then take pride in reaching it.

   Accept the fact that authors and production people have their own problems, and that your problem may be pretty far down in their priorities.

   Take time to enjoy what you are doing. If this is your chosen work, presumably you like doing it, or at least most of it. Yet some of us are so tense, so upset over every trifle, that the job sounds like punishment. We need to establish that sense of perspective.

   And, always, we need to keep an eye out for the funny side.

"How Do You 'Be' an Editor?"

by Mara T. Adams

With this question, a participant in one of EEI's seminars condemned me to hours of philosophical contemplation. What did she mean? What could she have meant: How does one set out to become an editor? How does one act as an editor? What is an editor? How does an editor think? Metaphysics aside, the question of how one "be's" an editor is intriguing because, as all editors know, the roads that lead to the practice of our craft are as various as its tasks and skills. I have chosen to interpret "be" in the sense of essence.

Temperament

Editors are seekers of that perfect harmony that Renaissance philosophers called "the music of the spheres." They are critics in the purest sense. But if you lack the inborn quirks of character that combine diffidence with arrogance, poetry with logic, and flexibility with compulsion, the best you can hope for is to be a grammarian. Given grammatical knowledge of the language, the editor must also possess two other qualities: an intuitive understanding of how words work together to achieve their best expression and an implacable conviction that the piece of writing does not exist that cannot be improved.

The occupational hazard of most editors is that they may never stop working—reading for pleasure is to them both the ultimate redundancy and the ultimate contradiction in terms. Yet common sense and authors' sensibilities demand that the editorial workhorse wear fetters. The editor therefore needs the sense of proportion and of balance that translates into knowing when to stop. Hence the lesson every editor must learn: Not every piece of writing needs or deserves the same level of editorial attention.

Training

Editorial training begins with an emotional attachment to the written word. By that I mean, the natural editor will read anything—poetry, history, trash novels, maps, dictionaries, comic strips, and the backs of cereal boxes—for the sheer joy of reading. Word games (remember "Botticelli"?) and crossword puzzles add to the cache of minutiae editors love to squirrel away. Acquiring the elements of style, consistency, accuracy, and clarity is simply a more elaborate word game, whose rules are set forth in dozens of reference works and whose object is to achieve encyclopedic knowledge of the lore of putting words on paper properly. (A college roommate once paid me the compliment of saying I possessed the largest store of useless information she had ever encountered.)

There is no one perfect way to train an editor, any more than there is one perfect way to train roses or children or puppies. Some cut their teeth directly on a manuscript, others on charts and tables, still others on verifying citations. For many, it's a matter of luck—landing in the right place at the right time; getting to know an old-fashioned editor who is willing to teach; reading, reading, and reading some more; or simply being thrown into the soup and finding the way out by instinct.

Whatever the method, the education of an editor is never complete. Every new manuscript, every new author, every new book has something to teach, and the natural editor is panting to learn it. In his wonderful little book, *The Elements of Editing*, Arthur Plotnik explains the compulsion that drives the editor:

> The art of editing has most to do with felicity—with making just the right improvement to create light, joy, song, aptness, grace, beauty, or excitement where it wasn't quite happening.

Not even the prestigious Radcliffe Publishing Procedures course can teach you that.

The Acrobatic Apostrophe

by Dianne Snyder

"You find not the apostrophes and so miss the accent"—thus the schoolmaster in *Love's Labour's Lost* criticizes a curate who has just read aloud a love letter intended for someone else. The schoolmaster's concern with apostrophes should come as no surprise in a Shakespearean play whose very title contains two of them. Those of us who work with words know whereof he speaks.

With the possible exception of the comma, no mark of punctuation is more misunderstood. And none provokes the level of editorial consternation that a wrongly used apostrophe does: "The company went broke, in 1990, it's fifth year in business." Readers might forgive the unnecessary comma skulking on the baseline but not the errant apostrophe bold as a flagpole-sitter or a high-wire artist.

The Source of Apostrophic Conventions

The conventions governing the apostrophe distinguish three usages:

- To show possession (*her mother-in-law's house*)

- To show omission and elision of letters or numbers (*isn't, o'clock, the '90s*)

- To denote certain plurals (*1980's, learn your ABC's*)

The last is a matter of style; some style guides prescribe the apostrophe while others omit it except when needed for clarity, as in "dot your i's." The second usage is uniformly accepted and rarely misused. The first usage—to show possession—is where most questions arise.

Scholars believe that these conventions all emerged from one primordial bog. When the apostrophe was originally introduced into English in the 16th century, it was used simply to show omission. As English began to drop its inflected endings, the apostrophe was used to mark the omission of *e* from *es*, the Old English genitive (possessive) singular ending (*scipes = ship's*). It was later similarly used with certain nominative plural nouns (*foxes = fox's*) and more commonly with words ending in a vowel (*comma's*). Shakespeare would have been familiar with both usages, though neither was consistently applied until the 18th century.

Gradually, the use of the apostrophe to mark the possessive spread to include all possessive nouns (with or without *e*'s), while the plural usage ceased with the few exceptions noted earlier. Perhaps a remnant of that ancestral apostrophe remains imprinted on our genes and causes some of our present-day confusion.

A comprehensive discussion of the apostrophe could end up back at the bog. Although usage to show possession is now clearly differentiated from usage to show omission, the boundary between possessives and plurals remains uncertain. What follows is a discussion of the main areas of dispute, along with some guidelines and caveats for sorting them out.

Strunk and White's Rule Number One Updated

Form the possessive of singular nouns by adding 's, said Strunk and White's first rule of usage. "Follow this rule whatever the final consonant," they advised, although, like most rule givers, they granted a few exemptions (*for conscience' sake, in Jesus' name*). The trend today, however, is to exempt many more.

Increasingly, the *s* is being dropped after all multisyllabic nouns ending in an *s* or *z* sound (*Horowitz' piano*). Some styles drop the *s* even after monosyllabic words where speakers normally pronounce it (*my boss' husband*). Fortunately, the question of *s* or no *s* is easily resolved by recourse to a style guide or one's ear. The main thing is to be consistent.

The more thought-provoking part of the Strunk and White rule comes at the beginning: "Form the possessive. . . ." In a world populated by the likes of *Teachers College* and *users manual*, what in fact constitutes a possessive noun?

Can False Possessives Be Forgiven?

"I sank back on the Cadillac's plush seat for an hour's nap." If possessive nouns are defined as nouns that show ownership—the standard definition— a fair percentage of them are what Wilson Follett, in *Modern American Usage*, calls "false possessives." Inanimate objects used as possessives are the main offenders; strictly speaking, inanimate objects can't own things.

According to Follett, constructions such as *the Cadillac's plush seat* or *Florida's governor* are false because they're descriptive, not possessive. "The error . . . is to assume that Florida's governor means the same thing as the governor of Florida," Follett states, ruling that the possessive apostrophe should be reserved for "ownership by a person." (It's not clear where that leaves either the cat's whiskers or its pajamas.)

Other authorities are more indulgent. Theodore Bernstein, in *The Careful Writer*, dismisses Follett's reasoning as pedantry. "If the purists are going to insist on their rule, perhaps we shall have to rewrite our national anthem to get rid of 'dawn's early light'. . . ." Bernstein observes that "we seem to be approaching a stage where genitives with lifeless things are acceptable except when they sound unusual enough . . . to call attention to themselves."

Another group of false possessives comprises expressions of duration (*one week's vacation, two hours' rest*). The usage is idiomatic; no real ownership is involved. Some authorities, including Fowler, note that these expressions could also be regarded as attributive nouns (nouns used as adjectives preceding another noun), in which case the apostrophe would be omitted. The consensus, though, is to treat expressions of duration as possessive.

Attributive Nouns Come with Strings

Nouns used to modify other nouns have a long history in the English language, but their proliferation in recent years has been striking on two counts: Many of these newer descriptive nouns have been pluralized (*funds solicitation*), and often the nouns they modify are themselves used attributively (*funds solicitation planning committee*). In a rush to condense that would do the *Reader's Digest* proud, nouns, phrases, and even clauses piggyback and fuse into dense strings.

One effect of this proliferation, aside from raising editors' eyebrows, has been to diminish the supply of inanimate possessives. Thus, *Florida's governor Lawton Chiles* has become *Florida governor Lawton Chiles*. If you object to the idea of possessive inanimate objects, the missing apostrophe may count as progress, but clarity is frequently traded for brevity, particularly when a long noun string is formed. Is a *young adult fiction writers workshop* (a) a workshop for people who write fiction for young adults or (b) a workshop for young adults who write fiction?

Writer's Center? Writers' Center? Writers Center? The distinction between a possessive noun ("a center created by or belonging to writers") and a descriptive one ("a center created for writers") is often so fine that the question becomes one of nuance. Do we want to encourage an individual sense of belonging or a collective sense (*'s* or *s'*)?

Do pluralized attributive nouns have a place in good writing? Most authorities, while conceding that they do, voice concern about ambiguity, loss of clarity, or unholy combinations of sounds. *Weapons systems* may be defensible on military grounds, but on grounds of euphony it deserves execution.

Double Genitives

That moth-eaten old coat of my father's has got to go! Sentences that show possession in two ways are termed double genitives. In this sort of construction, the *'s* is redundant since the *of* already implies possession. Nevertheless, most authorities accept the usage as idiomatic.

Follett, in *Modern American Usage*, points out that the *'s*, redundant or not, is often needed for clarity. Without it, for example, we cannot differentiate *a portrait of Mary Cassatt's* (a painting done by her or possibly a painting owned by her) from a *portrait of Mary Cassatt* (a painting of her done by someone else). Of course, we can write around the ambiguity by using *a portrait by Mary Cassatt* for one she painted.

Possession with a Gerund

The church bell's tolling interfered with his hearing our song. Using the possessive with a verbal noun (or gerund) is standard practice, and some authorities view it as the only acceptable construction to use with gerunds. But, in fact, the usage has been disputed among grammarians for more than three hundred years. Should it be *the bell's tolling* or *the bell tolling*? And does the clamor interfere with *his hearing* or *him hearing*?

Webster's Dictionary of English Usage points out that for centuries good writers have used either construction depending on what they want to emphasize. Among many contrasting examples cited are two from Flannery O'Connor's letters:

> She approves of this one's being a girl.

> ... I can't see me letting Harold C. condense it.

In the second example, *Webster's* notes, the use of *me* instead of *my* emphasizes the pronoun by making it the object of the verb, whereas in the first example the whole phrase "this one's being a girl" is the object of the verb and "one" needs no emphasis.

Webster's accepts both constructions and provides these general observations:

1. Personal pronouns used with a gerund are usually possessive but may be objective if the writer intends special emphasis.
2. The possessive is less frequent with nouns. Writers often drop the possessive if the noun ends in an *s* sound: *The twins shouting woke us up.*
3. The possessive may be dropped if the noun or pronoun is followed by a modifier: *I worried about Sebastian perhaps not having enough to eat.*
4. Some nouns and pronouns simply resist the possessive form: *The odds of that occurring are one in ten.*

"The possessive," *Webster's* concludes, "will almost always be safe for pronouns and will probably work most of the time with nouns."

Whither the Apostrophe?

Did the fortune cookie saying "You are the center of every groups attention" portend the future of the apostrophe? It is omitted with many attributive nouns, but educated writers and editors are unlikely to relinquish the mark itself as a routine sign of possession. Perhaps it will come full circle and be used simply to mark omission and elision. More likely, the apostrophe will continue to be used and flagrantly abused, in all its variety.

In Search of Editorial Absolutes

by Mary J. Scroggins

I was once a humble editorial trainee. Like most new editors, I had no formal training in writing or grammar and only a vague idea of what an editor was. I ventured into this new profession anticipating that I would be privy to all the editorial secrets and dictates contained in the 2,003 resource books (a conservative exaggeration) dumped on my desk by the training manager. These books surely had the definitive answers to all my questions on writing, editing, and the English language. I was entering the land of "absolutes."

I had the good fortune to train in a company with a style guide that could hold its own against the *U.S. Government Printing Office (GPO) Style Manual* or *The Chicago Manual of Style*. Little could be left to choice or free will, I thought in my naiveté. I assumed that everything would fit neatly into a mold, pattern, style, or system. Surely these books contained rules to fit every need of every manuscript I would ever encounter.

Much to my dismay, aside from strict rules of grammar and widely accepted points of style, the number of "absolutes" decreased as my editing skills increased. Reality set in; I had to think, make choices, and do more than flip to page 204 and follow example 4.3. The resource books and house style guide served as the framework for my task of clarifying the language.

Recently—and not for the first time—a participant in an editing workshop that I conducted for Editorial Experts, Inc., asked for the answer after almost every exercise. My answer—"That's good" (meaning, "You have improved the sentence and made it easier for the reader to understand. There are other ways to approach it, and we'll explore a few.")—would not do. I almost always followed my answer with a question: "How did other people in the class handle this sentence?" Again and again, this persistent woman, new to editing and still in search of absolutes, said, "Those are the choices; what's the answer?" The first few times she asked this, I responded with a lecture on the wonder, beauty, choices, and variations of the language. Note the emphasis on "choices" and "variations."

Those lectures can be summed up briefly: "There are no absolutes."

The lectures did not do the trick. During the wrapup portion of the class, the woman noted that she had enjoyed the workshop but that she was disappointed because I had given few absolutes.

Not to be outdone, I went into a long discussion of absolutes and the flexibility of language and style. It went something like this:

Good editors are not obsessed with commas, spacing around headings, or parallelism. We are obsessed with readers and their ability to understand printed words and thoughts as effortlessly as possible. We advocate clarity, consistency, correctness, conciseness, and other tangibles—some of which do not even begin with "c." That obsession compels us to weed out wordy constructions, untangle convoluted sentences, unpack noun strings. We do these things even before we know what to call them; we seem instinctively to know that readers will not be best served by certain constructions, phrasing, and word choices. That instinct is guided by a feel for the language, the precision of one word over another, and the tones and hues provided by various choices. This "talent" should be continuously improved and strengthened. The instinct cannot be bought, taught, traded, or willed, but it can be enhanced. It does not take well to absolutes. It thrives on diversity and choice, within the confines of a given discipline or stylistic framework.

The answer does not exist in matters of style and preference (by definition). There are many ways of accomplishing the editor's goal—clear, concise, consistent, correct communication. In training new editors and evaluating new and experienced ones, supervisors frequently make the mistake of insisting on adherence to their preferences or the ways that they would handle the sentence. The implication is that the editor being evaluated has handled a problem incorrectly, not simply differently. Personal and style preferences should not be stated as absolutes; choices should be allowed. We are generally taught to prefer the active voice over the passive, but not necessarily to choose it. Therefore, the use of the passive voice is not absolutely incorrect. However, if we encounter a singular verb with a plural subject, a discussion of absolutes is in order; that is, "they is" is always incorrect. That is a point of grammar and is an absolute.

Remember, editors are the readers' advocates. As such, we search for words, phrases, and stylistic techniques that allow readers to understand exactly, not partially, what the author intended. Editing is not an exact science; it is an art guided by instinct and enhanced by training and the tools of the trade.

So, will I bend, go against all my principles, and endorse the answer (otherwise called "my personal preference")? Absolutely not.

(© 1988 Mary J. Scroggins; reprinted with permission)

The Considerate Editor: The Art of Criticizing Colleagues

by Catharine Fishel

Professional writers and editors try to grow thick skins that will blunt the sting of criticism when it eventually comes, as it must. But the truth is, it's always painful to be edited by peers with whom one must maintain a working relationship—especially that particular peer whose edits make you want to stuff a dictionary down her throat. Could *your* editing of *her* work be what makes her so nasty? People on small staffs such as my own often edit each other, and it can get ugly.

You may be on the other side of the red pen someday soon, and what's good for you—tact, respect, support—is good for the people you edit. Whether you work on-line with embedded queries or mark hard copy for the writer to revise, consider practicing the small niceties listed below.

- Don't be pedantic, no matter what your mood. Being "objective" is not the same as being rigid—equating the two is a bad professional sign. Experience and education should make an editor flexible. (I can recall one editor who carefully typed long passages from the *Chicago Manual of Style* and taped them to my manuscripts. I don't miss him.)

- Craft your criticisms so they are positive and constructive. A successful editor is one whose suggestions are given close consideration and implemented; negative comments are likely to be resisted. Put yourself in the writer's place. Would you prefer to hear "Long direct quote is good, but interrupts the flow—let's trim," or "Delete! Confusing!"

- Provide positive feedback as well as identify problems. Almost every piece of writing has *something* good about it. A "Nice!" or "Interesting" (if you mean it) can go a long way toward getting a better reaction to your corrective edits.

- Don't mix messages. People are not fooled by such manipulative statements as "This is a good analogy, but it's probably not necessary." If it's so good, why is the editor suggesting cutting the analogy out? Be straightforward.

- Don't be patronizing. A good writer or editor will be as offended by a gratuitous compliment as a callous edit. Using a note or query to flash one's training makes it hard for a writer to be grateful for the attempt at improvement. Anybody would balk at absorbing a comment like "Nice try, but I'm wondering whether you're familiar with the rhetorical flaw of tautology?"

- Pick your battles, especially when someone's trying to engage you in Style Wars. You can build a fortress around your desk with reference books to defend your work, but daily full-scale battle is tiresome. Save your energy for the big things. This advice is predicated on a reasonable definition of what the big things *are*. Has the meaning of the sentence been compromised? Then fight for repunctuating, or a rewrite.

- Address the big issues in person, not on paper. Written criticism can sound harsher than you intend it to, but respectful, concerned inflection and informal body language can soften the implications of criticism. Friendly laughter and self-deprecating humor on the part of the editor are legitimate ways to make straight shooting less painful. However, some writers have no sense of humor about being edited, so be careful.

- Examine your own editing style. If you are routinely unnecessarily critical, you may be inspiring tit-for-tat editing of your work. The result is a stressful competition to find fault—and that ante only goes up.

- Phrase edits in the form of questions rather than imperatives when you can. But avoid cryptic wording. Try, for instance, "Sentences seem to be backward—can you rework?" instead of "Rework" or "Logic?" Nobody likes being on the receiving end of commands, and it's frustrating to be left wondering what a one-word comment means. Better yet, wherever possible rework the passage yourself.

- Resist the temptation to use underlines, exclamation points, un-smiley faces, and anything else that may rub salt in the wound. These little graphic inflections don't make editing seem more human: They make criticism seem more personal.

- Be tidy. Some edits are hard enough to swallow as it is. Spare the recipient time spent squinting to decipher what, after all, is an error message.

- Consider the cumulative effect on a writer of several tiers of editing comments. In my office, we use different colors so we can identify comments from different editors. Fortunately or unfortunately, I wield the wicked red pencil, so I try to keep my marks small and restrained. Although writing small doesn't necessarily indicate tact, it's symbolically a smaller mote in the eye.

- When edits are many and serious, soften the blow by jotting a quick note at the top of the manuscript enumerating its better points. It costs nothing to be nice, and the return in goodwill is worth the effort many times over. One of these days when you're on the receiving end of a stem-to-stern, you'll be glad to see a few kind words prefacing your own bout with humility.

The Editor as Seed Crystal

by Bruce O. Boston

On the theory that editors are just as narcissistic as the general population, and that we enjoy talking about ourselves just as much as failed actors and newly engaged couples, this article holds up the mirror to our sacred profession. The question is, what do we actually do?

First, since the glass doesn't lie, let's admit the truth. Despite the justifiable pride we may take in our craft, the living of an editor, like that of a book reviewer, is basically derivative. If it weren't for writers, most of us would be slinging hash instead of ink. Nonetheless, our profession does have standing of its own. There is some comfort, for example, in learning that—in English, at least—the verb *edit* did not come first, followed by the noun *editor*, as one might think. *The Oxford English Dictionary* (OED) reveals that *edit* is a back-formation from *editor*. (The OED's first usage citation for *edit* is dated 1793; the first citation for *editor* is dated 1648.) This chronology does not necessarily mean that who we are takes precedence over what we do. It only revalidates the eternal truth that the ways of language are mysterious and there is no accounting for how some things get started.

A New Profession

Which brings us to point number two: Compared with a number of other professions, editing hasn't really been around all that long. It is only since the early eighteenth century that editors have been understood as persons who prepare the literary work of others for publication by a process of selection and revision. For about 150 years before that, editor was synonymous with publisher. Apparently, the assumption was that authors didn't need any help with their writing, only with the less savory task of getting it before the public. Thus, from the beginning, we editors have been in the mercantile mire. Knowledge of one's origins is a great antidote for professional hubris.

But like any useful new idea, the notion of an editor has caught on and gone from strength to strength. Like engineering, medicine, law, and theology, editing has proliferated specializations, continually rejustifying its precarious existence on the fringes of literature. There are acquisitions editors, line editors, copyeditors, photo editors, technical editors, abstract editors, style editors, story editors, general editors, and, to supervise them all, editors-in-chief. Thus, editors have become like doctors; you don't know without asking what any of them really are.

Dinner with the Queen

What most editors mostly do (we're talking here about the ones who do not get to take authors to lunch at Elaine's or the Four Seasons) is to read manuscripts with pencil in hand, correcting the errors of organization and presentation that may confuse a reader, offend the canons of standard English usage and grammar, or aggravate the ulcer of a printer.

If that sounds like a piece of cake, you either do not understand editing at all or have not been doing it very long. The main problem with our profession, as William Bridgewater, former editor-in-chief of Columbia University Press has pointed out, is that it is a task without thoroughly set limits. In other words, in editing, as in dressing to go to dinner with the Queen, it's hard to know when you're "ready." And, truth to tell, more than anything else, what defines "ready" is that your manuscript, like your person at the palace, has a time beyond which, if it doesn't show up, it embarrasses everyone connected with the enterprise. You most of all.

Message and Medium

My own view of editing is a little more exciting than that, however. For me, editing is an immersion in the endlessly fascinating chemistry of the English language. I have yet to meet the editor who is really as self-absorbed as my tongue-in-cheek introduction to this column makes out. In truth, there is nothing editors care about so much as the endless possibilities for combination and recombination in language, and finding the right set of combinations for a particular manuscript. This passion is usually put in terms of the editor's responsibility to the author; what we really must care about is creating that arrangement of the author's words that best expresses the author's intention. What we seek is a kind of harmony, a crystallization in which message and medium merge.

When we do our jobs right, editors are like seed crystals. In chemistry, crystals are regular forms that seem to arise spontaneously and then replicate themselves in a stable manner. What sets this process off is a "seed crystal," which, when inserted into an assortment of molecules, brings those molecules together in a unique formation. Once the seed crystal is inserted, the molecules buzz around until, almost miraculously, they find the perfect arrangement to express exactly what they are. The result is maximum order and stability, in which all the molecules are organized in a way that leads to their continued existence. That's a job description for an editor if I ever heard one.

(© 1985 Bruce O. Boston; reprinted with permission)

Weeds

by Bruce O. Boston

If a weed is only a plant growing somewhere you don't want it, then jargon is the weedpatch of language. Thus, I don't hold with Fowler, who defines jargon as "talk that is considered both ugly sounding and hard to understand." Ugliness is in the eye of the beholder, and although a word like *byte* may be ugly to some, it is elegant to a computer programmer, for whom it expresses a precise and therefore clear meaning. It isn't that jargon is noxious in itself, it's that, like crabgrass, the dratted stuff keeps rooting where it doesn't belong.

Jargon creates two difficulties, both of which endanger clear understanding. The first is seldom mentioned: jargon deflects the attention of the reader away from the subject at hand and onto the writer. And, truth to tell, this is why most of us lapse into jargon; we succumb to the temptation to parade our command of various and arcane vocabularies. But the business writer who lapses into computerese while discussing marketing risks losing the reader's attention and respect. Or, as Dick Cavett puts it, "Anyone who uses the words 'parameter' and 'interface' should never be invited to a dinner party."

The Style of Jargon

The second difficulty is a more common complaint. Jargon, because it is language misdirected, soon becomes soporific and finally narcotic. It depends on a prose style that sooner or later becomes a candidate for the putdown C. Wright Mills made on the writing of fellow sociologist Talcott Parsons: "Talcott writes with ink of opium on pages of lead." Jargon prefers the noun to the verb; its building blocks are smothered verbs and the prepositional phrases that trail in their wake. Among the most common constructions of jargon-laden writing is the all too familiar: "the (choose any verb)-tion of (choose any noun)." Thus, like the builders of the Tower of Babel, the architects of jargon court the confusion of tongues as they stack their nominalizations one atop another. The style of jargon uses bricks without the mortar of thought; in the end, the sentences and paragraphs simply collapse.

On examination, both these problems turn out to have a moral dimension; both are a refusal to apply standards, in the one case to the writer and in the other to the product. Allowing the weeds of jargon to grow all over the garden is basically a refusal to say that this is good writing and that is bad writing. The writer's willingness to make such distinctions and the implicit trust of the reader that the writer will make them are part of the moral bond between them, and jargon threatens the integrity of this bond.

Two Responses

The conventional response to the moral problem of jargon is a kind of moralism, a "tsk-tsk-ing" of the kind that most of us learned from our eighth-grade English teachers. We hear their echoes today in the tough cadences of those Kojaks of the English language, Edwin Newman and John Simon. But the cure of moralism is no cure at all and is often worse than the disease. It changes so little and risks so much good will from people who might otherwise be disposed to curb their jargoneering; self-righteousness is a taste only angels can afford to cultivate.

But there is another way. Richard A. Lanham, in his intriguing little book *Style: An Anti-Textbook* (New Haven: Yale University Press, 1974), suggests that a more fruitful approach is to think of jargon as an effort toward a real style, however clumsy. His point is not that we indulge ourselves in a kind of linguistic Grundyism, but that we start translating jargon into real English, and thereby get some fun out of all the special little lingoes all of us dabble in from time to time. His advice is to stop being linguistic police and to start becoming connoisseurs of jargons.

Perhaps Lanham is right. Once we start thinking of jargon not as a collection of misplaced weeds but as a garden of metaphors, waiting to be dug up and repotted, we might just begin to get a new perspective and spread a little beauty around the place. There are plenty of flowerbeds out there, and, who knows, by transplanting a weed or two, and indulging in a little cross-pollinating, we may discover something new. Perhaps we need to take seriously the possibility that Gregor Mendel and Luther Burbank can be our role models as well as E.B. White and Lewis Thomas. Nothing immoral about that.

(© 1984 Bruce O. Boston; reprinted with permission)

What Editors Need to Know About Desktop Publishing

by Jayne O. Sutton

Editors are accustomed to seeing to it that what shows up on paper is a coherent, logical flow of ideas. But how about what's on the disk? The copyediting step—perhaps the last time a manuscript is gone over painstakingly, word by word—is especially significant in the desktop publishing (DTP) environment where the manuscript is formatted in paragraph units. Even editors who do not work on-line can no longer afford to ignore the mechanics of the electronic production process and the capabilities of word processing and DTP software. Establishing a checklist of details that can be systematically and routinely dealt with in every manuscript is central to the copyediting step and can help editors head off format and style errors early in the process. Adapting to the electronic environment may seem to demand more from editors early on, but the payback is a more effective system that allows them to concentrate on real editing.

Before Electronic Production: Clean Up the File

Even in cases where manuscripts are formatted to some degree during the writing and editing process, some "debris" is usually left over and some typographic details will still need to be taken care of. The process of creating a manuscript is messy—false starts, writing and rewriting, adding, deleting, moving, cutting—and its paramount goal is, of course, clear and effective communication. Even editors who are experienced software users may insert erroneous or extraneous codes and characters into the files when they are focusing on tone and content, and borderline users can make some truly admirable messes. Obsolete conventions, such as double paragraph returns and two spaces after periods and semicolons, are still a reflex for many of us who learned to type BDTP (before desktop publishing). These bad habits can throw a monkey wrench into electronic production or, at the very least, result in a sloppy page layout.

But marking or manually correcting each instance of these and other format glitches is drudgery and (more important) an unnecessary diversion from editing the words. One of the editor's most powerful helpers, search and replace, can streamline the process enormously. (The next step up, macros, can add jet propulsion.) See p. 325 for details that should be at the top of any checklist for global screening of documents.

When preparing a text file to be imported from a word processing program into page layout software, it's a good idea to strip page formatting codes out of the file. Even plain vanilla word processing files may contain some formatting information—for headers and footers and font changes, for example—that may conflict with or corrupt DTP command codes.

Finally, it's a waste of time for editors working in a DTP environment to mark draft copy for things like spacing, indents, and justification. DTP programs work with chunks of text separated by hard paragraph returns and apply typographic and layout formats to these units. The formatting information includes typeface, size, spacing (above, below, and between lines), margins, alignment and justification, indents and outdents, hyphenation, tab settings, and often such special touches as bullets and drop caps.

After Electronic Production: Checking Manuscript Pages

Once the various typographic and layout treatments are defined, they do not require editorial oversight; the editor need only identify by means of a "tag" or format name the type of treatment that is to be applied to each unit of text. If the DTP layout will be done by someone other than the editor, a short conference can clarify what can be handled consistently by the electronic style sheet or template and what needs to be treated on a case-by-case basis. For example, some programs can set capitalization (all caps, initial caps, or all lowercase) as part of a format; in others, capitalization must be changed and checked each time.

Even in its simplest applications, word processing software provides the full range of characters in a type font, in addition to keyboard characters. But most authors don't incorporate such characters electronically as they write because of the extra time and effort involved. Some coding for these characters can be written into a preliminary formatting program similar to the cleanup already discussed, and some is more efficiently handled during editing. In either case, the editor should see to it that during final production the desktop publisher makes the following translations from conventional typescript to take advantage of full typographic capabilities:

- *Em-dashes and "real" quotation marks.* The double dash (--) and straight quotes (") from the keyboard are not used for anything else in a DTP format, so searching for and replacing them is pretty straightforward. As a matter of fact, most DTP software can now automatically convert double dashes and straight quotes.

- *Single quotes and apostrophes* in typescript are represented by the same straight keyboard apostrophe, so they can't be universally replaced by the proper "real" character. Replace hyphens that have been used in word processing to take the place of en-dashes with coding for the special character (–). Check quotes carefully after formatting; in cases of complex combinations of punctuation (single quotes beginning or ending within double quotes) or unusual spacing, some marks can slip through uncoded.

324

- *Non-keyboard characters.* Some special characters can't be coded automatically because they can appear in different ways in text, thus making an electronic search impractical. Editors should check to see that they are set properly in each case. Besides the obvious examples of **math symbols** and **Greek, accented, and other foreign-language characters**, the following are non-keyboard characters that contribute to a professionally typeset look:

  - *Ellipsis points*—they are set as a single character, not just three typed periods;

  - *Fractions*—again, they are single characters, not two numbers separated by a keyboard slash; and

  - *Trademark, registered, and copyright symbols*—they are more properly rendered as superscripts in a smaller font, not as full-sized letters between parentheses or other workarounds.

- *Italics, boldface, and super- or subscripts* will usually come across from material specified in word processing to DTP software, but you should always check these words or phrases carefully. You might want to mark these treatments on a printout of the original word processed draft—for instance, with a highlighter—as a reminder that they shouldn't be changed but will need to be checked.

Prevent Format Glitches with Global Screening

Watch for these format problems in DTP copy:

- *Extra spaces* after final punctuation (and anywhere else). Delete them.

- *Double paragraph returns.* Delete them.

- *Manually inserted (or "hard") hyphenation* (use the "search with confirm" option). End-of-line hyphens—unless they are holding together the parts of a compound word or standing in for an en-dash—should always be left alone until the very final tweaking of line breaks in finished pages.

- *Tabs.* Weed *multiple tabs in tabular copy* down to one, so that the final formatting can take care of how the tabs should be set. And get rid of *paragraph indent tabs* altogether, since a DTP format will usually have indents built in.

- *Convert underscoring to italics.* Writers often do not consistently underscore punctuation following underscored words. The ending punctuation will not be properly translated into italic unless it has been underlined *before* it is translated into italics.

- *Special treatments like italic, boldface, and super- or subscripts.* If your software's conversion process drops word processing codes for these treatments, search and replace them with DTP codes to make sure they come across correctly.

Wish a Rote Task Would Disappear?

There's no way around it: Editors need to take some time to learn about the particular strengths of the DTP program used to produce the manuscripts they edit. Software developers are pouring a lot of money and effort into making their products stronger, smarter, and faster, and they are integrating an astounding array of editorial tasks. Just let yourself start thinking about how automated features could free up your time and allow you to focus your attention on real editing rather than on housekeeping.

In essence, the job of copyediting is very much the same as it has always been: to polish a manuscript and prepare it for final form. In the DTP environment, sometimes it seems that we're losing some of the niceties and details as we move from manuscript to final pages. But for those who take the time to harness the electronic workhorse, the potential is there for doing (Dare I suggest it?) an even better job of it than in the days BDTP.

In Defense of the Passive

by Mara T. Adams

Have you ever wondered why some editors rigorously excise passive constructions wherever they turn up, regardless of sense or sensibility?

Recently, I was asked to review an article for publication. The article was a delight—it had rhythm, style, variety, imagination, and elegance of expression—in its unedited state. The editor, in a fit of conscientiousness (perhaps brought on by having read the advice of too many proponents of the short and simplistic), had diligently changed all passive voice constructions to the active, with the result that the author's vigorous style was drained of vitality.

Now, the editor cannot be held entirely to blame. Any "effective writing" manual you pick up—starting with the estimable *Elements of Style*—tells you to prefer the active voice. The key word here is *prefer*, which means "like better; choose above another," not "adhere to mindlessly." Yet many editors respond to passives with a pencil-jerk, apparently not pausing to consider that the language probably would not contain a passive voice if it were never to be used.

All right, you challenge, give me one good reason for using the passive. I'll give you several.

First, the active voice, as we all know, is strong because it allows an actor to do something. But sometimes your sentence simply does not need an actor—as illustrated in the previous paragraph in the clause "the language probably would not contain a passive voice if it were never to be used." If the infinitive phrase were rendered in the active voice, the only possible actor would be the ubiquitous "one" (as in "if one were never to use it"), and "one" is overworked to begin with.

Second, the passive voice can be used to describe a situation in which the thing acted upon is more important than the actor. "The enormous diamond had been given to her on her 40th birthday, but she chose not to wear it until her 75th." Certainly the sentence would make sense if it began, "She received the enormous diamond . . . ," but that would shift the focus away from the stone which, in this case, is the more important element in the sentence.

Third, the actor may be obscure, unknown, or unimportant or may wish to be anonymous or transparent. This kind of passive construction occurs most often in scientific or technical material, as in, "The mice were fed a solution of gin and vermouth and were observed to behave in bizarre ways." The passive should be allowed to stand, except when it gets in the way of comprehension or produces absurd constructions, such as "It was felt that the mice were drunk."

And fourth, sometimes a passive construction can help you achieve a desired cadence. Robert Frost could have written, "I took the road fewer people traveled," but that's hardly as rhythmic as, "I took the one less traveled by." In deciding whether to change passive voice to active, be guided by your ear, as well as by your training. Read the sentence out loud. If you can't understand it, it may need the active voice (and perhaps much more). But if the rhythm is pleasing and the sentence makes sense, leave it alone.

Passive constructions are not evil in themselves; only the misuse and the overuse of the passive have given it such a bad name. Remove it carefully and with much thought; you may be pulling up a wildflower instead of a weed.

Who Said That? On Handling Quotations

by Edward D. Johnson

Did Virginia Woolf write that James Joyce's *Ulysses* has genius, but of an inferior kind? Yes, she did. But did Virginia Woolf write *"Ulysses* has genius, but of an inferior kind"? No, she didn't. To be precise, she wrote, *"Genius it has, I think; but of the inferior water."*

That is the difference between a paraphrase and a true quotation.

If we use quotation marks, we are promising our readers that we are reporting Woolf's words exactly as printed. If we don't use them, we are not making that promise. In both cases, however, there is an implicit promise that we are reporting the *meaning* accurately.

In nonfiction, indentation (that is, block quotation) usually replaces quotation marks for quotations of more than a few lines. A block quotation makes the same promise of strict accuracy that quotation marks do.

The following block quotation is a larger slice of Woolf's diary entry for September 6, 1922, which I will use to illustrate some of the fine points of fair quotation.

> I finished *Ulysses* and think it a mis-fire. Genius it has, I think; but of the inferior water. The book is diffuse. It is brackish. It is pretentious. It is underbred, not only in the obvious sense, but in the literary sense. A first-rate writer, I mean, respects writing too much to be tricky; startling; doing stunts. I'm reminded all the time of some callow board-school boy, full of wits and powers, but so self-conscious and egotistical that he loses his head, becomes extravagant, mannered, uproarious, ill at ease, makes kindly people feel sorry for him and stern ones merely annoyed; and one hopes he'll grow out of it; but as Joyce is 40 this scarcely seems likely.

Quoting Fairly

"Genius it has," said Woolf of *Ulysses* is obviously an unfair use of quotation; it gives a false impression of Woolf's opinion. It is also more casual in form than it should be, especially if the context is a scholarly study of Woolf's writing, because it gives no indication that Woolf's sentence continues. Adding points of ellipsis to the quote—

"Genius it has . . ." said Woolf

—would at least provide the information that Woolf had more to say on the matter, but the quote would still be misleading.

Note that including Woolf's comma in the original (*"Genius it has, . . ."* said Woolf) is correct but fussier than necessary in most contexts; punctuation within a quoted passage should not be changed or omitted, but punctuation at the end can usually be dropped or changed to suit the enclosing sentence. Note also that if words are omitted not at the beginning of a quotation but in the middle, points of ellipsis are not optional—they *must* be used:

Woolf commented, "Genius it has . . . but of the inferior water."

The entire extract here is a fair use of quotation, although even it does not communicate everything Woolf had to say about *Ulysses*—the passage goes on to admit that she has spent little time so far on the book, and she takes the subject up again in subsequent diary entries.

But we can be fair without quoting the whole thing. Perhaps all we want from Woolf is the gist of her opinion, in which case the freest paraphrase would suffice:

> Woolf reported in her journal that she considered *Ulysses* a pretentious failure.

Or perhaps we want to report only a specific comment, in which case a short quotation and straightforward attribution may be best:

> Woolf wrote, "The book is diffuse."

Often, though, rather than rely on bland paraphrases or simple attributed quotations, we want to work quoted material into our own sentences, enlivening our text and giving our readers direct contact with our source. That's fair—but it should be done properly.

Extracting Only the Words We Want

What about compiling a direct quotation from several sentences? To write

> Woolf considered *Ulysses* "diffuse, brackish, pretentious, and underbred"

might be fair enough as far as the meaning goes, but it is not true to the actual words. Those four damning adjectives have been extracted from their separate sentences and put into a series, and the quotation marks promise the reader falsely that Woolf had them all in a single sentence.

A trivial lie? Maybe, but still a lie. Misreporting the sentence structure of the source is as irresponsible as misreporting the words. The quotation could be rendered truthfully this way:

> Woolf considered *Ulysses* "diffuse," "brackish," "pretentious," and "underbred."

That may look fussy, but it doesn't really bother readers—and it doesn't lie to them. If we really want to avoid the multiple quotation marks, we could use points of ellipsis:

> Woolf considered *Ulysses* "diffuse . . . brackish . . . pretentious . . . underbred."

Note that neither way of extracting words tells readers the whole truth that the four adjectives come from separate sentences—they just let it be a possibility. The conventions of quotation have their limitations, but we at least can make sure we don't tell lies.

Making Just a Tiny Change

How literally must a quotation be rendered? The sentence

> Woolf wrote that she "finished *Ulysses* and thought it a misfire"

is, again, fair to the meaning but not a proper direct quotation. By changing *think* to *thought*, the writer has made it an **indirect quotation**—a kind of paraphrase in which the choice of words remains pretty much the same, but person and tense are changed to suit the enclosing sentence. Indirect quotations should not be in quotation marks.

In addition to changing *think* to *thought*, the example in the preceding paragraph changes Woolf's hyphenated *mis-fire* to *misfire*. In principle, closing up *mis-fire* corrupts the quotation, and no corruption is permissible in some kinds of writing, such as scholarly studies of literary texts. But trivial changes like this one are defensible much of the time.

Variant spellings are distracting, and a writer or editor who judges such a variation to be of no possible significance to the reader—in this case, for instance, *mis-fire* is just a quirky spelling, not a British variant—may rightly decide to eliminate the distraction. I myself would hesitate to change Woolf, but in another case—for example, a modern writer published in a poorly edited periodical—I would certainly correct such a variant and might change number style, capitalization, and even some punctuation to suit my own conventions.

Quotation vs. Paraphrase

A direct quotation often has a punch that an indirect quotation or a free paraphrase does not, but it may take some effort to fit the borrowed words into good sentences of our own. Paraphrase is sometimes a better choice. Here is a passage from a later diary entry, after Woolf had discussed Joyce with T.S. Eliot:

> Tom said, "He is a purely literary writer. He is founded upon Walter Pater with a touch of Newman." I said he was virile—a he-goat; but didn't expect Tom to agree. Tom did, though; and said he left out many things that were important. The book would be a landmark, because it destroyed the whole of the nineteenth century. It left Joyce himself with nothing to write another book on. It showed the futility of all the English styles. He thought some of the writing was beautiful. But there was no "great conception"; that was not Joyce's intention.

Woolf makes skillful use of direct quotation (*Tom said, "He is . . ."*), of standard indirect quotation (*I said he was virile. . . . [Eliot] said he left out many things that were important*), and of a looser indirect quotation that probably departs considerably from Eliot's diction but is doubtless an accurate paraphrase (*The book would be a landmark. . . . It left Joyce himself with nothing to write another book on*).

The last sentence of the passage, although itself a paraphrase, has *great conception* in quotation marks. Perhaps they indicate that the phrase was Eliot's, but more likely they are "raised eyebrow" quotation marks—suggesting irony or some insinuating qualification, just as we do with voice and facial expression when we say something scornful like *I suppose you think this piece of yours is "great literature."* Like scorn itself, this use of quotation marks can be unpretty; often it seems jeering and mean-spirited. But Woolf, of course, is showing scorn of her own expectations as a reader and critic, if anything. Her criticism of Joyce is not insinuated with raised eyebrows but stated bluntly.

Common Quotation Errors

Suppose a writer wants to give a brief account of Woolf's reaction to *Ulysses*, using Woolf's own words as much as can gracefully be done. Here is a beginning that makes two common errors:

> When she first read *Ulysses,* Woolf wrote in her diary that "The book is diffuse," that it "reminded her all the time of some callow board-school boy."

The first quotation is a complete sentence, initial capital and all, and it should not be introduced by *that* but by a comma or colon:

> . . . Woolf wrote in her diary, "The book is diffuse."

or

> . . . Woolf wrote in her diary: "The book is diffuse."

The *that* should alert readers to an indirect quotation or to a direct quotation of a sentence fragment that has been incorporated into the writer's own grammar. (The indirect quotation can, of course, go on to include a direct quotation, just as Woolf included the raised eyebrow quotation *"great conception"* in her paraphrase of Eliot.)

The writer could, however, retain the *that* and simply lowercase Woolf's *The* to make it clear that even though the quotation is a grammatically complete sentence, it is not being presented as one but included as part of the writer's own sentence. If the writer considers it important to indicate any change that has been made to the capitalization of the first word of a quotation to fit the context, the lowercase letter that is supplied can be put in brackets:

> Woolf wrote that "[t]he book is diffuse."

Just as points of ellipsis are mandatory to indicate the omission of words in the middle of a quotation, brackets are mandatory to mark any additions or changes to a direct quotation beyond capitalizing or lowercasing an initial letter.

The phrasing *Woolf wrote that . . . it "reminded her . . ."* is a giveaway; obviously the writer has taken some liberty with Woolf's words, because she would not have referred to herself in the third person. This error could be repaired by putting *her* in brackets to indicate that the writer is supplying the word, but it would be smoother either to move the opening quotation mark to *all* or to change the enclosing words to accommodate the grammar of Woolf's words. Here is a corrected version:

> When she first read *Ulysses,* Woolf wrote in her diary that the book was "diffuse," that she was "reminded all the time of some callow board-school boy."

The Cost of Truth-in-Borrowing

An editor can't always do much about inaccurate quoting, which may be neither intentional nor apparent, or clumsy quoting, which may be impossible to improve without complete rewriting or extensive research. But it's an editor's specific responsibility to understand the mechanics and to make sure the accepted rules are properly applied. For their part, writers who are careful to quote fairly will agree with Ralph Waldo Emerson's judgment: "In fact, it is as difficult to appropriate the thoughts of others as it is to invent."

Cracking the Code: Making Verbs Agree with Collective Nouns

by Dianne Snyder

In 1961, when I arrived in New York, college bound, the main landmark of the upper West Side was a huge black sign with grimy white letters that covered the side of a tall building: THE WAGES OF SIN IS DEATH. The words, visible for blocks, made me uneasy as I walked with my fellow freshmen (this was in the days before "first-year student" became required tactful usage) down a seedy stretch of Broadway. I hadn't sampled much sin yet, but I *was* planning to be an English major. Why, I wondered aloud, did *wages* have a singular verb?

"Because it's the wages of sin," the lone sophomore among us replied. "In New York, sin is collective."

My friend, I now realize, had a better grasp of metaphysics than grammar. Still, in her fumbling way she made me aware that certain nouns have a dual nature: They take a singular or a plural verb depending on their meaning, not their form.

Over the years, I've developed a set of mental pigeonholes for these nouns and collected some rules of thumb to guide me in using them. The nouns fall roughly into three groups:

1. Collective nouns or, more specifically, a subset of them that Fowler, in *A Dictionary of Modern English Usage*, calls "nouns of multitude"
2. Nouns expressing number or quantity
3. Nouns ending in *-ics*

This discussion primarily treats collective nouns, but questions of subject-verb agreement commonly arise with all three types; the final arbiter is common sense.

1. Nouns of Multitude

Fowler defines a noun of multitude as "a whole made up of similar parts." Words such as *company, government, family*, and *committee* generally take a singular verb but sometimes take a plural one. The general rule is to treat these nouns as singular if they refer to the group as a whole and plural if they refer more to the individual members than to the group.

> As the defeated crew rows back to the boathouse, the crowd straggle back to their cars.

The crew is acting as a unit, but the members of the crowd are dispersing separately; the reference to *their cars* reinforces the plural sense. Adding "members of" to emphasize the individuals in the crowd would make the sentence less jarring.

> As the defeated crew rows back to the boathouse, members of the crowd straggle back to their cars.

Loose usages. The words *number, total,* and *variety* are often used in a loose sense to mean "some" or "many." These words are governed by two easy rules of thumb:

- When preceded by the indefinite article *a,* these words are being used loosely and take a plural verb.

    A variety of spicy dishes were served.

    A number of guests have complained of heartburn.

Here, the emphasis is placed on the plural noun in the prepositional phrase rather than on the collective noun that is the grammatical subject.*

- When preceded by the word *the,* these words are being used more specifically and take a singular verb.

    The number of guests complaining of heartburn has embarrassed the hostess.

Here, the emphasis is placed on the collective noun *number* rather than on the plural object of the preposition ("guests").

Similarly, *majority* can be used both specifically and loosely.

- When *majority* refers to the number of votes cast or to a party or group acting as a body (usually in an electoral sense), *majority* takes a singular verb.

    Her majority was a slim 2 percent.

    The majority has swung its support to Carrington.

- When *majority* refers to members of a group acting individually, the verb is plural.

    The majority of residents of this neighborhood attend St. Michael's Church.

Churchgoing is something they do individually. *Majority* is being used loosely here to mean *most.*

A simple way around these sometimes delicate distinctions is to avoid using *majority, number,* and the like loosely and to substitute modifiers such as *most, many,* and *some.* Not only are they more specific in meaning but, as adjectives, they leave no doubt that the verb should be plural.

    Most residents of this neighborhood attend St. Michael's Church.

Duos, trios, and quartets. Words such as *couple, pair,* and *trio* follow the general rule for nouns of multitude. Where people are concerned, however, the rule is not always easy to apply. *Is the couple married* or *are the couple married*? Opinion is divided, but most authorities favor the plural. "It is difficult to see how a writer can go wrong by treating *couple* as a plural," Theodore Bernstein notes in *The Careful Writer,* but adds that "treatment as a singular could be defensible sometimes." Roy Copperud, in *American Usage and Style,* states flatly that both *couple* and *pair,* used "in reference to people," should take a plural verb.

Whatever the usage, it should be consistent throughout the sentence; pronoun referents must agree with noun and verb. No one should accept split formulations such as *The couple is on their way to a honeymoon in St. Croix and Disney World*. (This sentence can be fixed by changing "is" to "are.")

2. Nouns of Number and Quantity

Like collective nouns, numbers or quantitative expressions pose questions of subject-verb agreement that sometimes require making fine distinctions. Again, rules of thumb will help.

Less than a whole. With fractional numbers and percentages the rule is this:

- The noun in the prepositional phrase that follows the fractional number, or is understood to follow it, determines the verb.*

> One-fourth of the members have already left, one-fourth are still debating, and the rest are milling about the hall.

Members determines the number for all three verbs.

> Ninety percent of the vines have been picked clean.

Vines determines the number for the verb. The sense of number resides in the prepositional phrase—what has been "picked"—rather than in the grammatical subject—the percentage of "pickedness."

- What if the noun following the fractional number is collective? In that case the complement may determine the verb. Edward D. Johnson provides this example in *The Handbook of Good English*: "About 50 percent of the population is rural. About 50 percent of the population are farmers."

- Quantitative expressions such as *some of, most of,* and *all of* follow the same rules as fractional numbers.

> Some of the children are getting impatient.

> Most of the baked goods were made from scratch.

Whole numbers. Sums of money, weights, and distances, though plural in form, are generally considered as a unit and given a singular verb.

> Is thirty dollars too much to pay for this shirt?

Here, the total is more important than the dollars. But in another example, the individual units are more important than the total.

> Thirty parkway miles cut through the heart of a hardwood forest.

Usage is divided on how to treat abstract numbers used in arithmetic. In the following examples, either is correct, although the singular is preferred:

> Three plus three is six.

> Three plus three are six.

3. Nouns Ending in -ics

Nouns such as *politics, economics,* and *athletics,* though plural in form, take a singular verb when referring to a body of knowledge or a profession.

> Though economics is his major, politics is his real love.

These nouns take a plural verb when referring to separate activities, facts, or attitudes.

The economics of the proposal don't support your assertion.

His politics stink.

What About the Wages of Sin?

Where does "the wages of sin" belong in all this? Ninety-nine percent of the time, *wages* behaves like any ordinary plural noun. Only when it is used in the sense of recompense ("getting one's just desserts") does it take the singular. That usage is now so rare as to be an endangered species. (Even my old stomping ground on Broadway no longer has its biblical admonition. Is there no one left to redeem?)

In that sense, my sophomore friend was right. *Wages* is singular because it's the wages of sin. I reserve judgment, however, on whether sin in New York is collective.

The Eye hopes readers understand that in no other case is the subject's number "determined" grammatically by the noun that follows it in a prepositional phrase. Such nouns that come between the subject and verb should, in fact, normally be ignored when determining subject-verb agreement. Loosely used collective nouns and fractional numbers are special cases where you can use the more readily discernible number of the modifying prepositional object as a reliable clue to get at the sense—the logic—of whether the collective noun subject should be treated as singular or plural.

Editing a Moving Target

by Mary Stoughton

Does this scenario sound familiar? It's 3:00 p.m. and a proposal due at close of business the next day finally arrives for editing . . . . Or how about this one? It's 9:00 a.m. and the CEO asks for copies of your annual report to take to the board meeting that night. Now you have eight hours to finish what you expected to have three days to do.

I'd like to assume that most of us find ourselves having to edit a moving target only occasionally, but from the horror stories I've been hearing, it seems that more and more people are being expected to edit well in a ridiculously short time.

What matters most when the deadline's too soon?

There's no simple answer to this question. To illustrate why, take a look at the following list of basic editorial flaws. In theory, everything matters, but different people would prioritize these things differently. Try numbering them on the basis of their importance to you.

- **Content**

    A wrong total in a table of numbers

    An illogical conclusion

    Redundancy

- **Typos**

    An error in the spelling of your company president's name

    A word that's spelled correctly but is the wrong word

- **Grammatical problems**

    Subject-verb disagreements

    Misplaced modifiers

    Unnecessary passive voice

- **Format**

    Too much white space

    Paragraphs that seem endless

- **Stylistic errors**

    Inconsistent number style or capitalization

    Abbreviations defined more than once in a chapter or section, or not defined at all

What's involved in editing a moving target?

We're going to look at things from two points of view: that of the editor and that of the project manager who are deciding what to fix and what to leave alone.

These two people usually come at the problem a little differently although their interests naturally converge. To some managers, editing looks expendable until the company's major stockholder opens the report to page 29 and finds that the net profit line is missing a zero. To some editors, a document isn't presentable until every flaw, however minor, has been eliminated.

In the best of all possible worlds, every document gets the attention it needs, but in reality what gets fixed depends on the priorities mentioned earlier, as well as on the answers to the following questions.

If you're the project manager . . .

Here are the questions you need to ask:

- **How large is this document?** Even if it's small, you may still have a problem: You may have only half an hour to check a brochure full of addresses and prices. But you can usually fix a small piece even if you're already in final pages. It's just going to cost you. If it's large, however, how much of a problem you have depends on the answers to the questions that follow.

- **How visible is it?** Is it just an internal report or is it going to the media and members of Congress? Obviously, there's a lot in between. An internal report should be fixed as much as possible in the time you have because, after all, it reflects on you and your organization. But if there are errors in it, only your company will know. If the report is going to be seen by others, the question is, Which others?

- **Who is the audience?** Are your readers researchers, policymakers, stockholders, clients, people in the publications field, or the public in general?

For researchers and other technical specialists, you can assume that they're more interested in the content than in the style or format, so you really need two edits—a content review and a style edit. If you were planning to skip the review by a subject-matter expert, think again. The two edits can and should proceed simultaneously, but in this case the style edit is much less important than the content review.

If this document is meant to convince policymakers, persuade your clients, or inform your stockholders, you pull in every available resource on the premise that *everything* is important. And if by any chance there are publications specialists in your audience, they'll find every extra space and misplaced comma.

So you may have no choice: You have to do a full edit because the document is highly visible or because the audience demands it. But another factor has a bearing here: the production cycle.

- **Where are you in the production cycle?** Are you working with draft copy, or are you already into formatted pages? If the document went directly into final format, then the first thing you need to do is accept the fact that the production cycle imposes certain time constraints. The second thing you need to do is vow that this will never, ever happen again: Editing early in the cycle saves a lot of grief later on.

Now take a realistic look at what's there in terms of the complexity of the text; the number of pages; the number of tables, figures, or references; and the absolute drop-dead deadline. Remember too that you have to allow time to incorporate the corrections and proofread them. To determine just how much time you need to get the document into final form, the rule of thumb is to allot half of the total time for editing and half for correcting and proofreading.

Next, see whether there are any shortcuts you can use to streamline production and buy some time: Can you get a few extra days added to your other deadlines and set those projects aside temporarily? Can you authorize overtime? Can you set up an assembly line (that is, divide the work into batches and have several people editing, making corrections, and proofreading at the same time)?

Once you've tentatively decided on the level of edit and determined how much time you have, you need to find an editor who can do the work. Also, you need to find someone who can take that person's calls and pick up the other work that will languish in the meantime. This brings us to the last question.

- **Is there someone who can drop everything and work on this job exclusively?** You need to find the right person for the job. It may be that you have only one in-house editor and no money to hire a temp or freelancer, and so you have no choice. Let's assume, however, that you do have a choice. How do you decide which of the available editors to choose?

Some people have only one speed; doing something "quick and dirty" goes against their nature. Perhaps they're perfectionists, or perhaps they can't compromise or make quick decisions. Save these people for the day-to-day work that still needs to be done while your chosen editor focuses on the moving target.

Sit down with this lucky editor and decide on some ground rules. Discuss the level of edit you've tentatively decided on and make sure that the editor thinks it's appropriate for the document in terms of what it is, where it is in the production cycle, and how much time you have left.

Once you've done everything you can to make the production end of things go smoothly, step back and give your editor some room to work, but make sure you're available to answer questions.

If you're the editor . . .

Somehow you have to pull this off:

- **Psych yourself up.** The first thing to do is realize that this project will consume you for the next few hours or days. If you have personal plans, cancel them. If you're going to be working through the night, try to go home and change into comfortable clothes and grab a few hours of sleep before you start. Lay in a supply of coffee and sandwiches to keep you going.

- **Determine the level of edit.** Now you need to look at the document realistically and decide what you can do in the time you have. It may be that you physically can't do what the project manager wants, in which case negotiations are in order. Don't jump to conclusions, though. Remember that tasks often look insurmountable until you get started.

Approach the job by deciding that it *will* get done but that it's up to you to figure out how. To determine the level of edit you can do in the time you have, edit the first few pages at your best speed (as fast as you can do them accurately). Then take into account that you need to make more than one pass and that you'll have to go more slowly as you get tired so you don't make mistakes. If this exercise tells you that you can't edit in depth, scale back.

In any case, go over the first part of the document—the abstract, the executive summary, the introduction—and the conclusion meticulously on the premise that people tend to read the beginning and the end of a document. Also pay close attention to the rest of the front matter. No one will thank you if you find a minute error on page 20 and leave a typo on the cover.

- **Pace yourself.** As you work, try to set a rhythm; don't get bogged down. If something is badly worded and the fix doesn't come to you right away, mark the passage and come back to it. Try to work as long as you can at a stretch, but remind yourself to get up once in a while. Look away from the copy or the screen once in a while so that your eyes don't give out before you're done.

If you've decided to edit on-line, remember that the speed of an on-line edit depends on your keyboarding skills and those of the person who created the electronic file. For example, if hard spaces were used for indents and formatting, a handsome document will rewrap in strange ways when you start making changes. Then you'll have to add reformatting to the list of tasks you're already hard-pressed to finish.

- **Can you get help?** Can any revisions be made automatically? If you're editing on paper, don't waste your time marking things that can be fixed globally, like spacing or capitalization or particular terms that need to be changed. Can someone else check the format while you fix the words? Can other editors help with sections? (You would have to review their work and make sure everything is consistent.)

Whatever you do, keep moving—and above all, keep thinking. Work with one eye on the clock and the other on the copy. Ask another editor or the project manager to take a quick look at what you've done before you turn it in for corrections.

A postmortem now can save you out-of-body experiences later

When the dust has settled, hold a postmortem so that everyone on the project team can learn from this experience. If you're the project manager, write things up while they're still fresh in your mind, and try to see patterns. If editing is always an afterthought, you have serious problems with your production cycle.

Whether you're the project manager or the editor, don't berate yourself for missing things that you ordinarily would have caught. After all, editing, like politics, is the art of the possible. If you follow these guidelines, you'll be doing the best you can in the time you've got.

Are Editors on Their Way Out?

by Priscilla S. Taylor

Richard L. Peters of Germantown, MD, recently sent up a flare for help. "This is a request for a reality check," he wrote. "My question is simple: Are editors an endangered species?

"Based on the trend where we work (a large engineering corporation), based on what we read and hear generally, and based on the quality of what we see more and more in print, my co-editors and I are feeling akin to the little Dutch boy, with our fingers in the dike trying to hold back the floods of . . . what, we are not sure: ignorance, indifference, the bottom line? It is as if the whole world is rapidly coming to the conclusion that there is no value added by the services of a good editor.

"So, not only are we apprehensive that our department's days are numbered, but we are also starting to wonder if our very profession's days are as well. Anything you might be able to say to dispel at least the latter concern would be most welcome. Sans that, we are open to suggestions regarding suitable life jackets for when the dike bursts."

If it's any comfort, people have been predicting the end of editing and editors for as long as I can remember, certainly since the dawn of the computer age. How could any mere mortal compete with the mechanized wonder of spell check, electronic thesauruses, and, later, grammar programs?

Well, as we all know, it's not that simple. Although nobody doubts that ignorance is increasing, it can be argued that this situation will dictate more emphasis on careful editing rather than less. Of course, the extent of reader indifference may be the key to the future of editors, but I can't help feeling that although nobody wants to pay editors a living wage, everybody wants the published product to be perfect. Some publishers care enough to pay for near-perfection (as we all know, perfection comes only with the second edition).

We hear a lot about how editing and editors are vanishing: Fewer editors do actual correction of manuscripts—more simply oversee the production process; many editors in government offices and elsewhere are not replaced when they retire; and more offices are expecting everyone who writes a document to edit it as well. And we all see shoddy products from publishing houses we used to respect.

At the same time, to take only one person's experience, my husband has been surprised, and pleased, to have his work edited more carefully by the publishing houses with which he has dealt as the years progress (and, he thinks, as he has improved as a writer!). Charles E. Tuttle, in 1961, and W. W. Norton, in 1970, published his first two biographies without changing a word. In contrast, Doubleday, in 1989, had his biography of a general edited by a military specialist; and both HarperCollins, in 1991, and Brassey's, in 1994, had two other biographies edited by freelancers.

The main problem is that more publishers are looking for the cheapest editor they can find, and this means freelance rather than on-staff. As long as there are good freelancers available—who are paid by the job or the hour and work at home, perhaps sporadically or temporarily in an office, on varied projects and for varied employers—staff editing jobs may indeed be unable to compete when an employer's paramount concern is economy. At the same time, on-staff editors acquire expertise that may be difficult to duplicate outside the office, especially in a technical field such as yours.

In sum, I think the extent to which editors are an endangered species depends—on the priorities of the employer, the health of the company's finances, and the skills and adaptability of the editors. As long as people desire not to look ridiculous in print, there will be a need for editors, but whether editors will be able to feed their families on what they get for saving others from embarrassment is another question.

Editorial Consistency Enhances Readability

by Mary J. Scroggins

One of the words that I use most frequently when talking and writing about editing or conducting editing or writing workshops is "consistency." For me, editing and consistency are inevitably connected. Editing clarifies the language, making it more concise, correct, clear, and consistent; consistency provides logical connections between the ideas and parts of any thoughtfully written and edited manuscript.

The English language is rich in stylistic and grammatical variations and choices. Consistency dictates that this richness not clutter a piece (and thus interfere with correct communication) by giving the readers an overabundance of choices.

Readers ought to be able to depend on consistency in editorial style, usage, and format for guidance to the writer's intentions and interpretation. Consistency can hold together a less-than-superior piece that has substance, and it can add polish to a really fine piece. However, imposing a consistent style and format on a poorly written piece with little substance will not make it worth reading even if the piece becomes more tolerable.

Consistency dictates not that the writer or the editor make a *specific* choice of one capitalization scheme over another (for example, "the Institute" rather than "the institute" when referring to an institute previously mentioned by its full name), one plural form over another, one hyphenation pattern over another, or one style over another, but instead that the writer or the editor make *a* choice (either "the Institute" or "the institute") and stick to it. The writer or editor who fails to make choices, in effect, tells the readers, "I have given you several choices. You make the decisions. I am too careless, too lazy, or too unskilled to handle the abundance of choices." Inconsistency then flourishes, frustrates the readers, and undermines the effectiveness of the manuscript and the credibility of the writer or the project's sponsor. The work is devalued.

Inconsistencies can damage and even destroy credibility. For example, readers are often confused by inconsistencies in hyphenation, such as "two signal analyzers" versus "two-signal analyzers." Hyphenation is used to avoid confusion and ambiguity and chiefly to establish or clarify relationships between words. If hyphenation is inconsistent or haphazard, readers must guess at relationships. They might logically assume that the writer or project's sponsor is unsure of the relationships or does not care whether the readers understand the relationships. If the writer or editor does not take pains with such obvious matters as hyphenation, number style, spelling preference, capitalization, and abbreviations, how can readers be sure that appropriate care was taken with less obvious details such as accuracy of data collected and thoroughness of research? Inconsistency hangs about such a piece of writing like a sign that warns, "Reader Beware."

Inconsistency may also divert readers from the writer's purpose. In the struggle to decipher the puzzle of choices, readers may misinterpret, overlook, or completely ignore important information. If readers must decide whether "site," "facility," and "center" refer to the same location or whether the variable on page 2 is the same as the one on page 10, even though one has a capital C and the other has a lowercase c, energy that should be used to absorb information must be used to consider the probability of intent.

Clearly, consistency should be imposed by the writer and the editor, never the readers. Consistency indicates the writer's and the editor's common respect for the readers and concern for the importance of correct, expedient communication.

Titles and topics invite readers to read; consistency encourages them to continue to read and allows them to understand the message with as little effort as possible. Consistency is the glue that binds the parts without question of interpretation or confusion.

Learning to Edit Long Documents On-line

by Mary Stoughton

As a working editor, I know how difficult it is to edit long, technical documents on-line. That said, let me note that, whether we like it or not (much less whether we learn to love it), on-line editing is the way of the future.

Let me summarize the pros and cons. First, on-line editing has real advantages:

- It streamlines the process; the same person can decide on the changes, key them, and proofread them if necessary.

- It allows several people to work on the same document at the same time.

- It minimizes the need for hard copy.

- It creates a file that can be sent electronically for typesetting or approval.

- It provides helpful editorial features such as search and replace, spell check, and word counts.

- It lets editors move large blocks of copy instantly.

- It facilitates global changes necessary to accommodate style decisions made late in the process.

- It lets editors embed queries in the text (either visibly or using the hidden text option) or print them separately.

- It lets authors review clean copy without the distraction of editing marks and spares them the pain of seeing their writing chopped up and dissected.

On-line editing is extremely useful for stylistic edits and for substantive edits or rewrites. You can move, copy, and delete with amazing rapidity, but problems do remain. Some of the pros have a flip side that can turn them into cons, and you need to be aware of them. See p. 348 for some ways to counter these and other disadvantages:

- On-line editing streamlines the process, but that may mean that no one checks behind the editor.

- Several people can be working on the same document, but they can be working at cross-purposes. Having several people working on a document also means that the chance of their using the wrong version or creating multiple versions increases greatly. Most of us are reluctant to destroy earlier versions—especially for documents that have to pass committee scrutiny—but tracking versions can become a nightmare. (As programs like the Quark Publishing System become more common, this problem will become less serious.)

- Many editors find it difficult and tiring to do everything on screen. Having a full-page monitor helps, but checking complex format, equations, or head levels still presents problems, eyestrain among them.

- It can be difficult for authors to track extensive editing changes.

Some Ways to Make On-line Editing Less Wearing

- Editing on screen doesn't altogether eliminate the need for hard copy; you'll still want to print pages to check format or head levels or to correct equations.

- If you're trying to learn the software by the seat of your pants, you may need to ask your supervisor for formal training. Most of us use only a fraction of the features our word processing programs have. You'll be a lot less frustrated if you have a grasp of more sophisticated features like creating macros, coding equations, using table mode, and so on. If you're a rotten typist, swallow your pride and take a basic course in keyboarding, or buy a software package such as "Mavis Beacon Teaches Typing."

- If several people are working on a document at the same time, use the date/time feature to put a header or footer on each page to be sure that everyone is using the correct version.

- Take the time to read the document through before you start, even if it's long. Take notes and get a feel for the author's style and for the main arguments or findings. You'll make fewer mistakes that have to be undone later.

- Develop habits that take advantage of the shortcuts and avoid the drawbacks of working on-line. Try to work on long documents in sections, and take a break every hour. Get up and walk around. Print pages once in a while, especially where you've made extensive changes, as a stimulus and a checking step. Embed notes to yourself in the text (preface them with your initials or else use QQQ as we do at EEI) and switch back and forth between screens to keep your style sheet and acronym list current as you work.

- Display the document double spaced and change the font if necessary so that you can see the whole line at once. Most word processing programs can change the display without changing the underlying font.

- Allow time for review by another editor or else be sure you print and read the document yourself when you're through. This is time well spent.

If You're Still Not Convinced

Here are some commonly heard concerns about on-line editing:

- *How do editors avoid turning into keypunch operators?* Editors are editors, whether they edit on screen or on paper. The decisions they make are what defines their position and their function—not whether they put pencil to paper. Those decisions can be made at a keyboard as well as a desk. For those of us who write, making editing corrections on-line is nothing new and adding formatting to the revision cycle just means another step. When I edit on-line, I try to avoid printing out just to check corrections. I just did a 95-page report completely on-line. The format wasn't complex and I made my changes on screen. My review editor didn't print either. There was no need to.

You can't think just in terms of the editor's time—it's everybody's time. It may be more efficient for one person to do all the steps, or it may be that administrative staff are nonexistent or busy with something else. It may take the editor longer or it may not, but the choice is made in the context of the whole operation. Basically, what do we want to pay the editor to do? If the editor's job is being redefined, then there's the answer. Streamlining the operation eliminates management time and layers of responsibility. Those are hidden costs too.

- *How do you effectively use on-line editing in an environment in which the editor's substantive changes and queries must be approved by the author?* First, remember that not all authors have veto power over changes made to their documents. In many cases, once they turn those documents in, they see them again in print. If they do need to approve changes and answer queries, however, you can precede queries with a locator like QQQ and embed them in the document; the author can then search for them. Changes can be made in boldface, and the author can review them; the same applies to the editor. If you must have a paper trail, the current state of the art leaves something to be desired. Most of the on-line editing we do at EEI is just that—there is no paper trail. In this case, authors have to review their work carefully to be sure that the meaning has not been changed and that no errors have been introduced.

Like it or not, we authors and editors will have to relinquish our dependence on hard copy eventually. Also remember that nothing is static; computer technology is turning over every 18 months or so. Seeing and reviewing changes is going to get easier, not harder.

- *What's the best way to use on-line editing for a long document (more than 50 pages)?* For substantive editing, I think it's much easier to move copy around on-line rather than on paper. Nothing says you can't read the document first on paper, make some notes, and validate your thinking before you turn the computer on. As for flipping screens to check consistency, I use the search feature for that. Checking numbers in tables against the text or the appendixes is easier with hard copy, and that's the way I do it.

What then are my suggestions for a long document? Read it through first, work on it in sections, take breaks, change the font size so that you can see a whole line on your screen, and allow enough time for review.

Editing electronic files is the norm for many journals; it works best if the editor can simply present the author with clean copy. Trying to preserve an electronic trail, given the current state of the art, is often counterproductive. Existing software packages work well for stylistic or simple edits; they're less helpful for complex edits where a line may have many changes. Programs like CompareRite work for short, relatively simple documents, but no one will have the fortitude to plow through its "markup" of 200 pages of extensive changes. If editors have to move into the 21st century, so do authors. For them, electronic editing means that they'll have to take the time to review the editor's work carefully to make sure that the meaning hasn't been changed.

Finally, remember that on-line editing is only as good as the person doing the work, no matter how computer literate he or she may be. A bad editor is a bad editor, whether that person works on screen or on paper.

Not by Intuition Alone: Taking Stock of Editing Habits

by Diane Ullius

It's surprising how many editors rely on their intuition and how few seem aware of their editing techniques. The habit of editing by hunch is common to new editors as well as to those who have been editing for years and now work almost automatically. But editing is like performing: Doing it well requires both art and craft, innate skill and training.

I was reminded of this connection recently when I attended a performance of Jim Cartwright's play, *The Rise and Fall of Little Voice*. The main character is a young woman who sings brilliantly and ingenuously, with no sense of her own artistry. Another character asks her, "How do you do it? You wouldn't know, would you? The true performer never does." Natural talent obviously comes into play. But with editing, as with singing, intuition alone is not enough to sustain a career unless every assignment calls for the same approach.

Because most editing jobs require making reasonable (and defensible) judgment calls, I encourage the students in the workshops I teach to take editing out of the realm of pure intuition. I urge them to look for general principles and specific rules by asking them such questions as, "How did you know it needed fixing?" and "What made you choose this solution instead of that one?" The education of an intuitive editor—and of a veteran editor—can be undertaken on two levels: by using consistent work habits and by resisting the occupational hazards of introversion and stagnation.

How Can Editors Develop Organized Habits?

- **Make multiple passes.** One of the most reliable techniques is to make multiple passes through a manuscript. Susan Colwell, associate technical editor for *Byte* magazine, says, "I used to try to do everything at once, but I've realized that I do better by focusing on certain things individually." Colwell now uses her first pass to correct style problems and her second to address the content; other editors attend first to substance, later to style. Many make a separate, quick pass to review head levels, check figure titles and sources, or examine the format of lists.

The point is not that "Thou shalt only edit thus"; as long as your technique works well, it's legitimate, but be aware of what it is. You can always deviate from your standard if the document warrants it—for instance, when editing a short brochure—but only if you have a conscious standard to begin with can you avoid getting sidetracked in large, complex, or dense editing jobs.

- **Use flags for different types of problems.** It's also helpful to develop a system to make the most of the manual or electronic tools that can help organize a job. Many editors use self-stick notes to flag the problems in a document; later they find themselves pawing through pages bristling with yellow in the vain hope of finding a certain query. Why not invest in a rainbow of colors? Use one for queries, another for statements to be checked, a third for format inconsistencies to be resolved later, and so on, and you can then focus on particular problems systematically.

Electronic markers—"hidden comments" or notes and queries entered directly in the text—should also be used consistently. Mark them with a unique combination of characters, such as **??** or **xxx**, so that you can search for them easily.

- **Use a style sheet.** Maintaining a record of editorial decisions—a style sheet—is one of the best ways to deliver editorial consistency. But have you examined your criteria? Some editors record virtually every decision they make; others enter only issues that are not specifically treated in their main style guide. In any case, start the style sheet during the early stages of editing, scan it before your final read of the document, update it, and file it for future reference.

Again, there are many reasonable approaches. The exact format of the style sheet matters less than using it each time as a matter of objective quality control. Readers notice inconsistency.

- **Use an editorial checklist.** Perhaps the best tool is a comprehensive checklist. The kind of publications you edit will determine the items on the list, and not all items will be checked for each job. For a book you might include reminders to complete the permission forms, check pagination for the table of contents and the index, and cross-check the acknowledgments against the bibliography. A checklist for a brochure might include a reminder to verify the address and to cross-check the order form with product prices in captions. There are two basic kinds of checklists:

  - One checklist can be used at the start of a job to define the appropriate level of edit for a specific manuscript or client. An editor may be directed to impose a certain format on bulleted lists but to refrain from changing first person to third. This approach starts a job off on the right track and avoids wasted effort. (EEI fills out this kind of checklist for each project.)

  - A second checklist, used for quality control, can save editors from their worst nightmares. This out-the-door checklist is the last chance to correct the things that can sabotage a completed manuscript: copy repeated or left out, incorrect color specs, transposed placement of photos and captions, and the like. Even if you consider yourself a careful worker, never assume that you will always remember to check for everything. We all need memory aids.

How Can Editors Keep Learning—About Everything?

- **Remember that no editor is an island.** Especially if you're an introverted sort (true for many of us in this field), bringing the "people" part of the publishing equation into the open can be a big help in managing the editorial process successfully. And we can learn from our mistakes.

Consider, for example, the project that Carmen Drebing, of Sandia National Laboratories, says "almost crashed before I could get a good grasp on what was happening." Drebing, a technical writer responsible for editing and co-ordinating a major report, realized with dismay that she and the lead writer simply weren't on the same wavelength. "I wasn't getting the detail I needed, and the writer kept thinking that I should know where to put the various elements." All ended well, but only "after we each became aware that the other person wasn't wrong, just different." Adds Drebing ruefully, "The traumatic experiences are the ones you learn from."

- The more insular your work environment is, the more important are outside sources of knowledge and stimulation. I'm always surprised that editors don't make more time for general reading—science fiction, cookbooks, history, political essays—for pleasure or professional development.

  - Outside reading can provide perspective (both benign and malignant) while adding to your knowledge.

  - Professional reading should be regular fare. Some editors set aside time to actually read reference books, beyond just looking things up to document specific decisions. Reviewing a section of a particular usage manual each Friday afternoon almost surely will help an editor spot a useful rule or explanation that escaped earlier notice.

- **Get back to, and away from, the basics.** Regardless of the subject matter, a class can provide the benefit of cross-pollination that comes from ex-changing viewpoints with like-minded colleagues. The best editor is often a generalist. So why not stretch your muscles? An advanced grammar class will arm you with technical explanations you had forgotten and enable you to make decisions more expeditiously. A writing class will re-new your appreciation for the writer's task and help you develop judg-ment about style and organization. A computer or design course will open your eyes to a world of form beyond page margins.

(This article was the basis for the text used in the copyediting exercise in chapter 12.)

Fair Use and Copyright: An Unanswered Question

by Mara T. Adams

What is copyright? Who owns it? How does an author or publisher obtain copyright? What are the exceptions to copyright protection? What is eligible for copyright protection? How much of a work may be quoted or reproduced without copyright infringement? What effects has new technology had on copyright? Of all these questions, fair use is the greatest source of consternation for authors and editors.

Fair Use

Fair use is the major exception to the copyright law. That is, whatever the copyright owner decides is a fair quotation from or use of the protected material does not constitute copyright infringement. The current copyright law recognizes that the printing press is no longer the primary medium of communication, and fair use now covers phonorecords and reproduction copies, as well as printed materials. The law also specifies the legitimate boundaries of fair use: "criticism, comment, news reporting, teaching (including multiple copies for classroom use), scholarship, or research."

It is this element of the copyright law that has been so troublesome to authors, editors, and publishers. Just what constitutes fair use? The law remains vague on this point, leaving definition up to the copyright owner.

For people who want to quote the material of others, this lack of definition is a source of worry and frustration. The law says that many factors must be considered in determining fair use, including these:

- the purpose and character of the use, including whether such use is of a commercial nature or is for nonprofit educational purposes;

- the nature of the copyrighted work;

- the amount and substantiality of the portion used in relation to the . . . whole; and

- the effect of the use upon the potential market for the copyrighted work.

This means that the use a second author makes of copyrighted material may in no way compete with or diminish the market value of the original work. Many publishers believe 250 words to be fair use of copyrighted material— that is, quotable without permission. But suppose an author quoted 250 words from a 500-word article. Clearly, this kind of quotation would diminish the value of the original work.

Sometimes an author will object to having too little quoted. The chief book reviewer of the *Washington Post* recently took exception to a publisher's use, in promoting a trashy novel, of just two words from his review of the book, quoted out of context. The generally unfavorable review had been made to appear an unqualified rave because of the purpose and character of the publisher's use of the quotation—obviously commercial in nature.

A sampling of a cross section of publishers turned up a general policy of requesting and requiring permission for everything quoted. Most publishers want to know how the quoted material will be used, whether the person requesting permission will be charging a fee for the publication in which the material will appear, and whether such use will be in direct competition with the original work. To be on the safe side, ask permission in writing for anything you want to reprint.

New Technology and Copyright

An important recent amendment to the law, closely related to fair use, has to do with reproduction, xerographic or otherwise, of a copyrighted work. The Copyright Act provides that libraries and archives may make one copy or phonorecord of a work and disseminate such single copies under certain stringent conditions. The reproduction must be made without any purpose of commercial advantage; the collections of the library or archive must be open to the public or available to all persons doing research in a specialized field, not just those affiliated with the institution; and the reproduction must include the copyright notice. These rules apply only to unpublished works such as letters, diaries, journals, theses, and dissertations.

The Newsletter Association of America (NAA) contends, in its newsletter, *Hotline* (vol. 6, no. 17), that libraries are abusing this section of the act. Citing a report done for the Copyright Office, *Hotline* says that "the majority of users making library photocopies are either unaware of copyright notices or presume that duplicating of copyright materials is permitted for educational or research purposes." In particular, NAA says that databases "use (copyrighted) materials without permission, under the guise of abstracts."

To combat this abuse, at least one computer-based permissions system has appeared—the Copyright Clearance Center in Salem, Massachusetts. The center is set up, according to its promotional material, to protect copyright holders from both deliberate and inadvertent infringement. The center uses coded publication registration forms, similar to those for copyright registration, to collect royalty fees and convey permissions on behalf of its participating publishers.

Another instance of the effect of communications technology is a provision in the current law for payment, under a system of compulsory licensing, of certain royalties for the secondary transmission of copyrighted works via cable television.

Background on Copyright

The first legislation on copyright was an act of Parliament passed in Britain in 1709, aimed at preventing unscrupulous booksellers from publishing works without the consent of the authors. It provided that the author of a book had the sole right of publication for a term of 21 years; the penalty for infringement was a penny a sheet. The British copyright law was amended in 1801 (the fine went up to threepence a sheet) and again in 1842. In 1887 a group of nations, excluding the United States, ratified the Berne Union

Copyright Convention, which required members to have minimum standards of copyright protection and to apply them equally to citizens of all the nations represented.*

In the United States, copyright found protection in the Constitution, Article 1, section 1, clause 8, ratified in 1789. In 1790, separate legislation on copyright was enacted. The copyright law was revised in 1831, 1870, 1909, 1976, and 1978; and the 1978 law was amended in 1980. According to *The Nuts and Bolts of Copyright*, a pithy booklet published by the Copyright Office of the Library of Congress,

> Copyright is a form of protection given by the laws of the United States . . . to the authors of "original works of authorship" such as literary, dramatic, musical, artistic, and certain other intellectual works.

The owner of the copyright has the exclusive right to reproduce, distribute, display, or perform the work, and to prepare derivative works based on the original.

Copyright Ownership

Only the author or persons to whom the author has given or assigned the rights to the work may claim copyright. Among those other than the author who may legitimately claim copyright are an employer whose employee has created a copyrightable work as a result of his or her employment (work for hire); a publisher to whom the author has relinquished the copyright or who has paid the author to create the work; someone who has commissioned a work such as a sculpture, painting, or piece of music; or someone who has asked the author to contribute his or her work to a collective endeavor such as a motion picture, a translation, or an anthology, or as a test or instructional materials. It is important to note that the owner of a manuscript, or original sheet music, or a painting, for example, is not necessarily the owner of the copyright to those works.

To obtain copyright protection, the originator of the work need only attach to it a notice of copyright, the form of which is specified in the law. The notice must contain the symbol © or the word *Copyright,* or the abbreviation *Copr.;* the year of publication; and the name of the copyright owner: for example, " © *John Doe 1980.*" The notice of copyright must appear in a prominent place in the work to be protected. This element is important in light of the 1978 revision of the copyright law, which specifies that any work published before January 1, 1978, without such notice permanently forfeits copyright protection in the United States. This notice is all that is required to obtain copyright protection. Registration of copyright means filling out a series of forms and sending them with a fee and two copies of the work to the Copyright Office. The copyright owner need not register the copyright with the Library of Congress; however, if a lawsuit should ever arise over the work, the registration is necessary to prove ownership.

Summary

On fair use and reproduction of copyrighted material, the copyright law undoubtedly raises more questions than it answers. It does try to address sophisticated electronic methods of infringing on copyright, and it spells out in more detail than ever before the boundaries of fair use. But it still is not prescriptive in the area of fair use, and that section of the act will continue to confuse authors and publishers and to provide fertile ground for legal and judicial debate.

---

*Since this article appeared, the United States has agreed to join the Berne Convention. President Ronald Reagan signed the ratification in November 1988.

Index

in notes, 223
and quotations marks, 143, *149*
in tables, *231*
Pilcrow, 19, 24
Place of residence, punctuation, 139
Placement notations, 23-24
Plain English movement, 194. *See also*
  Concise language; Wordiness
Pluralization
  numbers, 166
  use of apostrophe, 139, 140, 166, 167
Possessive case, 91, 92-93
  abbreviations, 166
  adjectives, 91
  punctuation, 139-140, *147*, *148*, *149*,
  166, 167
Possessive pronouns, 140
Postal Service abbreviations, 162, 163
Predicate, definition, 67
Predicate adjectives
  hyphens, 150
  parallel construction, *11*
  and possessive case, 93
Predicate nominatives, 91
Prefixes, hyphenation of, 150, 164, 165
Prepositional phrases
  and passive voice, 81, *84*
  punctuation, 69
  and subject-verb agreement, 67, 69, *78*,
  79
Prepositions
  inserting into noun strings, 174,
  175-179
  and objective case, 91, *96*
  parallel construction, 111
Production process, 3
Pronouns
  antecedents, 7, *10*, 62, **97-99**, *100-107*
  cases, **91-93**, *94-97*
  relative, 92, *96*
  verb agreement, 67
Proofreading
  definition, 2
  editorial marks, 15
  in production process, 3
  of retyped manuscript, 38
Proper names, capitalization of, 156
Protection copy, 37
*Publication Manual of the American
  Psychological Association*, 155,
  162-167, *170*
Punctuation, **133-144**, *145-153*
  acronyms and abbreviations, 133
  appositives, 136, 137, *147*
  citations, 133, 219, 220, 221
  compiling a style sheet, 157, 158
  compound sentences, 135
  compound subject, 79
  compound verbs, *11*
  conjunctive adverbs, 142, *148*, *149*
  copyeditor's role, 2, 3, 58, 59
  direct address, *136*, *149*
  and editing software, 240
  first reading, 37
  introductory adverbial clauses,
  137-138, *146*, *148*
  lists, 110-111, *116*
  nonrestrictive clauses, *149*
  in notes, 223

numbers, 139, 151
  parentheticals, 136, *149*
  possessive case, 92, 139-140, *147*, 148,
  149, 166, 167
  separating compound verbs, *11*
  style issues, 156, 157, 166-167
  tables, 230, *231*, 237
Punctuation marks
  adjectives, 138
  apostrophes, 139, *147*, *148*, *149*, 166,
  167
  braces, 16, 19
  brackets, 134-135
  colons, *12*, 141, 143, *148*, 157
    capitalization, 162, 163
  commas, 135-139, 143, *146*, *147*, *149*
    serial, *148*, 151, 157, 166, 167, 207
  dashes, *149*, 150-151, *152-153*, 166, 167
  editorial marks, 21-22
  en-dashes, 21-22, 150-151, *152-153*,
  166, 167
  exclamation points, 143-144, *147*
  hyphens, 150, *152-153*
  parentheses, 134
  periods, 133-134, 143
  question marks, 143-144
  quotation marks, 143-144, *147*, *149*, *150*
  semicolons, 139, 142, 143, *148*, *149*

Query sheet, 159-160
Querying
  abbreviations, *215*
  circling queries, 17
  on content of text, *55*
  cover memo, *159*, 160
  jargon, 173
  mathematical discrepancies, 223, *235*
  quotation marks, *206*
  unclear antecedents, 99
  unclear or missing material, 3
Question marks
  editorial mark, 21, 22, *47*
  and quotation marks, 143-144, *150*
*Questions You Always Wanted to Ask
  About English*, 93
Quotation marks, **143-144**, *147*, *149*,
  150
  in citations, 222
  and editing software, 240
  editorial mark, 21, 22, *47*
  vs. italics, 165
Quotations
  capitalization, 133
  changing, 49
  copyeditor's role, 58
  ellipsis indicating omission, 133
  quotation marks, 143-144
  use of colons, 141

Ragged right margin, 61
Readability, 240
Red pencil, 37
Redlining, 239-240
Redundancy, *187-194*, *206*, *207*, *209*,
  210, *212*, *214*, *216*
  copyeditor's role, 173
  modification of absolutes, *11*

modifiers, 179
Reference books, 303-304
References, **219-223**
  en-dashes, 151
  format, 2
  speed of editing, 58
  in tables, 230, 233
Relative pronouns, 92, *96*
Reorganization, copyeditor's role, 2,
  59, 64
Repeated word, *47*
Replace, editorial mark, 18
Reports, in citations, 219, 222
Resolutions, 141
Restrictive appositives, punctuation,
  136
Restrictive clauses
  parentheticals, *149*
  punctuation, *53*, 138, *148*
Restrictive modifiers, 119-121, *121-123*
Retyping manuscript, 38
Revisions, 2
Rewriting, copyeditor's role, 2, 59, 64
Roman numerals, 163, *213*
Rounding disclaimer, 223
Rules, 224, *230*
Run-in heads, *45*
Run on, editorial mark, 19
Runover lines, *233*, *235*

Salutations, 141
Schematics, 224
Scientific writing, and passive voice, 82
Second person construction, *128*
Semicolons, **142**, *148*
  editorial mark, 21, 22
  and quotation marks, 143
  run-on sentences, 139
  vs. comma, *51*, *53*, 142
Sentence fragments, *147*
Sentence structure
  copyeditor's role, 58
  first reading, 37
Sequences, 59
Serial commas, *47*, *49*, 135, *148*, 207
  style comparison, 166-167
  in tables, *231*
  vs. em-dashes, 151
Series of items. *See also* Lists
  punctuation, 142, *148*
Sexist language, 58, 62, *88*, 99
[sic], 135, 165
Signature lines, 17
Slash marks
  in redlining, 239-240
  to replace letters, 18
Small caps
  abbreviations and acronyms, 17, 156
  editorial mark, 17, 27
Smothered verbs, *53*, 62, 109, **182**,
  183-186, *190*, *191*, *213*
Soft hyphen, 60-61
  editorial mark, 21, *25*, *26*
Software
  editing programs, 239-240
  hard and soft hyphens, 61
  making revisions, 15
  search-and-replace, 157, 239

EEI (formerly Editorial Experts, Inc.) is a technical services consulting firm based in Alexandria, VA. EEI's editorial and production services include writing, editing, proofreading, word and data processing, design and graphics, indexing, workshops for publications professionals, and temporary placement in the publications field. EEI also publishes the award-winning *Editorial Eye* newsletter and professional books for editors and writers. Other books written by EEI staff or published by EEI include

The New York Public Library Writer's Guide to Style and Usage, edited by Andrea J. Sutcliffe

Error-Free Writing: A Lifetime Guide to Flawless Business Writing, by Robin A. Cormier

The Expert Editor, edited by Ann Molpus

Mark My Words: Instruction and Practice in Proofreading, by Peggy Smith

Letter Perfect: A Guide to Practical Proofreading, by Peggy Smith

Stet! Tricks of the Trade for Writers and Editors, edited by Bruce O. Boston

For complete information on EEI's services, publications seminars, and books, please write to

EEI
66 Canal Center Plaza, Suite 200
Alexandria, VA 22314-5507
Attn: Publications Division
703-683-0683/800-683-8380
FAX 703-683-4915
e-mail books@eei-alex.com